ZOROASTRIANISM
Its Antiquity and Constant Vigour

Columbia Lectures on Iranian Studies
Ehsan Yarshater
General Editor
Number 7

Zoroastrianism

Its Antiquity and Constant Vigour

Mary Boyce

Professor Emerita of Iranian Studies

University of London

Mazda Publishers

in association with

Bibliotheca Persica

Costa Mesa, California and New York

Library of Congress Cataloging-in-Publication Data

Boyce, Mary.
    Zoroastrianism: Its Antiquity and Constant Vigour / Mary Boyce.
      p. cm. -- (Columbia Lectures on Iranian Studies: No. 7)
    Includes bibliographical references and index.
    1. Zoroastrianism. I. Title. II. Series.
    BL1571.B67   1992   92-25267
    295--dc20   CIP

ISBN:0-939214-89-x
ISBN:0-939214-90-3 (pbk.)

Cover: "Farvahar, 88." Original art by Massoud Arabshahi.
10 9 8 7 6 5 4 3 2 1

Mazda Publishers   **1992**

To the memory of

DELPHINE MENANT

who studied the Zoroastrians with
learning, respect and affection as
bearers of an ancient and still
living faith

TABLE OF CONTENTS

Foreword

Zoroastrianism was the official faith of the ancient Iranians and is still professed by Zoroastrian communities in Persia, India, Europe, the United States, Canada, Australia, and elsewhere around the world. For centuries it symbolized the Iranian ethos, embodying its social, political, and spiritual values and thus affording coherence and stability for Iranian society. Despite the glories of art and literature produced by the Iranian peoples, the Zoroastrian religion must be acknowledged as their greatest cultural and spiritual achievement.

The present work originated in a set of lectures in the Columbia Lecture Series in Iranian Studies, which Professor Mary Boyce, a leading authority on the Zoroastrian faith and its traditions, delivered in 1988. Drawing upon a great store of knowledge, she provides here an authoritative account of the origins and essential tenets of Zoroastrianism and traces its continual development down to the present day, incorporating new information and fresh interpretations.

Professor Boyce received her Ph.D. in Oriental Studies from Cambridge University in 1945. She was appointed Lecturer in Iranian Studies at the University of London in 1947 and Professor in 1963. Her numerous publications have contributed substantially to our knowledge of the religious history and practices of the Zoroastrians, Middle Iranian languages, and Manichaeism. Her publications include *The Manichaean Hymn Cycles in Parthian* (1954), *A Catalogue of the Iranian Manuscripts in Manichaean Script in the German Turfan Collection* (1960), *The Letter of Tansar* (1968), *A History of Zoroastrianism*, in Handbuch der Orientalistik (3 vols. to date, the last in collaboration with F. Grenet, 1975-91), *A Reader in Manichaean Middle Persian and Parthian* (1975), *A Word-List of Manichaean Middle Persian and Parthian* (1977), *A Persian Stronghold of Zoroastrianism* (1977, 1989), *Zoroastians: Their Religious Beliefs and Practices* (1977, 1984), and *Textual Sources for the Study of Zoroastrianism* (1984).

She has received many honors for her contributions to Iranian studies, among them the Burton Gold Medal for work among the Zoroastrians of Iran, the Sir Percy Sykes Memorial Medal, an invitation to deliver the Ratanbai Katrak Lectures at Oxford in 1975, and a two-volume festschrift, *Papers in Honour of Professor Mary Boyce*, published in *Acta Iranica* in 1985.

With the present work, the culmination of years of research and numerous earlier publications, Professor Boyce has placed all students of Iranian religion and culture in her debt.

Ehsan Yarshater
General Editor

PREFACE

This book is based on five lectures given in 1985 at the invitation of Professor Ehsan Yarshater in the series "The Columbia Lectures on Iranian Studies". The lectures had the general title of "Zoroastrianism: three thousand years of faith", which has been changed for the book in order to give a clearer indication of its two main themes. The book's title is in part an adaptation of Cardinal Newman's dictum that one indication of the validity of a religion is its "chronic vigour". He was speaking of Christianity, for which it is often claimed that it and Judaism are the only survivors from among the many religions of the Near East in Roman imperial times. But Zoroastrianism, which was old before Christianity was born, also still exists today, and the present work is in part an attempt to account for its remarkable longevity and strength.

The first two chapters form a necessary prologue to such an attempt, in that they are concerned with the question of the religion's actual age. By now the spurious dating of Zoroaster to the sixth century B.C. has been generally abandoned by scholars, after having troubled Zoroastrian studies for over a hundred years; and a consensus appears to be forming that the prophet lived over half a millennium earlier, around 1200 B.C. The sixth-century dating had made him a contemporary of Cyrus the Great, which meant that the founding of his religion supposedly took place at about the same time as the founding of the Achaemenian empire. The earlier dating sets over six hundred years between the two events, thus placing the prophet in a far remoter age. The attempt has accordingly been made here to study his teachings in the setting of his own ancient society. The development of his religion is then traced, as far as can be known or reasonably surmised, through the following centuries, for which there are no written records, and among the historically known Achaemenian and Sasanian Persians. The final chapters bring an outline study of Zoroastrianism in Muslim Iran down to the mid twentieth century, thus following the survival into modern times of Zoroastrian orthodoxy and orthopraxy. (By these terms are meant here the essential teachings and observances attributable to Zoroaster himself.)

A good deal of what is treated selectively here has been dealt with at greater length by the writer in the three volumes which have so far appeared of *A History of Zoroastrianism* (the third in collaboration with Dr. Frantz Grenet). These are accordingly frequently cited. A number of points made in the two earlier volumes, some of them important, have called for revision; but she has found no reason to alter the main lines of interpretation offered there. It is hoped that the present small work (which contains some wholly new materials) will make a slight further contribution to counter-balancing the academic tendency (grown very marked in recent decades) to break Zoroastrianism up into almost disjunct phases, these corresponding with the periods of its long existence which happen to interest individual scholars. This tendency is readily explicable, since there is not a single post at any university in the world specifically for the study of Zoroastrianism, which is therefore often pursued more or less incidentally by scholars with widely differing specialities. But though explicable, it plainly does not favour a comprehensive or consistent treatment of Zoroastrianism, or its study for itself as a religion, rather than the use of its ancient texts as a quarry to be dug into from time to time for data to aid in philological, mythological, literary, archaeological, ethnographic and other pursuits. Such explorations have steadily extended understanding of details of the texts; but sometimes in the course of them rather wild surmises are made about the Iranian religion by scholars who may be of high standing in their own fields, but have perhaps no natural bent for the study of religions, or any great knowledge of Zoroastrianism from other aspects or at other periods. The fact that in putting forward narrowly based theories individual scholars often contradict one another is salutary, but not conducive to clarity or progress in real understanding of this ancient and by no means simple faith.

In a work such as the present one which, though small, traverses many centuries proper names inevitably occur in changing forms. Thus that of Zoroaster's God is to be found here as Ahura Mazda, Ahuramazda, Ohrmazd, Ormazd. It is hoped that such developments (brought together, with cross-references where necessary, in the index) will cause no trouble to a general student of religions. With some less prominent and less frequently occurring names (such as that of the Zoroastrian World Saviour, the Saošyant), the Avestan form has been retained throughout for clarity; and the familiar Middle Persian form of the Evil Spirit's name, Ahriman, has been kept rather than the recently proposed Ahreman (except in an occasional citation of a Middle Persian text). Simplicity has been aimed at also in transcription. In the text almost the only special character used in Iranian words and proper names is š for internal *sh*, since this has its convenience in avoiding sometimes awkward clusters of consonants (as in Khšathra). All Avestan nasals are rendered uniformly by *n*, and indeterminate short vowels generally by *e*, and only occasionally, with particular terms, by inverted *e*. Special characters are thus restricted ordinarily to quotations from texts. Length marks over vowels are also confined to such quotations, and to the index.

It is a pleasure to express my gratitude to Professor Ehsan Yarshater both for having invited me to give the lectures, and for allowing me to postpone preparing them for publication until another work was finished. To the publisher, Mr Ahmad Jabbary, I am indebted for his general helpfulness.

Mary Boyce
January 1992

ABBREVIATIONS

For abbreviations occurring after an author's or editor's name see under that name in the Bibliography. There are apt to be small variations in the spellings of the titles of Pahlavi books and Persian proper names.

Acta Ir.	Acta Iranica
Air. Wb.	see Bibliography under Bartholomae
AN	Ataš Niyayeš
Av.	Avestan
AVN	Arda Viraz Namag
AZ	Ayadgar i Zareran
BAI	Bulletin of the Asia Institute
BSOAS	Bulletin of the School of Oriental and African Studies
BSOS	Bulletin of the School of Oriental Studies
CH Inner Asia	The Cambridge History of Inner Asia, see Bibliography under Sinor
CHIr.	The Cambridge History of Iran, see Bibliography under Yarshater (Vol.III) and Frye (Vol.IV)
Dd.	Dadestan i denig
Dk.	Denkard
DkM	Denkard, ed. Madan
EIr.	Encyclopaedia Iranica
GBd.	Greater Bundahišn
HdO	Handbuch der Orientalistik
HZ I, II, III	see Bibliography under Boyce and Boyce-Grenet
I.E.	Indo-European
IIJ	Indo-Iranian Journal
J	Journal
JA	Journal Asiatique
JAOS	Journal of the American Oriental Society
JCOI	Journal of the K. R. Cama Oriental Institute
JNES	Journal of Near Eastern Studies
JRAS	Journal of the Royal Asiatic Society

MPers.	Middle Persian
MX	Menog i Khrad
Ny.	Niyayeš
OAv.	Old Avestan
Pahl.	Pahlavi
Pers.	Persian
PRDd.	Pahlavi Rivayat accompanying the Dadestan i denig
Riv.	Persian Rivayats, see Bibliography under Dhabhar and Unvala
RSO	Rivista degli studi orientali
SAA	South Asian Archaeology
Saddar Bd.	Saddar Bundaheš
SBE	Sacred Books of the East
St. Ir.	Studia Iranica
Stronghold	see Bibliography under Boyce
Sources	see Bibliography under Boyce
TVA	see Bibliography under Kellens-Pirart
Vd	Vendidad
VDI	Vestnik Drevnej Istorii
WZ	Wizidagiha i Zadspram
Y.	Yasna
YAv.	Young Avestan
YHapt.	Yasna Haptanhaiti
Yt	Yašt
ZDMG	Zeitschrift der deutschen morgenländischen Gesellschaft
ZVYt	Zand i Vahman Yašt
ZXA	Zand i Xwurdag Abestag

CHAPTER ONE

Zoroaster's Supposed
Time and Homeland:
A Confusion of Fabrications

To explore the question of Zoroaster's homeland calls first for the hacking away of a tangle of legends, false claims and fanciful speculations which grew up around this matter long ago, and which cast deep shadows over it. The reason why there could be a luxuriant growth of this kind was the lack, apparent already in ancient days, of exact knowledge. For this lack the prophet's own community cannot be blamed, for (as it is hoped to establish in the following pages) Zoroaster lived at a time when the "Airyas" (as his people identified themselves)[1] inhabited a region of the Inner Asian steppes which they knew as "Airyana Vaejah of the Vanhvi Daitya", often abbreviated to Airyana Vaejah (later Eranvez). After they had moved away southwards from there they continued to speak of their old homeland by this name; but it was one unknown to others, and gradually it ceased even for them to correspond to an identifiable locality, only a tradition about its general direction being for a long time preserved.[2]

Since only those Avestan texts survive which are used devotionally, this name rarely appears in them; but it occurred more frequently in the legendary life of the prophet, contained in the *Spend Nask*, and in other Avestan works describing the world and its creation. This fact is attested through the *zand* or exegesis of these lost texts, i.e. their Middle Persian translation, with glosses and commentaries.[3] The *zand* has perished with the Avestan originals, since

1

the two were written together; but a number of surviving Pahlavi writings either contain citations from it, or consist wholly of excerpted passages. In using these it is essential to try to distinguish the *zand* translations from the glosses and commentaries, which carry less authority and may be relatively late - even in some instances as late as early Islamic times.

The name "Airyana Vaejah of the Vanhvi Daitya" has been explained as "The *vaejah*, belonging to the Airya, of the good Daitya". Young Avestan texts make it clear that the Daitya (Pahlavi Daiti) was a river, and its *vaejah*, it seems, was the stretch or expanse of land watered by it at seasonal overflowings.[4] In the surviving Avesta Zoroaster is said to have been "famed in Airyana Vaejah";[5] and passages of *zand* translation tell how he received enlightenment on the bank of the Daiti,[6] and how it was in Eranvez that he first taught his new religion.[7] According to the Avestan *Vendidad*, when later the Evil Spirit was about to assail him, the prophet prepared himself by sacrificing "to the good waters of the good Daitya",[8] while in *Yašt 5*, by what is clearly a late adaptation, it is to the river Yazata, Aredvi Sura Anahita, that he sacrifices in "Airyana Vaejah of the good Daitya".[9]

For Zoroastrians generally Airyana Vaejah was therefore a holy land; and in time it became for them a semi-mythical place, set at the very centre of the earth, and lying accordingly at the foot of the world-mountain, "high Hara" (*Hara berezaiti*), around whose peak the sun circles, making night and day.[10] In Airyana Vaejah all the great acts of myth, legend and early religious history had taken place. According to passages of *zand* translation, it was there that Ohrmazd created life in the forms of a single Plant, Bull and Man. The Bull he set on the right bank of the Daiti, the Man on the left.[11] After Ahriman killed the Bull, its seed was taken up to the moon to be purified, and was then scattered in Eranvez, where it produced all the species of creatures that there are.[12] Thereafter, when men and creatures and plants had flourished and increased, then, according to the *Vendidad*, "the Creator, Ahura Mazda, famed in Airyana Vaejah of the good Daitya, held an assembly together with the immaterial Yazatas. ... To that assembly came shining Yima, possessed of good herds, famed in Airyana Vaejah of the good Daitya, together with the best of men".[13] Yima was the mythical first ruler over men, and the first man to die; and the phrase "famed in Airyana Vaejah", used thus of God, his prophet and this figure of ancient, pre-Zoroastrian myth, was evidently a fixed element in early Zoroastrian oral literature, going back to the time when fame within Airyana Vaejah, their own territory, was all-important to the Airyas and their poets.

No identifiable place-names occur in Old Avestan - that is, in Zoroaster's own utterances;[14] but in two much discussed passages in the Young Avesta there is mention of places that can be located, some of their names persisting indeed into medieval and even modern times. All these places are in the sphere of eastern Iranian settlement, that is, in terms of modern geography, in Soviet Central Asia, Afghanistan and eastern Iran. In the hymn to Mithra, verses describe how that Yazata, taking his stand each day at dawn on the peak of Hara, surveys "all the region dwelt in by Airyas" *(vīspəm ... airyō.šayanəm).*[15] This region is described as having high mountains rich in pastures, and many lakes and rivers. Its separate lands, which are then named, represent the upper valley of the Helmand, Gor, Herat, Marv, the area around Samarkand between the Amu Darya and Sir Darya (ancient Sogdia), and that along the lower course of the Amu Darya and the south shore of the Aral Sea (ancient Khwarezmia).[16]

All these lands except Khwarezmia appear again in the first chapter of the *Vendidad.* [17] This lists the sixteen lands created best by Ahura Mazda, with the particular afflictions visited on each by Anra Mainyu. The first to be named is Airyana Vaejah; and the other fifteen, it is generally assumed, are those settled lands in which Zoroastrianism was early established. To those listed in the *Mihr Yašt* are added others from further east and south, notably Harahvaiti (Arachosia to the Greeks), Haetumant (Drangiana, modern Seistan) and Hapta Hendu (the Punjab). There is no mention of any region north of the Sir Darya (the ancient Jaxartes), nor of any western Iranian place. (It has been convincingly shown that the Ragha of *Vd* 1:15 was a region of eastern Iranian settlement, not to be identified with the Median city of Raga[18].) There is only one land which is named in the *Mihr Yašt* but not in the *Vendidad,* and that is Khwarezmia. Why this is so is a puzzle; but the explanation once offered, that it was because this was in fact the original Airyana Vaejah, and appeared under that traditional name in the latter text, is now rejected.[19]

There is no suggestion in the *Vendidad* that any one of the fifteen lands - some qualified with a brief description, others not - was holier than the rest, or of special importance in the history of the faith. Instead, in the opening section, devoted to Airyana Vaejah as the first created and best of places, it is said that Ahura Mazda made these other lands only to prevent all living creatures wanting to go to it. But the Avesta of these lines is poor, and they are thought to be a late addition,[20] made perhaps so that the holy land should not lack mention. In order to assimilate this addition to the rest of the text, even it is said to suffer an affliction from Anra Mainyu, in its case "demon-created winter" *(zyqm .. daēvō.dātəm).* There follows what is held to be an Avestan gloss on this, in which Airyana Vaejah is said to have had ten months of winter and only two of summer. It seems odd, at any stage, to attribute such a climate to the best of all lands; but it is comprehensible if there were a persistent tradition that Zoroaster's homeland lay far away to the north.[21] In general the north is regarded by Zoroastrians as the inauspicious quarter, where hell was thought to gape; and it is therefore striking that the implications of these *Vendidad* lines are supported by a passage in the *zand* translation of the legend of the prophet's life, where he is said to have dreamt, just before his enlightenment, that the people of the world would congregate in the north (*be ō abāxtar*), led by his cousin Medyomah, who was to be his first convert.[22] What was presumably an accurate memory among the first generation of migrant "Airyas" of the harshness of the winters in Airyana Vaejah, exaggerated in length in *Vendidad* I, thus persists as a fixed tradition side by side with the transformation of their old homeland into a mythical paradise on earth, the two concepts remaining characteristically unreconciled.[23]

In one of the *Gathas*[24] Zoroaster speaks of being rejected by his own kindred and community. In another he has converted Kavi Vištaspa, the chief, it seems, of another group of "Airyas".[25] How far he journeyed to reach Vištaspa is in no way indicated; but allusions in two late verses in the *Yašts* show that their composers thought that Vištaspa and the other *kavis* (chiefs and heroes among his predecessors) also lived in Airyana Vaejah[26]; and a Parthian Manichaean text states; "A peaceful ruler (was) King Vištasp in Aryan Waizhan" (*rāmgar šahrdār [bū]d šāh wištāsp [pad aryā]n waižan*)[27]. This accords with the fact that nowhere in the Avesta or the *zand* translation is a link made between Vištaspa and the *kavis* and any named place within the settled Iranian sphere.

In the Young Avesta a truly Zoroastrian association with an identifiable place is that of the myth of the future World Saviour, the Saošyant, with Seistan. This is attested in *Yašt* 19, which is largely devoted to the celebration of *khvarenah*, the fortune or grace sent down on chosen and just mortals from on high. In one of its verses it is declared that *khvarenah* will accompany the victorious Saošyant "when ... he comes forth from the Kansaoya water".[28] This is clearly an allusion to the belief that the seed of the prophet is miraculously preserved in the depths of a lake, and that one day a virgin, bathing there, will conceive his son, the Saviour.[29] Another verse in the same *Yašt* says that the "fortune of the *kavis*" (*kavaem khvarenah*) "accompanies him who rules there where is the Lake Kansaoya, [which receives] the Haetumant".[30] The Haetumant is the modern Helmand, so this identifies Kansaoya as the Hamun lake, into which that river flows. In the verse which follows eight other rivers from the same region are named,[31] showing that this area (ancient Arachosia-Drangiana) played an important part in the transmission of *Yašt* 19, or at least this part of that hymn, with verses being composed there to celebrate local places and a local ruler.[32] Expectation of the Saošyant continued to be linked with the Hamun lake (which in the past was a huge sheet of water) and with the mountain that rose out of it, named the "Hill of the Lord" (*Kuh-i Khwaja*), down the centuries and indeed far into Islamic times;[33] but when the belief itself took shape, and whether it was from the first attached to this place, there is no means of knowing. In character the myth is fully in accord with Zoroaster's teachings, which were focussed on the salvation of the world. The prophet even, it seems, himself alluded to the part to be played in that salvation by one who would come after him, a noble and truly righteous man.[34] The fabulous element in the actual myth shows, however, that it evolved some time after he lived. The great importance which the Iranians gave to lineage evidently led his community to hope that the new leader would be descended from Zoroaster himself, and this hope was then transmuted into belief in the coming of his miraculously conceived son.

The link of the myth with the Hamun lake was not apparently accepted as certain truth by all Zoroastrian scholastics at all times; [35] but it undoubtedly gained general credence. A part seems likely to have been played in this by the nameless prince who is said in *Yašt* 19 to have been accompanied by "the fortune of the *kavis*". This phrase does not mean that he was of Vištaspa's line, for, as *Yašt* 19 itself abundantly illustrates, *kavaem khvarenah* had become a stock phrase which might signify no more than "royal fortune", possession of which meant divine approval.[36] Very possibly the Seistani prince earned this eulogy from the local priests because he had been active in supporting their claims concerning the Saošyant and Lake Kansaoya, and so had helped these to become widely acknowledged.

A noteworthy point about this Seistani claim is that it is in its way a modest one; for profoundly important though the expectation of the Saošyant is in Zoroastrianism, in its developed form the belief is clearly secondary. There is no suggestion in *Yašt* 19, or anywhere else in the Avesta, that Zoroaster himself lived in Seistan, or that this was the homeland of the *kavis*. The contrast in this respect with more extravagant later pretensions suggests the strong probability, supported by *Vendidad* I, that when the Young Avestan texts were composed a genuine tradition still existed among the eastern Iranians that the prophet's homeland lay far away to the north, and that this knowledge inhibited false assertions.

It was only later - in what for our present purposes may be called "post-Avestan" times - that such assertions came to proliferate, with the example being almost certainly set by a western Iranian region, Azarbaijan. The evidence for its claims comes from a variety of sources: verse 5 of the fifth *Niyayeš* (the prayer to fire), put together from scraps of older Avestan texts, probably in the Sasanian period; statements in Pahlavi books taken from glosses or commentaries in the *zand*; passages in Firdausi's *Shahnama*, which derives very largely from the lost Sasanian royal chronicle, the *Khwaday Namag*; and information recorded by early Muslim geographers and historians.[37] Together these sources show that a clear positive claim was made for Azarbaijan that it was Airyana Vaejah, and that it was there that Zoroaster spent his life. The town of Urmia, about half way up the western shore of Lake Urmia, was said to be where he was born. This town was described in medieval times as a pleasant place set among vineyards, with a stream flowing through it down to the lake;[38] and presumably this stream was identified as the

Dreja, beside which, according to the *Vendidad*, Zoroaster's father lived.[39] Later, according to the legendary life of the prophet, he left his parents' home in quest of enlightenment; and the Azarbaijani claim was that he went then to Mount Sabalan, the highest peak in that region. This mountain may have received accordingly an Avestan name, as did a more modest eminence on which was built the temple of a much venerated sacred fire, famous in Sasanian times as Adur Gušnasp.[40] The hill on which it burnt was given the name "Asnuvant", that of one which occurs in a fairly lowly position among the mountains of the world enumerated in *Yašt* 19.[41] Adur Gušnasp is said in some sources to be "in" Ganzak, a town by modern Miandoab in the plain at the southern end of Lake Urmia; but this presumably means no more than that "Mount Asnuvant" was not far from that town, used thus as a point of reference.

The huge lake itself, despite being remarkably shallow, was renamed Chaechasta after the Avestan Chaechasta, which is described as deep;[42] and with this name came the story of Haosravah, one of the most famous of the *kavis*, who in the Avesta is said to have sacrificed by its shore. It was now told[43] how "Kay Khosrow" visited the temple of Adur Gušnasp and prayed there to be allowed to find his father's slayer, Afrasiyab (Avestan Franrasyan); how his prayer was answered; and how Afrasiyab was dragged from his hiding place in the shallows of "Chaechasta" and put to death on the lakeshore; and how Khosrow then returned to Adur Gušnasp and in thanksgiving lavished wealth and gifts on its temple and priests.

It is clear that these claims, however detailed, by a region of western Iran to be the homeland of Zoroaster and the *kavis* were false, since the whole tradition of the Avesta belongs to the eastern Iranians; and a set of circumstances is known which explains when and why they came to be made. Under the Achaemenians Azarbaijan had been no more than an obscure corner of the rich and strategically important satrapy of Media. It was old Urartian territory, and it was perhaps only around the fertile shores of Lake Urmia that it had been much settled by Iranians. Ganzak(a), the "Treasury", was its one important town; and nothing of any religious - or indeed other - interest is known of it at this period.[44] The holiest place of the Medes then appears to have been the ancient city of Raga (modern Ray, near Tehran). This stood on the Khorasan Highway, Iran's chief artery linking east with west, and was close to Media's border with Parthia; and it has been cogently argued that, despite the slightly different spelling of the name, it is this city, and not the *Vendidad* land of Ragha (for which, as we have seen, no particular claim to holiness is made) which is really the Ragha of a late passage in *Yasna* 19.[45] Small additions to Avestan texts can be shown to have been made for particular purposes as late as Sasanian times, but within certain conventions. No palpably new subject matter could be introduced (thus, for instance, there is no mention in the Avesta or *zand* translation of a fire temple, sacred edifices having been instituted only in the Achaemenian period); and what was newly said had to be expressed through adaptations or new combinations of familiar Avestan words and phrases.[46] Hence the mention of the virtually homonomous Ragha in the Avesta made it possible for Median priests to compose a brief Avestan passage to establish the holiness of their own city of Raga (which they evidently actually identified as the place mentioned in the *Vendidad*)[47], and to introduce this into the *yasna* liturgy.

Yasna 19 consists of a commentary on the greatest of Zoroastrian *manthras*, the *Ahunvar*; and in v.17 this prayer is said, in characteristic scholastic fashion, to have three measures, four classes and five "masters" (*ratu*).[48] This is then developed in v.18, where the first four masters are named, according to standard Young Avestan social divisions, as those of house, clan, tribe and country; and the fifth is declared to be Zarathuštra. This brief statement appears to encapsulate a general priestly claim that religious authority was greater than that of the king. Elsewhere for the fifth in this series the title *Zarathuštrō.təma* appears, "the one most like Zarathuštra", a title glossed in one place in the *zand* as "he who does the work of a Mobadan mobad" (*mardōm ī andar xwēškārīh mōbadān mōbad*),[49] that is, the chief ecclesiastic of Sasanian times. To this general statement in *Yasna* 19 a brief, awkwardly phrased particular one is then added: "(Thus) with (all) lands but Zarathuštrian Ragha. In Zarathuštrian Ragha there are (only) four masters. Who are its four masters? He of house, clan, tribe, and fourth Zarathuštra". The meaning of this seems to be that "Ragha", i.e. Median Raga, was at some time an autonomous holy city, governed by its chief magus in the role, as it were, of a prince-bishop.[50] This interpretation receives some support from the fact that Raga remained an important centre of Zoroastrianism down into early Islamic times (and indeed still possesses a famous shrine of Zoroastrian origin[51]). All this, together with its position as the first Median town to be entered by travellers from the east, led to the persuasive suggestion that Raga was probably the first western Iranian place to receive Zoroastrian missionaries from the east, becoming itself both a missionary centre and the religious metropolis of the Median magi.[52] Its holiness would thus have dated back to before the rise of the Achaemenian empire.

When eventually, after successive Macedonian conquests and reconquests, Seleucus established himself as ruler of Iran (around 305 B.C.), he refounded Raga, with all its strategic and commercial importance, as a Greek *polis*, which he named Europos.[53] Whether Europos was built beside the old Median town, or actually incorporated it, is not known; but this act clearly put an end to any civil authority being exercised by its chief magus, and brought an influx of infidel foreigners there, unclean in the eyes of a Zoroastrian priest. Before this Media itself, which under Alexander had still been governed by a Persian satrap, Atropates,[54] had been almost all assigned to a Macedonian, and Atropates was left with only its north-west corner, which became known thereafter as Lesser Media or Media Atropatene (later Atropatakan, Azarbaijan). There, though with wealth and power greatly reduced, he was at least able to make himself independent, founding a dynasty that lasted for several centuries; and for some time this was the only part of Iran that was under Zoroastrian rule. In all other regions the unbelievers were dominant.

What happened then in the religious sphere has to be deduced from subsequent developments. The chief magus apparently left Raga-Europos, with some of his priests, bearing with them their sacred fire,[55] and sought the protection of Atropates. That prince may be supposed to have been very willing to receive so distinguished a co-religionist, and to have granted him land near what was now his capital, Ganzak, on which to build a temple for the fire. The chief magus thus gained freedom from the neighbourhood and dominance of infidel foreigners, and was doubtless accorded every respect; but there were also clearly losses for him and his priests through their change of abode. Raga was a busy as well as a holy city, through which throngs of travellers passed; and in Achaemenian times these would have been predominantly Zoroastrians, bringing wealth not only to the town but also to its priests and shrines. There would also have been pilgrims coming seasonally. Some of the most devout among the latter were probably still prepared to make the longer journey to Atropatene, along emptier and perhaps more dangerous roads, to pay their respects to the chief magus and to worship at the sacred fire; but their numbers are likely to have been greatly diminished.

For the magi in Atropatene to redress this change in their circumstances, and to recover something of former wealth and prestige, was clearly not easy. Raga - where some priests had doubtless remained - continued to be regarded as holy; and for Atropatene to rival it in sanctity, and so to draw pilgrims in numbers, some large religious claim had to be made. The magi there chose accordingly the most impressive one possible, namely that this previously unregarded land was in fact the most sacred of all places for Zoroastrians, Airyana Vaejah itself. Plainly such a claim could only have been made because of the vagueness of the tradition as to where Airyana Vaejah truly lay. All that was known of it was probably, as we have seen, that it was in the north; and Atropatene was unquestionably to the north of Raga, indeed to the north of most of Iran. It was possibly this one simple fact which was taken as justification for identifying it as the holy land, and which doubtless soon allowed a measure of pious credulity to develop, even among the Atropatenian magi themselves.

Initially, however, there must have been more than a little pragmatism in the development of local associations to support the claim. Thus the story of Kay Khosrow and Adur Gušnasp reads very much like a carefully fostered shrine-legend, such as would have been told to those coming to worship at the great fire; for it not only enhanced the dignity of Adur Gušnasp through giving it Avestan connections, but emphasized its power to answer prayers, while providing a desirable pattern of behaviour in Khosrow's lavishness to the temple and its priests when his petition was granted. The legend would also have justified a visit to the shore of Lake Urmia to see the exact place where the wicked Afrasiyab had died; and looking out over that vast sheet of water would have been an impressive experience in itself, helping to make the pilgrimage memorable and worthy to be talked of to others on the return home. Ganzak no doubt exerted itself to receive pilgrims; and there was the further goal of the town of Urmia, to see where the prophet was born and to tread where he had trodden. Urmia is some distance from Ganzak, near which the Khosrow legend suggested that the *kavis* had lived; and conceivably it was fixed on as Zoroaster's birthplace partly to fit the fact that he left his own kindred and community to travel to the court of Vištaspa.[56]

For all these developments the Atropatids may reasonably be assumed to have given active patronage (like, probably, the nameless Seistani prince for the Saošyant legend); for clearly they too would have benefited from them, both by wealth flowing in and by the dignity of their small realm being enhanced. Political boundaries do not seem to have hindered the movement of travellers in Seleucid times, and once the holy legends of Atropatene were accepted Zoroastrians probably came there from all over Media, and even further afield.

It is thus likely to have been a combination of priestly and princely power, together with special political circumstances, which enabled little Atropatene to establish its audacious claim, at least as far as western Iran was concerned; for Persia, it seems, never seriously sought to vie with Media over possessing the older Zoroastrian tradition.[57] The eastern Iranian lands must have been aware, however, of having a longer religious history; and so it is hardly surprising that eventually several of them also put forward claims to have been the scene of the prophet's activity. The probability that these were made after the Atropatenian one, and in rivalry to it, is very strong. As we have seen, no such local claims are to be found in the extant Avesta, or in passages translated from lost Avestan texts; and it seems most unlikely that any could have established themselves under the Achaemenians. It is not known how far in their epoch Persian priests sought to control Zoroastrian affairs throughout the Iranian satrapies; but that they were able to exert some leadership, backed by the great king's authority, is shown, for instance, by the imposition then of changes to the liturgical calendar on the whole community. Close Persian surveillance of secular affairs is well attested; and any upstart claim concerning Zoroaster would inevitably have become known at court through the same channels, and would surely have been promptly dealt with.

Matters changed wholly in the religious sphere with Alexander's conquest, and the eventual establishing of Seleucid rule over Iran. The Macedonians generally were tolerantly indifferent to the religious affairs of their alien subjects; and with the destruction of a Zoroastrian central government the priesthoods of the different satrapies - which corresponded broadly with the territories of the different Iranian peoples - were free again to act independently of one another. When in the mid second century B.C. the Arsacids supplanted the Seleucids in Iran, the whole land came once more under Zoroastrian rule; but the Parthians permitted considerable local freedom under their hegemony, and it was not until the rise of the second Persian empire, that of the Sasanians, that there was again a strictly centralized authority which concerned itself with religious affairs. During "post-Avestan" times it was therefore only in the combined Seleucid-Arsacid epochs - a long period from the end of the fourth century B.C. to the early third century A.C. - that there was local autonomy in religious matters, and so no check on new and rival claims being put forward concerning the prophet.

The first of these rival claims was probably that advanced by the Parthians themselves. In the second century B.C. the Arsacids became overlords of Atropatene;[58] and it would be natural if their priests had not been best pleased to find their homeland outshone in sanctity by this small western vassal state. Parthia too had a great sacred fire, called Adur Burzen Mihr; and it was probably now that the holiness of this fire was strongly promoted, with the creation of a myth that its Spirit (Mainyu) had had a great part in the conversion of Vištaspa. It then, it was claimed, "revealed many things visibly, in order to propagate the faith and establish certainty, and to bring Vištasp and his descendants to the faith of God."[59] This statement occurs in a section of the *zand* devoted to temple fires, which, as its subject matter attests, embodies "post-Avestan" materials; and it is in conflict with one in the *zand* translation of the prophet's legendary life, which is obviously older and of better authority.[60] This says that among the three divine beings who took Vištasp in spirit up to heaven, so that the truth of the religion might be revealed to him, was the "Fire of Ohrmazd" (*ātaxš ī Ohrmazd*), that is, the Yazata Atar himself. By annexing this fundamental religious myth for their own great sacred fire, the Parthian priests were undoubtedly claiming greater sanctity for it than had their Atropatenian brethren for Adur Gušnasp, linked merely with the heroic Kay Khosrow, and so may be held to have outdone them. The Parthian legend went on to say that Vištasp, having thus been brought to adopt the religion, built a temple for Adur Burzen Mihr on "Mount Revant".[61] This is a name taken, like the Atropatenian "Asnuvant", from the Avesta,[62] and, like it, was evidently given to the actual hill on which the temple stood - in this case, it is thought, a spur of a range near Nishapur, the whole range being called the "Ridge of Vištasp", in Middle Persian *Pušt ī Vištāspān*.[63] These identifications too found a place in the *zand*, in an extension of "post-Avestan" times made to the list of mountains given in *Yašt* 19.

The fact that these Parthian claims, like those of Atropatene, were taken into the *zand* shows that they likewise succeeded in gaining wide credence; and in their case also the existence of a well-told shrine-legend is likely to have played an important part, with knowledge of it being carried far and wide by returning pilgrims. Moreover, success in establishing the great sanctity of this sacred fire was probably again achieved by a combination of secular patronage and priestly myth-making, with the Arsacid kings now taking the presumed part of the Atropatids and the Seistani prince. There is a parallel to this, geographically apt, with the Safavid Shah 'Abbas, who in the seventeenth century encouraged devotion to the tomb of Imam Reza in Mashhad - in old Parthian territory - and so drew pilgrim wealth to it and away from the holy places of the Arab world.

In Parthia, as in Atropatene, ancillary traditions grew up around the main shrine-legend, notably the claim that the famous battle for the faith between Vištaspa and the chief of another Iranian tribe, Arejat-aspa (Arjasp) had been fought on Parthian soil, on the plain below Mount Kumis at the western end of the "Ridge of Vištasp".[64] This battle is only just alluded to in the extant Avesta,[65] but is treated at length in the Middle Iranian *Ayadgar i Zareran*, and in the *Shahnama*. The *Ayadgar*, although preserved in Pahlavi, shows many traces of a Parthian transmission;[66] and it seems that tales of this holy war, with all the scope which these gave for describing heroic feats, were much celebrated by Parthian minstrels. It is therefore surprising that in the only passage with place-names in the *Ayadgar*,[67] Vištasp's brother Zarer is represented as summoning Arjasp from Khotan[68] to "Zoroaster's Marw" (*Morw ī Zarduštān*), "which (has) neither high mountains nor deep lakes. In that level plain (it is) to be decided (between) the horses and brave footmen". This, the only attestation in Pahlavi literature of a claim by Marw to a link with Zoroaster, flatly contradicts the Parthian one about the site of the great battle; and its occurrence in the *Ayadgar* well illustrates the confusion that developed, as time passed, through the proliferation of rival local claims to be the place of the prophet's activity.

No striking historical circumstances suggest themselves for the shaping of any of these claims other than those of Atropatene and Parthia; but clearly once priests of those two regions had adapted early traditions of the faith to enhance the sanctity and renown of their own shrines, then others were likely, in the absence of a restraining authority, to follow suit. Among the best attested, although only from late sources, is that of Bactria. There is no mention of this in the *zand*; but in the *Shahrestaniha i Eran*, whose existing redaction dates to early Islamic times, it is said that Vištasp's son Spendiyar built part of the city of Balkh (Bactria's capital) and founded an Ataš Bahram there.[69] This suggests yet another shrine-legend. Further, in the thirteenth-century *Zaratušt Nama*, whose author declares this to be the Persian versification of a lost Pahlavi work,[70] Zoroaster is said to have travelled from his (unnamed) homeland outside Iran to Balkh, to reach the court of "Guštasp" (i.e., Vištaspa).[71] This is, however, the only mention of Balkh in connection with Guštasp in the whole poem, and its name could well have been inserted here by the author on the authority, not of his Pahlavi original, but of the *Shahnama*.

It is in the *Shahnama* that Balkh's claim is most fully set out. But many streams of tradition met in the epic (as already in its main source, the *Khwaday Namag*); and in telling the story of Zoroaster's establishing the faith Daqiqi (who composed most of this section) blended together - or more probably found blended together - the rival Parthian and Bactrian claims. These are fitted into a continuous narrative with incompatibilities left unresolved. First it is told that Balkh was built by Guštasp's father Lohrasp (Av. Aurvat-aspa); and by a piece of total confusion this king is said to have founded there a great fire, "Adar Barzin", that is, the Parthian Adur Burzen Mihr[72] (and this before Zoroaster has even entered the story). Lohrasp then abdicates in his son's favour. Zoroaster appears at Guštasp's court in Balkh, and Guštasp and his people accept the faith. Then (and here events take a wholly Parthian turn) Guštasp establishes "Adar Mihr Barzin" in its temple, declared to be the first fire temple on earth, and the prophet plants before its gate a cypress.[73] A number of lines later this is referred to as the "Cypress of Kishmar", and a message concerning it is sent by Guštasp throughout his realm: "Where in all the world is there the like of the Cypress of Kishmar? God has sent it to me from heaven, he has said to me: 'Ascend to heaven from here!' Now listen, all, to my counsel, go on foot to the Cypress of Kishmar. Take, all, the path of Zoroaster!"[74]   These artless lines derive clearly from the legend of a particular shrine, giving authority for the merit of pilgrimage to it. The existence of a sacred cypress at Kishmar was later attested by two Muslim writers, Qazvini (thirteenth century) and Mustawfi (first half of the fourteenth century). According to the former the great tree flourished majestically until 861, when it was felled at the order of Caliph Mutawakkil, to the profound grief of the Zoroastrian community.[75] Kishmar is a village near Turshiz in former Parthian territory; and though there is no way of dating the origin of this legend about its holy tree, it seems likely that it developed during the later Arsacid period under the aegis of the shrine-legend of Adur Burzen Mihr, with which it is awkwardly conflated in the *Shahnama*.

The *Shahnama* then takes up the story of the battle with Arjasp. Its account agrees broadly with that of the *Ayadgar i Zareran*,[76] but here there is mention neither of Marv nor of the plain below Parthian Mount Kumis. Instead Guštasp sets out from Balkh with his army and meets Arjasp at the

Oxus (Amu Darya).[77] As in the *Ayadgar*, Arjasp, defeated, escapes with his life; but the *Shahnama* alone continues the story. It tells how later, when Guštasp had gone to "make the Zend-Avesta current" in Seistan, that is, to convert that region,[78] Arjasp attacked Balkh, killed the aged Lohrasp, sacked the fire temple and slew its priests. Firdausi (who has by now taken over the story from Daqiqi) recounts this incident twice, first as narrative, then as reported to Guštasp by his wife, who had escaped from the assault.[79] In the narrative it is said: "There were eighty priests ... They slew them all before the fire. ... The fire of Zoroaster died from their blood. Why the priests were slain I know not" (*hērbad būd haštād mard ... hamē pēš-ī ādar be kuštand-šān ... zi xūn-šān be murd ātaš-i zardhušt nadānam čerā hērbadrā be kušt*). According to the queen, Arjasp's men "went to Adar Noš. They beheaded the master and all the priests. The blazing fire died from their blood" (*... be nōš ādar šudand. rad u hērbadrā hamē sar zadand. zi xūn-šān farūzande ātaš be murd*). The name Adar Noš occurs here for the first time, the place of this fire having been usurped previously by the Parthian Burzen Mihr. The name is known indeed only from the *Shahnama*, but the fact that there in later passages oaths are sworn by this fire[80] (as elsewhere by Adur Burzen Mihr) suggests that it too was an actual one, presumably the Ataš Bahram of Balkh. The expression used of it, "fire of Zardušt" is echoed when the incident is spoken of once again, this time by Guštasp's daughters, who were carried off by Arjasp. They recall, when rescued, how their captor, among other villainies, "killed the Zoroastrian Noš Adar" (*nōš ādar-i zardhuštī be-kušt*).[81] The phrases "of Zardušt, Zarduštī" are understood to imply that the fire was established by the prophet himself, which suggests that in this the priests of Balkh sought in their turn to outdo the Parthians' claim for Burzen Mihr (established merely by Vištasp).

What is less convincing is the general assumption that the word "master" (*rad*) in the queen's account refers to Zoroaster himself, with the supposition that the prophet met his death in this attack.[82] He has not, in fact, been mentioned in the poem for a long time - not since the beginning of hostilities with Arjasp; and it would be very strange if he were suddenly brought back in this oblique and casual way, with the momentous event of his death not being spoken of at all in the main narrative, nor recalled by Guštasp's daughters, but being referred to only by his queen, and that without prominence given to it. When these facts are duly considered, it seems much more likely that Firdausi was closely following, even if at one remove, his Pahlavi original, and that *rad* (Av. *ratu*) here simply means the temple high priest, "master" of the other priests serving there.[83] The strong probability is that behind the fiction of Arjasp's sacking of Adar Noš was the reality of an actual nomad assault on Balkh, in which the temple priests did all perish with their high priest and the sacred fire; but whether this is so or not, the incident cannot reasonably be supposed to have anything to do with Zoroaster.

In the surviving Avesta nothing is said of the prophet's end, but in a Pahlavi passage from the *zand* his death is referred to in conventionally devout terms, as "the departure of Zardušt of venerated spirit to the Best Existence, when 77 years had passed from his birth" (*wihēz ī yašt-frawahr zarduxšt ō ān ī pahlom axwān ka uzīd ēstād az zāyišnīh frāz 77 sāl*).[84] Another text that draws on the *zand* sets out, as pseudo-prophecy, the deaths of the great men of the early days of the faith, beginning with the prophet himself; and for each the verb used is *widērēd* "he will pass away" - a standard idiom for dying. [85] There is just one interruption in the list, when by contrast six of the devout, it is declared, will be killed, the verb used then being *ōzan-*.[86] The tradition of the prophet's quiet end persisted, and in the late *Saddar Bundaheš* it is said that after Guštasp had accepted the religion and propagated it throughout the world, Zoroaster returned to Eranvez,[87] the implication being that he died a natural death there.

A story did nevertheless gain currency that the prophet had met a violent death, but this is more dubiously attested. The fifth book of the *Denkard* is a work compiled in the ninth century A.C. by the high priest Adurfarnbag i Farrokhzadan as an exposition of Zoroastrianism for a sympathetic unbeliever;[88] and in it national feeling is intermixed with theology and sacred legend. It was the Kayanians (that is, the *kavis*), Adurfarnbag declares, who maintained the chosen and superior Iranian people, and so helped them to preserve the revelation brought by Zoroaster. Among the passages exalting the prophet himself is one illustrating his powers of prediction; and one thing which he is said to have foretold is that he himself would die a violent death - in Adurfarnbag's words "the killing of Zardušt himself by the Tur, Bratrores" (*ōzadan ī tūr ī brātrōrēs ō xwad zarduxšt*).[89] The name of the imagined assassin, which recurs, is "variously written, and the exact form cannot be determined from the Pahlavi script."[90] Another allusion to this supposed event is in the *Greater Bundahišn*, in a chapter which belongs to Zoroastrian apocalyptic, and which again contains matter from the "national" tradition. Here the future appearance is foretold of the "dangerous-natured Malkus, of the family of the Tur, Bratrores, who caused the death of Zardušt" (*malkūs ī sēj-čihr ī az tōhmag ī tūr ī brātrōrēs, ī ōš ī zarduxšt [aziš] būd*).[91] Malkus, Avestan Mahrkuša, is an ancient name for an evil sorcerer who will cause many people and animals to die in harsh winters;[92] and linking him thus with the wicked Bratrores, as another destroyer, is clearly the work of a systematizer, not the reflection of a genuine tradition. In another apocalyptic work, the *Zand i Vahman Yašt*, Bratrores appears by implication as the archetypal enemy of Zoroaster, for Ohrmazd declares to the prophet: "If I make you immortal, O Spitaman Zardušt, then the Tur, Bratroš the *karb*, will (also) be immortal" (*ka tō rāy anōš bē kunēm, spitaman zarduxšt, ēg tūr ī brātrōš ī karb anōš bē bawēd*).[93]   In a parallel passage in the *Pahlavi Rivayat accompanying the Dadestan i denig* Ohrmazd identifies "the Tur, Bratrokhš the *karb*" as the man "whom Ahriman created for the purpose of killing you" (*ī ahreman ōzadan ī tō rāy dād*).[94] *Karb*, Avestan *karapan*, is the title given in the *Gathas* to, it seems, priests of the old religion who were hostile to the prophet; and it is accorded once again to his putative slayer by the high priest Manušchihr, who composed the *Dadestan i denig* in the latter part of the ninth century A.C. In it Manušchihr names among the seven greatest evildoers "the Tur, Bratrokhš the *karb*, of bad religion, the sorcerer, who put to death the best of men" (*tūr ī brātrōxš ī karb ī dušdēn ī jādūg, kē-š ān ī pāšom az mardōmān margēnīd*).[95] In a similar list in the *Saddar*, a work of early Islamic times, the villain appears as "the Tur, Bratrokhš, who killed Zardušt";[96] and in a passage on the early history of the faith in the *PRDd.* "the Tur, Bratreš", slayer of the prophet, is said to have been "like a wolf" (*pad gurg ēwēnag*).[97]

None of these passages suggests a genuine old tradition; and the fact that those in the *Greater Bundahišn* and *Denkard* both occur in sections which draw on epic materials makes it all too probable that the basis for this story of Zoroaster's violent death was simply the shrine-legend of Bactrian Adar Noš, incorporated with other north-eastern materials in the Sasanian *Khwaday Namag*[98]. As we have seen, the wording of the *Shahnama* verses which tell of the sack of Adar Noš suggests a close rendering by Firdausi's source of a Pahlavi original; and that original was apparently interpreted by some Zoroastrian scholastics themselves, in late Sasanian or early Islamic times, as telling of the death of their "master", Zoroaster - an interpretation prompted by the reference in the same passage to the "fire of Zardušt". Then, in the way of scholastics, they would naturally have sought to establish the identity of the man who struck the actual blow. In the Avesta Arejat-aspa is chief of the Hyaona tribe, and in the *Ayadgar* Arjasp is addressed accordingly as the Khyonan Shah,[99] and his followers are Khyons. But in the *Shahnama* he appears as the Turan Shah, or Turan Khoday,[100] that is, lord of the "Tur" people, Avestan Tuirya. There was a tendency in Zoroastrian tradition to regard the Tuiryas as the natural foes of the Airyas, because Franrasyan (Afrasiyab), the *kavis'* great enemy, was of that tribe; and early Islamic writers attest that Arjasp, as Kay Vištasp's opponent, was regarded by some as a kinsman of Afrasiyab,[101] and so as himself a Tur. Further, when in late Sasanian times Turks began to threaten Iran's north-eastern frontier, they and the Turs were confounded, and "the land of Turan" became the general name for non-Iranian Central Asia. From all this it follows that Zoroaster's putative killer, being one of Arjasp's army, could be classified as a Tur. But how then to identify him more closely? It would have been unacceptable to invent a name; but the legendary life of the prophet tells of two *karbs* who tried repeatedly to harm Zoroaster in his infancy. One was named Bratrores, the other Durasrab.[102]   The latter is more prominent, but he, it is told, perished in his malevolence.[103]   This then left Bratrores as the sole candidate for the part of implacable enemy still in the prophet's old age, the only adjustment needed being for him to become a Tur.   The fact that this wolf-like assailant would have had by then to have been at least in his nineties was evidently not considered.

That cross-influencing resulted thereafter, presumably through the work of copyists, is shown by the fact that in one place in *Denkard* 7, where the old infancy legends are told, the second *karb* is actually called "the Tur, Bratrores"[104].   The story of Zoroaster's death by violence thus proves quite worthless and late, the product of scholastic ponderings upon a misinterpreted passage of the "national" epic.   That it moreover failed, despite its dramatic character, to become generally known is illustrated by a reference to Arjasp's assault on Balkh in one of the *Persian Rivayats*:   "When the worthless and vile Arjasp killed King Lohrasp and sought (to extinguish) the fire, that Adur Burzen Mihr disappeared suddenly by its own power.   There is a place called Dašt-i Vištaspan.   There it settled ... They also call it ... Pušt-i Vištaspan."[105]   This story plainly represents an attempt to reconcile the confused legends about the Parthian and Bactrian sacred fires; but what is striking is that it could be told without any suggestion that not only Lohrasp but also Zoroaster himself had perished in Arjasp's attack.

The Bactrian legend of the founding of Balkh's sacred fire by Zoroaster thus had developments which its inventors could neither have foreseen nor wished.   In the *Shahrestaniha i Eran*, however, it is the claims concerning Zoroaster of Bactria's northern neighbour, Sogdia, which are given prominence.   In it it is said[106]   that Samarkand, the Sogdian capital, was founded by Kayus (Kavi Usan) and Siyavakhš (Kavi Syarvaršan); and that Siyavakhš established its Ataš Bahram.   It was in Samarkand that Zoroaster came to Vištasp; and there, at that king's behest, he inscribed the Avesta on tablets of gold and placed these in the treasury of its fire temple, where eventually they were found and destroyed by the accursed Alexander.   This particular legend resembles tales of Hellenistic times about divine revelations recorded on costly scrolls or tablets and kept concealed in temples,[107] and it fits well with the supposition that all these pious stories about the prophet, emanating, it seems, from local fire temples, came into being after Alexander's conquest.

There remain to consider the claims of Seistan.   It is understandable if that region, with its long-established tradition of especial sanctity, because of its association with the Saošyant, should have been unwilling to be outdone in holiness by these other places with their new pretensions to links with Zoroaster himself; and imbedded in a little Pahlavi text praising Seistan there is a statement that King Vištasp first began propagating the faith there, and only thereafter in other lands.[108] This statement follows others about the Saošyant which continue the local tradition celebrated in *Yašt* 19; and it flatly contradicts Balkh's claim in this respect, as recorded in the *Shahnama*, and may indeed have been made to counter it. These Seistani claims found acknowledgement in their turn, although not prominently, in the *zand*; but the statement there that Lake Frazdanu (by which, according to *Yt.* 5:108, Vištaspa sacrificed) was in Seistan has plainly no more factual validity than the other statement that Lake Chaechasta was in Azarbaijan.[109] This does not mean that the original Lakes Frazdanu and Chaechasta were therefore "mythical", but rather that their identification with lakes in the settled Iranian lands was secondary and relatively late, a product of the contending pieties of post-Achaemenian times.

It is noteworthy that, despite such rivalries, not a single one of these eastern Iranian lands put forward a claim to be Eranvez, Zoroaster's own homeland. It is Vištaspa and the other *kavis* who are locally annexed, while the prophet comes from elsewhere, explicitly said in the *Zaratušt Nama* to be outside Iran. This common reluctance to make the full claim to be the Zoroastrian holy land is in striking contrast to the boldness of western Atropatene, and suggests the persistence among the older communities of the east of a tradition that the prophet's home lay somewhere far away.

Just one group is known to have shared Atropatene's audacity, and they were not Iranians at all, but priests of Atargatis' great shrine at Mabug (Bambyce, Greek Hieropolis) in north Syria. They identified one of their many temple statues (originally, it is said, that of a god named Hadan) as representing Zoroaster; and they told how the Iranian prophet had practised the Magian craft there by exorcising a demon which haunted a well. They also claimed that it was in the forests around Mabug that he had wandered alone in his quest for enlightenment.[110] The Mabug legend too appears to have been invented in Hellenistic times, for in it Zoroaster is associated with Orpheus, seen as his fellow-magus. Atargatis' priests evidently had some knowledge of the legendary life of the prophet, and doubtless harboured some real awe of him as a remote, mysterious figure with occult powers. This was presumably a legacy from Achaemenian days, when Zoroastrian kings ruled Syria and Iranians and their magi settled there in numbers. After the Macedonian conquest descendants of these colonists continued to live there and in neighbouring Commagene and Cilicia, and the priests of Mabug evidently then felt free to try to attract them as well as all the others who visited their shrine. According to Lucian, writing in the second century A.C., pilgrims came even from Media, bearing gifts;[111] and no doubt they and their fellow-Zoroastrians were happy to be provided with a pious reason for travelling to so famous and splendid a sanctuary, and were probably not unduly troubled to find themselves in the footsteps of their prophet there as well as in Atropatene.

In Hellenistic times Zoroaster also came to be regarded as having belonged to Babylon;[112] but this idea does not seem to have been based on a claim put forward by the numerous magi who lived there, but to have developed rather in the thoughts of Greeks. They had come to consider the Iranian prophet as the great teacher of astronomy, a knowledge which they associated with both the native priests of Babylonia and the magi, who in this had been pupils of the former. So Zoroaster, being for them the first and greatest magus, was sometimes assigned to Babylon and called a Chaldaean.

During the Macedonian-Parthian periods - or to put it in terms more generally familiar, in Greco-Roman times - a whole set of conflicting legends thus came into existence about Zoroaster and the scene of his religious activity, those recorded within Iran itself being from Atropatene, Parthia, Bactria, Sogdia and Drangiana (Seistan), with a single trace of one also from Margiana (Marv). Plainly the local priesthoods which evolved these legends had no interest in seeking to reconcile them, each being concerned to promote the sanctity and renown of its own shrines; and this task was left to scholar-priests in the later Sasanian period. By then the revolutionary step had been taken of writing down the holy texts, and the compilation was in progress of the *Khwaday Namag*, "Book of Kings", a hugely influential work of religio-political propaganda on behalf of the Sasanian dynasty and Zoroastrian faith. To get materials for its early sections (in the absence of any historical records for pre-Achaemenian times) the compilers drew on ancient myths and legends, and more recent local traditions, the latter especially, as we have seen, from Media (geographically and historically close to Persia) and the north-east (an area then of lively political concern to the Sasanians).[113]

By recording these materials the compilers of the *Khwaday Namag* provided new data for those of their brethren who were studying and commenting on the Avesta. The latter were evidently conscientious and careful men, who were heavily handicapped by their lack of historical perspective and critical training. Systematization, and bringing together data which might aid understanding of the holy texts, were very much their preoccupations; and, as we have seen, it was their ponderings on the shrine-legend of Bactrian Adar Noš, and their combining of this with materials from the Avestan life of the prophet, which gave rise to the story of Zoroaster's death at the hands of Bratrores. Another matter that called for reflection was the incompatibility of the claims of Balkh and Azarbaijan concerning the prophet, and there are indications that some magi sought to reconcile them by saying that Zoroaster was born in Azarbaijan and journeyed from there to Vištasp's court in Balkh. This venture at explanation is clearly attested only by Muslim writers,[114] but in the *zand* indications for it come perhaps in connection with the two occurrences of the place-name Ragha, both of which the commentators took to refer to the Median city, Raga. At *Vendidad* 1:15 Ragha is glossed as

"Azarbaijan. Some say Ray. ... There are those who say thus, that Zoroaster was from there" (*ādarbādagān. ast kē rayy gōwēd .... ast kē ēdōn gōwēd, ē zardušt az ān gyāg būd*).[115] Then at *Yasna* 19:18 the statement that there Zoroaster was the fourth "master" (*ratu*) is explained as follows: "That is, when he was in his own land, then truly he took the occasion and was fourth over it" (*ē ka pad deh ī xwēš būd, a-š zamān grift-iz ud tasom abar būd*).[116] The implication of these commentaries appears to be that some thought that Zoroaster was "from", i.e. born in, Adarbayagan, otherwise Ray (which in the late Sasanian period belonged to the north-west quarter of Iran, named after its chief region, Azarbaijan);[117]   and that he revisited this, "his own land", on occasion, but was also active elsewhere - presumably Balkh.   In the *Shahrestaniha i Eran* it is said positively of Ray, without any of the caution of the Avesta commentators, that Zoroaster "was from that city" (*az ān šahrestān būd*).[118]

The attempt to harmonize the claims of Media and Bactria conflicted with another which tried to unite the Median sanctities of Ray and Azarbaijan. According to this, Zoroaster's father was from Azarbaijan, his mother from Ray. This explanation was based on the story in the legend of the prophet's life that his mother was driven from her family home by the plottings of demons, and made her way from there to the land of the Spitamas.[119] It is attested, however, by only one Muslim writer,[120] so there is no means of telling when it was first put forward, or how much credence it obtained.

With such use being made by Zoroastrian scholastics of the relatively late and conflicting legends evolved by temple priests, the confusion over Zoroaster's homeland and place of activity became complete. Muslim writers recorded much of the material, and the *Shahnama* contributed greatly to establishing Balkh's claim. Yet when, centuries later, modern scholars came to struggle with the problem, a majority at first accepted that of Azarbaijan, as the most detailed; and when in due course this was rejected as impossible, champions came forward for most other regions - Ray, Balkh, Marw, Seistan, even silent Khwarezm. The only land whose claim failed to win any serious advocacy was Parthia, although its legends are well attested. This was both because of the effectiveness of the anti-Parthian propaganda of late Sasanian times, and because in the *Shahnama* the Parthian legends are swallowed up by those of Balkh.

When all the data are gathered together, it is satisfying to be able to deduce that there is not in fact a scrap of historical truth in any of these claims. None of them can reasonably be held to go back to before the Macedonian conquest; and the scholastic use made of them in the *zand* and other Pahlavi works has merely given a spurious appearance of authenticity to these products of local myth-making. It is thus possible to turn back to the Avesta and to conclude from it, as a scholar concluded already over half a century ago, that the one genuine Zoroastrian tradition about the homeland of the prophet, Airyana Vaejah, was that this lay outside the settled Iranian lands, somewhere far away to the north.[121]

The harm done to the study of Zoroastrianism by the abundance of these regional claims has been considerable. Much scholarly time has been diverted into investigating them individually, and into championing now this one, now that; and together they have fostered for many the illusion that somewhere amid all this confusion and contradiction must lie the truth, hence that Zoroaster must have lived somewhere within the borders of Greater Iran. This supposition has then affected considerations about when it was that he lived. Over this there was much less concern in antiquity among the Zoroastrians themselves, for dates had no value in their tradition. Interest in chronology appears to have been restricted to priestly scholastics, and even for them it only developed, it is generally agreed, through contacts between the magi and Babylonians and Greeks.

When the Seleucids established the first fixed era in human history, dated from Seleucus' acquisition of power in 312 B.C., they gave a stimulus to chronological calculations generally; but the two dates proposed by the Greeks for Zoroaster were by origin independent of this. Towards the end of the Achaemenian period in the school of Plato the prophet had been assigned to "5000 years before the Trojan war", that is, to c. 6000 B.C., while during Hellenistic times another date gained credence of "258 years before Alexander", i.e. before the Seleucid era, that is, 570 B.C. The basis for this more modest reckoning, it has been convincingly shown,[122] was a fiction, most probably launched as such in the latter part of the fourth century B.C. by Heraclides of Pontus, that Pythagoras had studied with Zoroaster in Babylon. This fiction was then developed, it seems, as fact by Heraclides' younger contemporary, Aristoxenus, and was in due course incorporated in the general chronology created by Apollodorus in the second century B.C. It is to his system that, ultimately, the curious formulation that "Zoroaster was 258 years before Alexander" is to be traced. This date for the Iranian prophet evidently gained credence among those interested in chronological matters, and was eventually adopted by Magian scholastics themselves, doubtless to fill what they had come to regard as a lack in their own tradition. It accordingly underlies various chronological reckonings which appear in the Pahlavi books, where it was discovered for Western academics in the latter part of the nineteenth century. The contexts convinced some that this was a "traditional" date among the Zoroastrians, worthy therefore of acceptance,[123] while others rejected it from the outset as far too recent to be credible.[124] Again, therefore, valuable scholarly time was spent in barren controversy, with confusing distortions of Zoroastrian history being proposed to justify the 570 B.C. date.[125] But now that the wholly artificial nature of this date has been fully demonstrated, it is possible finally to dismiss it as being as worthless historically as are the various conflicting local claims to have been the scene of Zoroaster's activity.

NOTES

1 Since "Arya" (Av. "Airya") was the general name used for themselves by all the I.E. peoples of ancient India and Iran, it remains a problem why it should also have been used particularly by Zoroaster's people to distinguish themselves from other "Aryan" tribes. On the usages of the word see latterly H.W. Bailey, "Arya", *EIr.* II 681-3; R. Schmitt, "Aryans", ib., 684-7; Gnoli, *The idea of Iran*, passim.

2 Cf. Markwart, *Wehrot und Arang*, 126.

3 There had been an Av. *zand* of glosses, some of which survive through having become incorporated in the Av. text; and presumably there were *zands* in various Middle Iranian languages, of which only the Middle Persian one survives, being known therefore as "the" *zand*.

4 See E. Benveniste, "L'Ērān-vēž et l'origine légendaire des Iraniens", *BSOS* VII, 1934, 265-74; Gnoli, o.c., pp.38-40. Slightly differently K. Hoffmann-J. Narten, *Sas. Archetypus*, 85 n.32, who translate *vaējah* as "flood of water", although supposing a secondary meaning of "seasonally flooded plain". Vanhvi Daitya, apparently signifying "the good Law-Abiding-One", they explain by suggesting that the river earned itself this name by the regularity of its seasonal overflowing.

5 *Y.* 9:14.

6 *WZ* 21:1-8 (where "Ērān" is to be emended to "Ērānvēz"); 22:1, 7.

7 *GBd.* 35:54; *PRDd.* 47:3.

8 *Vd* 19:2.

9 *Yt* 5:104.

10 This Zoroastrian concept is reflected in a Sogdian Manichaean text, where "Aryan Waižan" is set at the foot of Mt. Sumeru, the Indian equivalent of Hara (W. B. Henning, "The Book of the Giants", *BSOAS* XI, 1943, 68 = *Selected Papers,* II 131). There is nothing to suggest that there was any geographical reality behind the idea. The concept of Hara was evidently deeply imprinted in Iranian imagination, and different Iranian tribes identified the world-mountain and its associated and equally mythical mountain chain with various high mountains and ranges which they encountered in their migrations, notably the "Alborz" (< *Hara berezaiti*) range in northern Iran, and, it seems, some peak in the Hindu Kush, according to the *Mihr Yašt*, v.13. Gnoli, arguing for Zoroaster's homeland having been in settled Iranian territory, regards the place-name Airyana Vaejah as a creation of the Young Avestan period, and sees it as having belonged originally to one of the lands dominated by this Hindu Kush peak (o.c., p.40 f.); and he suggests that its river and the peak of Hara shared (in Pahlavi texts) the epithet *dāidīg* "lawful" as "evoking the idea of the 'law' promulgated by the prophet". This hypothesis seems in every way shaky.

11 *GBd.* 1a:12, 13; *WZ* 2:8. Cf. *PRDd.* 46:15. There (46:13) the Plant is also explicitly said to have been created in Ērānvēz.

12 *GBd.* 13:4; *Ind.Bd.* 14:3-4; *WZ* 3:50-1.

13 *Vd* 2:20-1.

14   On the *YHapt.* as Zoroaster's own composition see below, p.87 ff.

15   *Yt* 10:13.

16   Ib., v.14.   These two verses have been much discussed.   See in detail Gershevitch, *AHM*, 172-6, Gnoli, "Airyō.šayana", *RSO* XLI, 1966, 67-75; *Sistan*, 83-4; *ZTH*, 84-90.

17   On this see principally Christensen, *Premier chapitre du Vd*; Gnoli, *ZTH*, 23-90 (with references to his own earlier studies); D. Monchi-Zadeh, *Topographisch-historische Studien zum iranischen Nationalepos*, Wiesbaden 1975 (discussed in detail by Gnoli in *ZTH*, Ch.I).

18   See Gershevitch, "Zoroaster's own contribution", *JNES* XXIII, 1964, 36-7; and most recently Gnoli, "Ragha la zoroastriana", *Acta Ir.* 24, 1985, 217-28.   Otherwise Humbach, *Western approach*, 18-19.

19   See Gnoli, *ZTH*, 88-127; *De Z. à M.*, 18-19; *Idea of Iran*, 42 ff.; Humbach, *Western approach*, 19-28, and "About Gōpatšāh, his country, and the Khwarezmian hypothesis", *Acta Ir.* 24, 1985, 327-34; MacKenzie, *East and West* 38, 1988, 81 ff.

20   See Christensen, o.c., pp. 23-8.

21   Humbach, *Western approach*, 15-16, suggested instead that this description referred to a part only of Airyana Vaejah, "a summer pasture high in the mountains not far from the source of the river Vanhvi", whereas Gnoli, *Idea of Iran*, 40 f., set the whole country high under the Hindu Kush.   Neither theory accounts for the fact that Airyana Vaejah was not given a place originally in *Vd* I among the other eastern Iranian lands.

22   *WZ* 20:2-3.   Another, later, version of this story in the *Zaratušt Nama* (ed. F. Rosenberg), 1.461 ff., is assimilated to the standard Zoroastrian concept of the north as wicked; for according to it Zoroaster dreams of a fierce army coming from the north, and another from the south which routs it.   The army from the north, it is explained to him by Ahura Mazda, represents the forces of evil, that from the south Medyomah who, accepting the religion from Zoroaster, will be able by reciting Avesta to defeat them.

23   E.g., strikingly, *MX* 44:17-35.

24   *Y.* 46:1.

25   *Y.* 51:16-18; 53:1-2.   Kellens-Pirart, *TVA* 9, by the strict application of a syntactical law to an admittedly awkward Gathic phrase (*Y.* 53:2b) deduced that Vištaspa was Zoroaster's son.   This comical flouting of the whole Zoroastrian tradition is irreconcilable with *Y.* 46:1, but this verse, they suggested (agreeing in this with Humbach), should not be understood to mean what it has generally been supposed to.

26   *Yt* 5:112; 9:29.

27   Henning, art. cit. in n.10, p.73 (text U 2-4) = *Selected Papers* II, 136.

28   *Yt* 19:91-2.

29   See the passages of *zand* translation in *GBd.* 33:36-8, 25:56-60; put together with comments in *Sources*, 90-1.

30   V.66 (*upaŋhacaiti yō avaδaṭ fraxšayeite yaθa zrayō yaṭ kạsaēm haētumatəm*).

31   V.67, on which see Gnoli, *ZTH*, 27-30; Monchi-Zadeh, o.c. in n.17, p.120 ff.

32   Such materials were naturally easily incorporated in the text as long as it remained in fluid oral transmission.

33   For references see *HZ* III 151 n.139, 452 n.447.

34   *Y.*43:3 (as tr. by S. Insler, *Gāthās*, 61); cf. also Lommel, *Rel.*, 229 on *Y.* 53:2.

35   See the commentary on the statement in *ZVYt* 7:2 that the first Saošyant will be

born at Lake Frazdan: "(Know that there was one) who said at Lake Kayansih. There was one who (said) in Kabulistan". *GBd.* 35:60 has the prophet's seed entrusted by Neryosang simply to Anahit, that is, to the Yazata of waters.

36 In *Yt* 19 it is indeed possessed by the *kavis* themselves, who are individually named (vv.70-74, 84), but also by the mythical heroes Haošyanha, Takhma Urupi and Yima (vv.26, 28, 31), as well as by Zoroaster (v.79) and by his future son, the Saošyant (v.89). Nevertheless, a number of scholars have been led by this expression, supported by the *zand* gloss in *GBd.* XI.c:5, *Ind.Bd.* XXI:7, to suppose that *Yt* 19:66 "recognizes that the Kavi dynasty came from Seistan" (Jackson, *Zoroaster,* 218).

37 For an analysis of these sources, with detailed references, see *HZ* III 71 ff. Much of the material is collected by Jackson, *Zoroaster,* 193-201. See earlier R.J.H. Gottheil, "References to Zoroaster in Syriac and Arabic literature", *Classical Studies in honour of H. Drisler,* New York/London 1894, 24-51; and, for the Muslim references only, C.E. Bosworth, *EIr.* III 225.

38 G. Le Strange, *Eastern Caliphate,* 165-6.

39 *Vd* 19:4. Cf. *GBd.* 17:16.

40 On this fire, with references for what follows, see Boyce, *EIr.* I 475-6; *HZ* III 74 ff.

41 *Yt* 19:5.

42 *Yt* 5:49.

43 This story, preserved in the *Shahnama* (Beroukhim ed., Tehran 1314/1935, V p.1386 ff.; tr. Warner, IV, p.259 ff.) appears to have evolved from *Yt* 5:49 and *Yt* 19:77 with *Yt* 9:18, see *HZ* III 73, and further below.

44 See W. Kleiss, *EIr.* III 219.

45 See above, p.3 with n.18.

46 E.g., *Ny.* 5:5, constituted to make possible the veneration liturgically of Adur Gušnasp. The Pahl. commentary makes clear the significance of the juxtapositions here of Av. phrases, see Dhabhar, *ZXA,* text p.38, tr. pp.67-8; Taraf, *Der Avesta Text Niyāyiš,* pp.98/99.

47 This is shown by the *zand* gloss to *Vd* 1:15, see pp.18-19.

48 The four classes are a mark of a later date, since the old social classification had only three.

49 See Bartholomae, *Air.Wb* 1677.

50 So Markwart, *Ērānšahr,* 122-3. Others, including Bartholomae (*Air.Wb.* 1671) have taken "Zarathuštra" here to imply the prophet's actual presence in Raga.

51 See Boyce, "Bibi Shahrbānū and the Lady of Pārs", *BSOAS* XXX, 1967, 30-44.

52 Nyberg, *Rel.,* 5-6, 46, 342-3, 396-7; Boyce, *HZ* II 8-9; Gnoli, *Acta Ir.* 24, 1985, 226-7.

53 The district around, from which it took its name, continued to be known as Raga (see Markwart, o.c., p.123), and indeed the town's own old name was never abandoned, being Rhages to the Greeks.

54 On him see M.L. Chaumont, *EIr.* III 17-18; Boyce, *HZ* III 69.

55 There was a tradition that Adur Gušnasp was moved, see Schippmann, *Feuerheiligtümer,* 354; Boyce, *HZ* III 75. This appears undoubtedly to have been the case in the 5th century A.C. (from Ganzak to Takht-i Suleiman). Whether there was an earlier move (from Raga to Ganzak) remains a matter for reasoned speculation; but the great

antiquity attributed to this fire suggests the likelihood that it was established already in or near Raga under the Achaemenians.

56   For a different explanation see Herzfeld, *Zoroaster*, I 65.

57   Claims to Avestan connections within Persia (see, e.g., Jackson, *Zoroaster*, 219-20) appear both sporadic and late, belonging to a period when such claims were being made almost automatically.

58   See K. Schippmann, *EIr*. III 222.

59   *GBd*. 18:14; cf. *WZ* 23:6; *PRDd*. 47:12.

60   *Dk*. 7:4:75-8 (Molé, *Légende*, 57/8).

61   *GBd*. 9:37; *Ind.Bd*. 12:34; cf. *WZ* 3:85; *PRDd*. 46:35.

62   *Yt* 19:6 (Raēvant).

63   The ruins of a fire temple have been partly excavated on the spur in question, but there is not the absolute certainty over their identification that there is over that of the ruins of Adur Gušnasp's temple on Takht-i Suleiman, where inscriptions with the fire's name have been found.

64   *GBd*. 9:35-7; *Ind. Bd*. 12:32 (West, *SBE* V, 40 with n.4).

65   *Yt* 5:109, 113, 116-17; 9:30; 17:50.

66   These are oddly ignored by its latest editor, D. Monchi-Zadeh (*Die Geschichte Zarēr's*, Uppsala 1981), but see the review of his book by D. N. MacKenzie, *IIJ* 27, 1984, 155-63.

67   *AZ* 19.

68   Monchi-Zadeh's interpretation, endorsed by MacKenzie, art. cit., q.v., pp.157-8, for the translation of the passage.

69   Markwart, *Provincial Capitals*, 8-9.

70   Ed. Rosenberg, ll.14-57. He probably in fact used more than one Pahlavi source, see West, *SBE* XLVII, xxiv.

71   Ib., l.442 (his wish to travel to Iran), l.728 (Balkh his goal there).

72   *Shahnama*, ed. Beroukhim, VI p.1446 ll.19-22; tr. Warner, IV pp.317-18. The Parthian fire appears variously in the epic, according to the exigencies of metre and rhyme, as Mihr Barzīn, Mihr, or Barzīn.

73   Ib., V p.1499 ll.61-2; Warner, V p.34.

74   Ib., V p.1499 ll.75-8; Warner, V p.35.

75   For references see Le Strange, *Eastern Caliphate*, 355-6. Qazvini's account was elaborated on in the 16th century forgery, the *Dabistan*.

76   A detailed comparison of the two accounts was first made by the Warners, V pp. 24-7.

77   *Shahnama*, V p.1514 l.309; Warner, V p.48.

78   Ib., V p.1551 ll.961-2; Warner, V p.85.

79   Ib., V p.1559 ll.1097-9, p.1560 ll.1112-13; Warner, V pp.92, 93. There are no significant variants in the Moscow edition (Vol. VI, pp.141, 142).

80   Ib., V p.1638 l.2505, p.1709 l.3748; Warner, V pp.173, 241. The name Noš Adar is given in the *Shahnama* to Isfandiyar's fourth son, and in one passage (ib., V p.1548 l.892, Warner, V p.81) this prince is said to have founded the great fire. It is, however, a well-attested usage of the Sasanian period to name children for sacred fires, as for Yazatas; and if, as seems likely, this son of Isfandiyar is a purely fictional character,

the practice may have suggested a name for him, for which subsequently a different explanation was found.

81   Ib., V p.1723 l.3997, Warner, V p.255.

82   This interpretation was made explicit in the prose *Shahnama*, see T. Hyde apud Jackson, *Zoroaster*, 130.

83   For instances of *ratu*, *rad* being used for one in ecclesiastical authority see Bartholomae, *Air. Wb.* 1502. The incident is referred to again by Jamasp, when he is trying to rouse the deeply devout Isfandiyar to avenge it (text, V p.1566 ll.1224-7, Warner, V pp.99-100); but even in those circumstances he speaks only of the deaths of Lohrasp and the 80 priests. Their *rad* was evidently not so significantly more important than they to be separately mentioned.

84   *Dk.* 7:5:1, cf. 6:1 (Molé, *Légende*, 62/3, 66/7). Passages concerning Zoroaster's death, in Pahl. and Persian literature, were brought together by West, *SBE* XLVII, xix; Geiger, *Eastern Iranians*, II 215-17; Jackson, *Zoroaster*, 127-32.

85   *WZ* 20:4-11.

86   The tense here too changes, with a clumsy past (*NKTLWNyhst*) instead of a future.

87   *Saddar Bd.* 35:3 (ed. Dhabhar, p.103; tr. Dhabhar, *Riv.*, p.527).

88   See J.-P. de Menasce, *Une encyclopédie mazdéenne, Le Dēnkart,* Paris 1958, 29-34.

89   *Dk.* 5:3:2 (Molé, *Légende*, 110/11).

90   A.V. Williams, ed., *PRDd.*, note to Ch. 36:6.

91   *GBd.* 33:30.

92   See Bartholomae, *Air.Wb.* 1147; West, *SBE* XLVII, 108 with n.1.

93   *ZVYt* 3:3.

94   *PRDd.* 36:6.

95   *Dd., Pursišn* 71 (ed. P.K. Anklesaria, London University thesis, 1958, 141, tr. West, *SBE* XVIII, 218).

96   *Saddar Bd.* 9:5 (ed. Dhabhar, p.8, tr. West, *SBE* XXIV, 267-8).

97   *PRDd.* 47:23.

98   Although the story of the sacking of Adar Noš' temple is known only from the *Shahnama*, the fact that Ṭabari and Masʿudi both say that it was in Balkh that Zoroaster found Vištasp suggests that the Balkh claim as a whole was incorporated in the *Khwaday Namag.*

99   *AZ* 17 et pass.

100   *Shahnama*, V p.1497 l.36 et pass.

101   See E. Yarshater, "Afrāsiāb" and A. Tafazzoli, "Arjāsp", *EIr.* II 570-6, 412.

102   The basic text is *Dk.* 7:3:20 ff. (Molé, *Légende*, 32/33 ff.)

103   *Dk.* 7:3:45.

104   *Dk.* 7:3:27.

105   Text and tr. in Dhabhar, *Riv.*, 72.

106   Paras. 2-5.

107   See Nyberg, *Rel.*, 425-6.

108   *Abdīh ud sahīgīh ī Sagestān* 9, *Pahlavi Texts*, ed. Jamasp Asana, p.26; tr. Bailey, *Zor. Problems*, 161; B. Utas in *From Hecataeus to al-Ḫuwārizmī*, ed. J. Harmatta,

Budapest 1986, 263.

109 *GBd.* 12:3, 6; *Ind. Bd.* 22:2, 5. On Lake Chaechasta's identification with Lake Urmia see in more detail in *HZ* III 73-4, 77-8.

110 The authority, Pseudo-Meliton, is a Syriac text held to have been composed at Mabug under Caracalla or Eliogabalus. See Bidez-Cumont, *Mages hellenisés*, I 39, II 94-5; A.H. Harmon, ed., Loeb ed. of works of Lucian, IV 354 n.; *HZ* III 356-7.

111 *De dea Syria*, 32.

112 See Bidez-Cumont, o.c., I 36.

113 E. Yarshater has convincingly argued (*CHIr.* 3(1) 390-1) that, contrary to the theory put forward earlier by the present writer, the Kayanian legend, mingled with Parthian traditions, had become widely known in Iran already under the Arsacids. Confusion between the shrine-legends of the most sacred Parthian and Bactrian fires can hardly have developed, however, before fairly late in the Sasanian period.

114 Mas'udi, *Les Prairies d'Or,* tr. Barbier de Meynard, ed. C. Pellat, Paris 1962-71, II 203 (para. 547). Similarly Ṭabari, *Annales*, Pt.I p.648. See further apud Jackson, *Zoroaster*, 199.

115 *Pahlavi Vendidad*, ed. B.T. Anklesaria, Bombay 1949, 10-11. In *GBd.* 31 (which consists of the *zand* of *Vd* I) in para. 28 the gloss on Ray is simply *ī ast ādarbādagān* "which is Azarbaijan".

116 *Pahlavi Yasna and Visperad,* ed. B.N. Dhabhar, Bombay 1949, 108.

117 Christensen, *Premier Chapitre*, 43-4.

118 Para. 60, ed. Markwart, p.23, with his judicious note, p.113.

119 *Dk.* 7:2:3-11. (Molé, *Légende*, 14/15, 16/17.)

120 Shahrastani, *Religionspartheien und Philosophie-Schulen,* tr. T. Haarbrücker, Halle 1850, repr. Hildesheim 1969, I 280.

121 So Markwart, see n.2.

122 See P. Kingsley, "The Greek origin of the sixth-century dating of Zoroaster", *BSOAS* LIII, 1990, 245-65.

123 See the admirably scholarly exposition by E.W. West, *SBE* XLVII, xxviii ff., with arguments, however, against its authenticity, p.xlii.

124 For a bibliography of some of the leading opponents of this dating, both 19th-century and more recent, see Gnoli, *De Z. à M.*, 38-9 with nn.26-30.

125 The most thorough attempt to reconcile this late date with other facts was that made by Darmesteter, who was driven thereby to suppose (*ZA* III lxxxv-xci) that the *Gathas* were composed in the 2nd century A.C. The startling nature of this conclusion by so great a scholar was in itself a demonstration of the impossibility of the 6th-century date.

CHAPTER TWO

Zoroaster's Actual
Time and Homeland

In 1897 a scholar who did much to bring the sixth-century date for Zoroaster to the attention of Western academics, being inclined to regard it as genuine, conceded nevertheless that "at present we have no really historical information about the origin of Zoroastrianism, and must still consider it as decidedly prehistoric".[1] Almost a century later this observation still holds good, with no possibility of discovering a precise date for its founder. All that can be hoped for is to establish approximate boundaries of time and space within which he is likely to have lived; but this endeavour, however limited its aim, remains vital for the understanding of his teachings, since every prophet belongs in large measure to his own place and age.[2]

The main source of information is the Avesta, and within it primarily the small body of Old Avestan texts, since these are Zoroaster's own utterances.[3] Data gleaned from them can usefully be correlated with others from the Rigveda, and with the ever more abundant discoveries of archaeologists and ethnographers.

To begin with the Avesta as a whole, it is accepted that this composite body of texts belongs to the "eastern" Iranians, that is, to those tribes which settled in the eastern parts of Greater Iran; for nowhere in it is any knowledge shown of western Iran or the peoples who settled there. As we have seen (in connection with Median Raga) the western magi, when eventually they received the faith from the east, appear not to have felt able to add any substantially new matter to its holy texts, and did not even introduce any direct references to major religious developments which took place thereafter. Instead they contented themselves, when they felt the need, with altering old texts in small particulars, or adding a few words or sentences here and there in halting or imitative Avestan; or, on a larger scale, with extending texts or creating "new" ones by repetition, or by putting ancient passages together in fresh combinations. The fact that they were prepared to do all this suggests that it was not piety alone which held them back from composing more freely in Avestan; and the probably explanation of their reserve is that they had no training in doing so - that Avestan was already a dead church language even for the eastern Iranians before the faith was carried to the west. This would mean that the texts which then existed were already all being memorized and transmitted in more or less fixed form (as distinct from being handed down in a fluid oral tradition, that is, partly composed afresh, from inherited elements, by each generation of priest-poets). The marked unevennesses to be found linguistically between different parts of the Young Avesta may therefore arise from the differing degrees of sanctity with which they were invested, those which were the most highly regarded being the most carefully memorized and often recited. Some presumably, like the *Gathas* and other Old Avestan texts, were learnt by all priests throughout the Zoroastrian community, whereas others were perhaps preserved only locally down to the third century A.C., when all the texts of the existing canon were finally collected together - still in oral transmission - under the first Sasanian king.[4]

It now seems probable that members of the Achaemenian family were Zoroastrians from at least the time of Cyrus the Great, that is, from the mid sixth century B.C.[5]   They, like other Persians, appear to have acquired the faith from the Median magi,[6] who can therefore themselves hardly have adopted it later than 700.   The Young Avestan texts must therefore have received their essential forms before that date, hence the language of those which were carefully memorized - notably parts of the great *Yašts* - must represent Avestan at a stage considerably earlier than the language of the Old Persian inscriptions. This is in no way surprising, since the latter is much more evolved. (This fact is not, however, in itself of strong evidential value, since even in the same area languages can develop erratically. Thus a number of western Iranian dialects maintain to this day linguistic features which are more archaic than corresponding ones in Old Persian.[7])

Some of the Young Avestan texts contain matter for which close parallels can be found in the Rigveda, and which must originate accordingly in proto-Indo-Iranian times.   These verses of ancient substance, expressing traditional concepts of the gods to whom they were addressed, form the core of the great *Yašts*; and to them other matter was presumably added by each generation of poet-priests, to become partly forgotten again in favour of still later verses, the process being one of gradual loss and slow accretion over centuries. In the surviving Avesta this process can be traced most clearly in the *Farvardin Yašt*. In this, among verses which appear very archaic (that is, pre-Zoroastrian) in character, is imbedded a muster-roll of names of individual Zoroastrians, illustrious upholders of the faith whose spirits, *fravašis*, are to be venerated. Few of the names recur in later Zoroastrian usage, and their unfamiliarity suggests the remoteness in time of those who bore them.[8]   Among them is that of Saena, son of Ahum-stut, to whose *fravaši* reverence is offered in verse 97. In verse 126 the *fravaši* is revered of a man who, it is reasonable to assume, was his great-grandson, namely Utayuti son of Vitkavi son of Zighri son of Saena.[9] Hence, allowing for the usual 30 years to a generation, verse 126 may be reckoned to have been added to the *Yašt* some ninety years after verse 97, with the composition of the whole list of names spanning a period of some 100-150 years.

In addition to archaic proper names, there occur in this and other old *Yašts* a number of tribal and place names which are otherwise unknown.[10] This is consonant with the verses containing them having been composed well before the eastern Iranians entered history through being absorbed into the Achaemenian empire. Among the regions which the Persians conquered in the sixth century was Drangiana, once ruled by the nameless prince of *Yašt* 19:66; but this prince himself is likely to have lived well before that event, to allow for the legend of the Saošyant (to which most probably he gave his patronage) becoming firmly attached to that locality during a time of its independence.[11] All this fits with the supposition that the great *Yašts* slowly acquired more or less their existing forms during the ninth-eighth centuries, becoming essentially fixed by the end of that period.

If then one seeks to estimate the time that elapsed between the *Gathas* and these Young Avestan texts, Saena son of Ahum-stut provides once more a point of reference. He was famed as the first teacher of the Zoroastrian religion to have had a hundred pupils, "from which we learn that there had been previous teachers in the period since Zoroaster". Moreover, "the religion must have had a considerable development for such a number to be possible".[12] How long this development took is necessarily a matter for reasoned guesswork, but an estimate of 150-200 years has been made, taking one back to around 1100 B.C. as the "lowest possible date for the founding of the Zoroastrian religion"[13] - that is, for the lifetime of Zoroaster.

The linguistic evidence suggests that this may indeed be an under-estimate; for the Old Avestan language not only appears considerably older than Young Avestan, but has a few traits which are archaic even in comparison with Vedic.[14] The composition of the Rigveda is as impossible to pinpoint in time as that of the *Yašts*, since its hymns too were the work of generations of priest-poets, and likewise, as we have seen, contain matter going back well into proto-Indo-Iranian times; but a broad, fairly generally accepted, estimate is that hymns beginning to take the form in which they are known were being composed from about 1800 B.C., and that the first collections of such hymns (that is, the oldest Rigvedic *Maṇḍalas*, II-VII), were made about 1500, with the whole collection being complete by about 900.   On the basis of linguistic comparison with the Rigveda, the first Western scholar to identify the *Gathas* as Zoroaster's own words held that the prophet could not possibly have lived later than 1000 B.C.,[15] and various estimates followed setting him between 1700 and 1000, no one, naturally, seeking a precise date. As far as the purely linguistic evidence goes, there is the possibility that Old Avestan evolved more slowly than Vedic, since it was, it seems, spoken in Zoroaster's day by a relatively conservative community on the Inner Asian steppes, whereas the composers of the Vedic hymns had already left their northern homelands far behind them, meeting new conditions which may have quickened change. The setting of their hymns is in the north-west of the Indian sub-continent, and their verses express no recollection of any other land.[16] This means that the society which they reflect resembles in some respects less that of the *Gathas* than of the *Yašts*, whose authors likewise belonged to communities which had left the steppes and settled in new lands, evolving there new ways of life. Any social traits delineated in the Old Avestan texts are thus no less important than their language for the approximate dating of Zoroaster.

These texts - that is, the *Gathas*, two brief *manthras*, and the short "Worship of the seven chapters", *Yasna Haptanhaiti* - yield in fact some significant indications about the society in which the prophet lived. This appears to have considered itself ethnically homogeneous. There is no reference (as, occasionally, in the *Yašts*[17]) to alien people, *anairya-*. The few proper names are Iranian in character, and, despite some religious divergences, worship and cult appear to have had a common basis.[18] There is a firm social order, repeatedly referred to, whose units are the family (*khvaetu*) settlement (*vərəzana*) and clan (*airyaman*), the land claimed by the clan as its own being called *dahyu*.[19] Whether Airyana Vaejah (not mentioned in these texts, which in general lack place-names) was a single *dahyu*, or comprised several, there is no means of knowing. Nor can it be proved that kinship ties linked the members of *khvaetu*, *vərəzana* and *airyaman* together, but this seems highly probable, with a tracing back to some remote, possibly hypothetical, common ancestor. There are recurrent references to power, *khšathra*, exerted presumably in varying degrees by the heads of each of these groups; and special terms for those who wielded it on a large scale. One is *sastar,* "giver of commands, commander". This occurs in the plural in the phrase "commanders of the land"[20], and so is likely to have been used for petty chieftains. In contrast a reference to those who are "bad rulers (*duškhšathra-*) of the lands"[21] suggests that each *dahyu* had its own ruler, one in supreme authority.[22]

There is a general term for men of wealth and power, *ahu*, usually rendered as "lord, master";[23] but Old Avestan, unlike Young Avestan and Rigvedic, has no terms for social classes linked with different callings. These callings in the two later-evolved societies are those of priest, warrior/nobleman, and herdsman/farmer; and it is significant that the Vedic and YAv. sets of terms for them are quite different: *brahman, kṣatriya, vaiśya* against *athravan, rathaeštar, vastryo.fšuyant*. Since the two languages share a fairly large inheritance of ancient words, it is reasonable to suppose that these two divergent sets of terms evolved independently some time after their separation, in response to a new complexity developing in their societies.[24] It is further striking that on the one hand in both India and Iran the scheme of these three classes (with the addition in each country of a fourth for labourers, respectively *sudra* and *huiti*), continued to function adequately for a very long time as a theoretic social classification; and that on the other the Old Avestan classless groupings of family and clan repeat themselves as the basic pattern for all later Inner Asian steppe-dwellers, of whatever race or tongue, this being the form of society dictated by the region itself and how life there was lived.[25]

In accordance with this essentially simple social structure, Zoroaster addresses his hearers plainly as "men, women",[26] and uses the word *vastrya,* "herdsman", for the men of the community generally.[27] He also employs an evidently archaic compound term, *pasu-vira*, a formal dual meaning "cattle-(and)-men", for the community as a whole, the collectivity of men and beasts which formed the unit for living. This term survives as a fossilized one in Young Avestan,[28] but the enormous importance given to cattle in the *Gathas* shows that it still had real significance in Old Avestan times. In addition to numerous references to cow and bull - it seems both factual and metaphoric - there is mention there of horses and camels; and out of the eleven personal names which occur (excluding that of mythical Yima) six are compounded with the words for one or other of these animals: one with *gava* "cow" (*Hvogva*), two with *uštra* "camel" (*Zarathuštra, Fərašaoštra*), and three with *aspa* "horse" (*Vištaspa, Dəjamaspa, Haechat-aspa*).[29] These are the names of a pastoral people; and although similar ones (again predominantly compounded with *aspa*) are to be found in the *Farvardin Yašt*, already there they form only a small proportion of those listed.

All the animals concerned, as well as the economically important sheep and goats ("small cattle", too lowly, it seems, to earn separate mention) had long been domesticated on the steppes; and in southern Central Asia the camel and ox had been used to pull carts with solid wheels from the third millennium, this form of transport having been adopted from the Near East.[30] It was not, however, until about 1800 B.C. that the chariot was evolved, a much lighter, swifter vehicle with spoked wheels, drawn by horses and used for hunting, racing and in war.[31] The earliest known remains of such chariots on the Inner Asian steppes are dated to around 1600,[32] and it was perhaps the swiftness and power of horse-teams harnessed to these vehicles which captured the Avestan people's imagination and led to "horse" names being so often given among them.[33]   Chariot-racing seems to have become one of their chief pastimes, with the length of a race-course providing the two oldest Avestan land-measures (hathra, čarətu);[34] and a famous chariot-race is twice referred to in the Yašts, the victor being Kavi Haosravah, of an older generation than the prophet.[35]   Allusions in the Gathas show that Zoroaster himself shared his people's delight in the contests and in the speed of the teams. He calls horses the "swift ones" (asu-, aurvant-), and uses as metaphor harnessed horses racing ahead,[36] or imagines such teams pulling the wind and clouds,[37] while the charioteer (raithi-) furnishes him with a symbol for control and mastery.[38]

There is no mention of grain or tillage in the Gathas;[39] but even if farming was relatively unimportant, yielding no imagery for the poet, there is nothing in the prophet's words to indicate that, as pastoralists, his people were nomads. The actual terms for their dwelling and abiding places, dəmana-, šoithra-, could refer either to tents or to houses, to seasonal encampments or to permanent villages or townships; but Zoroaster's expressed longing for "peace in the dwelt-in abodes (šyeitibyō vižibyō)" has reasonably been interpreted as implying fixed settlements.[40] This accords with the finding of Soviet scholars, that nomadism belonged to a later stage of life on the steppes, when chariot-driving by the few (for this was a relatively costly matter) had yielded to the general riding of horses. This development gave the steppe-dwellers more mobility, and they took to keeping larger flocks and herds and to migrating seasonally in search of fresh pastures for them. The "five animals" (cow, sheep, goat, horse and camel) remained those of the steppe people throughout history;[41] but with nomadism the number of cows declined proportionately, since of the five they are the least able to travel far or to fend for themselves in harsh conditions.[42]   It is therefore reasonable to conclude that Zoroaster's own people, prizing their cows so highly and driving, not riding, horses, were settled pastoralists, living in a well-watered region with its own sufficient pastures, namely Airyana Vaejah of the good Daitya. Yašt allusions to the feats of Kavi Haosravah show that within Airyana Vaejah there were also forests. The names are given of three of them. One, called the "Forest of All the Airyas", may, it has been suggested, have had within it a sanctuary of the old Iranian religion, held sacred by all the Airyas and so a general meeting place for them. Another, called the "Whitely Forest", lay within the "Whitish Forests". These last two names, it is pointed out, conjure up forests of white-stemmed birches, which are characteristic not of Iran but of the Inner Asian steppes.[43]

There are few social indications in Yasna Haptanhaiti, but such as they are, they are in harmony with those in the Gathas. Thus one striking passage attests both the immense symbolic importance of the cow, and a general feeling for the closeness of man and beast. "So we reverence the Soul and Maker of the cow. Then we reverence our own souls and (those) of domestic animals ... and the souls of wild creatures, in so far as they are not harmful".[44] These words convey not only a strong sense of the *pasu-vira,* the community of men and their domesticated animals, but also a respect for the wild life around it, such as is found in a number of ancient and "primitive" societies where man has not imposed himself on the natural world to any marked degree.[45] On behalf of the humans themselves there is a prayer to Lord Mazda to "make men just, desiring what is just, herdsmen inflicting no harm".[46] In this there is the same reflection of a pastoral society as in the *Gathas,* with the same dominant desire for justice and for peace. There is again no distinction of occupation or class,[47] and the worshippers ask for these gifts "likewise for families, likewise for settlements",[48] indicating the Gathic pattern of society. Women are mentioned several times as if on an equal footing with men, both in this world and that of departed souls;[49] but perhaps the prominence given to them owes something to Zoroaster's own convictions, and the equal hope which he held out to men and women alike of achieving salvation.[50]

This picture of Old Avestan society, yielded by the texts themselves, accords well with what is known of the peoples who lived in the second half of the second millennium B.C. to the north of the Jaxartes. The vast area of steppe and desert, birch-forest, river and mountain, which corresponds to modern Kazakhstan, is in extent "roughly equal to that of all western Europe".[51] Objection has been made to assigning the Old Avestan people to somewhere in this wide expanse on the grounds that this is to place them in unknown territory, indeed in "a kind of vacuum";[52] but although little is as yet known of its inhabitants during the Stone Age there (sixth to third millennia B.C.), Soviet archaeologists have by now gathered a substantial amount of information about them in succeeding times.[53] In the second millennium three closely related material cultures, termed Abachevo, Srubnaya and Andronovo, have been identified over an immense area of grassland and wooded steppe, from eastern Europe across to western Siberia. Srubnaya (Timber-Frame) is named from the character of its graves, the other two from type-sites. The Abachevo settlements and graves are concentrated in the basin of the Don and along the right bank of the Volga, the Srubnaya ones extend from the left bank of the Volga to the river Ural, and those of the Andronovo culture from the river Ural eastwards to western Siberia. All three cultures have, however, much in common, and often blend confusingly in the minor points which are supposed to distinguish them, so that some archaeologists treat this hugely extensive steppe culture as essentially one, which they term Srubnaya-Andronovo, treating Abachevo (like yet other local manifestations) as a subform of it.[54]

The bearers of these material cultures are held to be peoples of diverse ethnic groups, some of them closely intermingled; and among those on the

Kazakhstan steppes were, it is widely thought, proto-Indo-Aryans and proto-Iranians. (Some of the skeletal remains there have been identified as Indo-European in character.[55]) Their Andronovo culture is seen as characterized by a settled pastoralism, with individual communities established most often in river valleys. Here the earth, through seasonal flooding, was soft enough for hoe cultivation, and the pastures provided good grazing. A little wheat and millet were grown, but stock-breeding was the chief source of livelihood. Bones of sheep, cows and horses were found in abundance, as well as those of camels, with the remains of wild animals being relatively few. The settlements were usually between ten to forty large houses. These were rectangular buildings, partly sunk in the ground, and there were sometimes many layers of occupation, showing that a site had been lived in for generations. (In contrast, the settlements of the Abachevo people to the west, who appear to have kept more livestock and to have adopted a more roving existence, have relatively few occupation layers.) Within the houses there were plank beds along the walls, hearths and storage pits. The remains of many clay vessels are another indication of a sedentary way of life, since "pottery is not compatible with nomadism".[56] Some of the cemeteries are correspondingly large. These are always a little way from the settlements (in contrast with the practice of indigenous communities south of the Jaxartes, where often the dead were disposed of in or near houses.) The graves were usually simple trenches dug in the ground, often bordered by stone slabs and covered with blocks of stone.[57] There is regular evidence of animal sacrifice at or near them, and usually they were furnished with goods to accompany the dead.

It is often graves which provide the archaeologist with most data; but these Kazakhstan ones were in most cases looted (sometimes already in antiquity) before scientific excavation took place. This was because this period saw the coming of the Bronze Age to the steppes, and metal goods attract grave-robbers. Copper and tin had been in daily use in lands to the south - Anatolia, Mesopotamia, Iran - from the latter part of the fifth millennium,[58] and copper objects (probably imported from Iran) have been found from that time in southern Turkmenistan (the cultures of Anau and Namazga I-III) and Transcaucasia.[59] For some reason, however, the steppe peoples remained unaffected, maintaining a Stone Age culture into early in the second millennium. Then quite swiftly, it seems, from around 1700, they took to using first copper, and then bronze, for weapons and tools, passing from a brief Chalceolithic into a Bronze Age. They also learnt to mine and work copper and tin extensively. These metals were to be found in the Urals, in Kazakhstan and in the Altai Mountains, and in some places were exploited on a large scale. Thus at Jezkazgan and Kenkazgan in Kazakhstan it is reckoned that tens of thousands of tons of copper ores were extracted, and it is thought that here and elsewhere there were probably villages inhabited solely by miners and metal workers.[60] Knowledge of how to smelt ore (instead of, as previously, merely beating cold metal into desired, usually ornamental, shapes) led the Iranians to adopt the use of molten metal, poured on bare flesh, as one form of judicial ordeal by fire - a form which was apparently known to Zoroaster, and laid strong hold on his imagination.

The most interesting excavation from the point of view of evidence for a steppe society akin to the Gathic one is that of a settlement in northern Kazakhstan, set in a bend of the Sintashta river in the province of Cheliabinsk on the south trans-Ural steppe.[61] It is this settlement whose graveyard has yielded the earliest evidence for the horse-drawn chariot on the steppes, and it has other unique features. Its inhabitants depended on a well-developed pastoralism, tending sheep and a few goats, cattle and horses, and practising a little farming. A number of dogs were kept, presumably chiefly for herding (though the bones of wild boar suggest some hunting also). In the excavated part of the settlement ten large houses were found, sunk up to a metre in the earth. These were set close together in two rows, with one "great house" among them. On the north side of the settlement, well away from it and the river, was the cemetery, whose graves, remarkably for this region, were of Srubnaya rather than Andronovo type. They consisted of timber-lined pits of unusual size, which had been dug laboriously out of thick clay with sticks; and here and there traces of posts were found which had held up their wooden roofs. This feature, making them like houses sunk in the ground, enabled the excavator to trace a poetic reference to such a grave-chamber in the Rigvedic hymn X:18.[62] Within the tombs, the dead were disposed of in a variety of ways: the body extended or flexed, on back or side or (once) face, and with instances of excarnated dismembered bones neatly piled together. Horse-bones were found in some men's graves, together with the traces of five chariots;[63] but apart from this, none of the tombs appears to have been especially richly furnished, and in character they were broadly uniform. This seems to match the nature of the settlement, with its large closely-packed houses, presumably each for what the Gathic people would have called a *khvaetu* or extended family, the one very large one being perhaps for the village chief and his kinsfolk, and for communal gatherings. The tombs themselves had been plundered of old, but some scores of humbler bronze objects were overlooked - socketed axes, knives, spear-heads, fish-hooks, bracelets. It is however a bone one - a bridle cheek-piece - which is regarded as the decisive chronological indicator, since it belongs to a group of such artifacts dated to the sixteenth century B.C.[64] Taken all together, the surviving evidence suggests a fairly homogeneous society, with some differences of wealth (to support the owning of chariots) but no marked social distinctions.

Among other striking features of this Sintashta community is the number of remains of animal sacrifices at or near the graves. These are very rarely of wild animals; and this accords with the widespread belief (shared by the Indo-Iranians) that only an offering made to the gods from one's own possessions, and so entailing a measure of loss, was truly meritorious and hence effective. What impressed the excavator was that the Sintashta people, living, it seems, almost wholly from their flocks and herds, were able and willing to sacrifice so many animals "at the burial of almost every member of the community", with there being found at some graves "two, four, and in a collective burial even seven horses".[65] In some instances the entire skeletons of horses and other animals (sheep, dogs, a calf) had been put in the earth covering the burial chambers; but usually only parts of animals, notably the skull and leg-bones, were placed in the graves themselves. (The practice of preserving skull and leg-bones is held to be linked with belief in bodily resurrection, widespread among primitive peoples.[66]) In addition, two shallow pits were found, "completely crammed with bones",[67] from which it was deduced that the flesh of sacrificed animals was eaten at funerary feasts held near the graves. In one of these pits a large vessel had been put mouth downwards among the bones, which perhaps, it has been suggested, held drink for such a feast. Or this may be an instance of a chthonic offering, such as is elsewhere recorded among the Indo-Iranians[68] (although then one might expect the pot to be set directly in the earth).

This abundance of sacrifices, together with the unusually large, laboriously dug graves, suggests a community for which the afterlife was a matter of great concern. The variety of ways of disposing of the corpse would seem, however, to indicate speculation and perhaps controversy about the fate which awaited the departed soul. There are other signs of diversity in this community, notably the shape and decoration of the hundred or so pots discovered, which suggest the presence of three distinct cultural traditions.[69] Possibly, therefore, different groups had joined to form this settlement, with Iranians perhaps dominant, and the use of their language creating unity. That it is likely to have been Iranians rather than Indo-Aryans in north Kazakhstan at this time can reasonably be deduced from the pattern of the Indo-Iranian migrations: accumulated evidence shows that it was the Indo-Aryans who first moved into the lands to the south, and this suggests that the Iranians lived to the north of them before the great migrations took place.[70] This interpretation of events is supported by the presence of ancient Iranian loanwords in the Finno-Ugrian languages spoken by peoples of the forest zone to the north of the steppes.

The deep occupation layers at the Sintashta settlement, the large houses and abundant pottery, all indicate a settled pastoralism, with the Stone Age evolving here, it seems, peacefully into that of Bronze. Some archaeologists have nevertheless termed the chariots there war-chariots, and on this basis alone have characterized the Sintashta people as bellicose. The use of the light horse-drawn chariot is attested, however, elsewhere for racing and hunting, or its possession could be largely a matter of prestige;[71] and the *Gathas* bear indirect witness to the peaceful enjoyment of it on the steppes also, for it is difficult to suppose that Zoroaster, with his passionate rejection of the war-bands' predatory way of life, would have had his imagination fired by the sight of horse-teams galloping into an attack.

Inferences from limited data clearly cannot be too much relied on; but in general the material remains of the Sintashta people, and the indications which these yield about their social and religious life, accord remarkably well with the relevant facts which can be gleaned from the *Gathas*. These hymns, it has justly been said, although composed at a prehistoric era, can nevertheless be regarded as quasi-historical documents, emanating as they do "from a human society come to a critical moment in its existence".[72] This moment appears to have been a time of great stress within the community of pastoralists. Some among them, whom the prophet sees as wicked, had become "non-herdsmen among herdsmen" (*fšuyasu afšuyanto*), "non-pasturers" (*avastrya-*) in opposition to "pasturers" (*vastrya- fšuyant-*).[73] This choice of expressions suggests that for him these men defined themselves by abandoning the traditional duty of the tribesman to take his part in working with the cattle, and hence his proper orderly place in society. Further, these renegades "raise a weapon to the just man", harming the *pasu-vira*, the community of cattle and men.[74] They "destroy pastures"[75] - perhaps through firing summer grasses, maliciously or to check pursuit[76] ? - and shed blood.[77] They gather, it seems, in bands led by wicked chieftains or "lords" (*ahu-*), who devour the property of others and harm the life of the cow.[78] This was done, it appears, through raids, with the attackers working themselves up into battle fury. (The Spirit of fury, Aešma, is the only demon named in the *Gathas*, and remains one of the great agents of evil in Zoroastrianism.) Underlying the profoundly metaphysical *Yasna* 29 is, it is thought, the reality of such a raid as experienced by its victims, with terror and the brutal carrying off of hapless cattle.[79]

Help for interpreting these Gathic materials - always allusive, with multiple layers of meaning - is to be had from the Rigveda. The cattle-raid figures in a number of its verses, both as reality and in metaphor[80]; and whether raiding or fighting battles, the Vedic Indo-Aryans still used the horse-drawn chariot familiar to Zoroaster. A charioteer guided the team, the fighter himself, by now a warrior by calling, stood beside him. Hence in Young Avestan the word coined for such a warrior was *rathaeštar* , "one standing in a chariot".[81] A cattle-raid is, however, mentioned unambiguously only once in the Young Avesta, in verses in the *Mihr Yašt* which plainly derive from the *Gathas*.[82] In another *Yašt* a "chariot-stander" is visualized rather as amassing treasure, which he guards with his sword.[83] From this it appears that by the time of the final composition of the *Yašts* the eastern Iranians, settled in newer, richer lands and with life on the steppes far behind them, had so long abandoned cattle-raiding that this had ceased to figure in their thoughts, or even to provide their poets with an inheritance of imagery.

Although the Vedic Indo-Aryans continued raiding for cattle, there are striking differences between the Vedic and Gathic references to this practice. The victims of the Vedic raiders were not fellow-tribesmen but people whom they regarded as alien to themselves, the Dasa, whom most identify as the indigenous inhabitants of the north-west Indian sub-continent.[84]   To attack foreigners has usually been a straightforward action, widely practised; and the Vedic poets regarded such raids as admirable undertakings, carried out with profit by brave, adventurous men.   In the homogeneous Old Avestan society, however, Zoroaster saw the counterparts of these men as wicked and selfish, enriching themselves lawlessly at the expense of their more honest fellows. Both he and the Vedic poets lived in a Heroic Age; but whereas the latter perceived theirs from the point of view of the "heroes", bold warriors whom they as priests served, Zoroaster experienced the Iranian one from that of ordinary law-abiding people, whose traditional way of life these predators were destroying.   Clearly there were Iranian priests who served Iranian war-lords, and the hymns which they composed are likely to have resembled the Vedic ones much more closely than do the *Gathas*; but none of their verses has survived.

Although one has to be wary of seeking to deduce too much from the *Gathas,* the prophet's words undoubtedly suggest that the violent events which he witnessed were something relatively new, and that he could himself look back to a time - perhaps during boyhood in his own tribe, perhaps to memories of his father's generation - when life was still relatively peaceful and ordered.   Archaeology so far gives no help for tracing, let alone dating, the turbulence which evidently reigned for a while on the steppes, and which seems likely to have accompanied to some degree the great migrations also.   Linguistic evidence indicates, however, the presence of proto-Indo-Aryans in what is now western Iran from as early as the mid-eighteenth century B.C.[85]   There some probably took service as mercenaries with local rulers, and in the kingdom of Mitanni some had risen in the fifteenth century to high positions as "chariot-standing" noblemen.   Others - less successful, or more attached to their homelands - are likely to have returned to the steppes after a period of foreign adventuring, taking with them not only new technical knowledge (of chariotry and horse-management), and new and relatively deadly bronze weaponry,[86] but also their experience of life as professional fighters.   It would clearly have been hard for such men to settle back into the quiet rhythms of a pastoral life, with its regular activities and slow, predictable gains; and it was most probably they who introduced a new element of unrest among the proto-Indo-Aryan steppe-dwellers, which then infected the Iranians to the north of them.   To judge from the *Gathas*, such men not only failed to take up their traditional duty of working with the tribe's cattle, but also broke away from old kinship bonds, taking service with some war-lord. With him they could continue to live adventurously, with fighting, risk, and the chance of sudden wealth - even if here wealth was mostly to be won in the relatively humble form of cattle.

This reconstruction of events is based on the combined evidence of Mitannian and other written documents of the southern lands concerning the presence there of proto-Indo-Aryans, archaeological data which show bronze artifacts and technology reaching the steppes from around 1700, the *Gathas*, and the usages in the Vedas and Young Avesta of the word *marya/mairya*. This term goes back, it appears, to a proto-Indo-Iranian one applied to the young men of the tribe, aged between about fifteen and thirty, who in the Stone and early Bronze Ages would have been those who fought when there had to be fighting. It would have been from among them that the adventurers to southern lands, and in due course the "chariot-standers", emerged.[87] In what was presumably an interim usage, before the "chariot-standers" established themselves as a separate class with its own fixed designation, this old word *marya/mairya* came apparently to be applied especially to the members of warbands. Zoroaster does not himself use it, preferring, it seems, the pregnant circumlocutions of *avastrya, afšuyant*; but Young Avestan has certain fixed phrases, which may well go back in origin to his day, in which the *mairya* is linked with the wolf, indeed is called a two-legged wolf - presumably because for pastoralists of the steppes wolf and marauding warrior were the chief predators of their cattle.[88] In the Rigveda, by contrast, the word *marya* survives only used in laudatory fashion of chariot-riding gods, notably of the band of youthful Maruts. That the *marya/mairya* should be linked by one set of people with the dreaded wolf, by the other with worshipped gods, is another clear testimony to the great gulf in outlook between Zoroaster with his followers and the Vedic priest-poets.

The above interpretation of the data receives support from two facts. One is a particular one, namely that the Indo-Aryans and Iranians who reached the Indian sub-continent and Iran in considerably numbers in the second half of the second millennium were evidently led, in part at least, by chariot-warriors, who established themselves in both countries as a class of landed gentry. The other is general, namely that the commonest known cause for the genesis of a Heroic Age has been the return of ex-mercenaries to their own people after service in lands with more developed ways of fighting.[89] (One of the best documented instances is that of the Teutonic Heroic Age, generated in all its poetry and harshness by tribesmen returning north after serving in Rome's armies.) Ex-soldiers have moreover been identified as agents of unrest and change on the Asian steppes themselves in historic times.[90] It is the spurious sixth-century dating for Zoroaster, and the misplacing of his homeland, which together have prevented the events which he experienced being seen in this light.

Geography dictated, it is held [91], that the main movements of the proto-Indo-Aryans were from Kazakhstan south into Soviet Central Asia, whence some moved on into Afghanistan and northern Pakistan, others into eastern Iran and Baluchistan. These movements, beginning probably on a small scale in the eighteenth century B.C.,[92] had probably increased by the fifteenth to the point where locally their languages and culture had become dominant. On their heels came the first wave of Iranians, ancestors, it appears, of the Medes and Persians, who pushed more of the proto-Indo-Aryans eastwards, killing presumably or absorbing those who remained. After them, thrusting them away in their turn towards western Iran, came yet more Iranians who, spreading out, settled permanently in Central Asia, eastern Iran and the Indo-Iranian borderlands. In the latter regions too, it is currently thought, they again absorbed or drove out their close kinsmen, proto-Indo-Aryans who were there before them. One of the reasons for this assumption is that Avestan (the sole surviving representative of the ancient "Eastern Iranian" languages) contains (unlike Old Persian and Vedic) virtually no foreign loanwords. This is explicable, it is held, if proto-Indo-Aryan was already dominantly spoken in these eastern areas, since it would have been close enough to Avestan to be assimilated with barely a trace.[93] Other Iranian tribes remained on the Asian steppes, and their descendants enter history in the next millennium as Cimmerians and Sarmatians, Scythians (Sakas), Massagetae, Dahae, Alani and others.

This reconstruction of events receives only a little support from excavations in Central Asia itself, the presumed chief corridor for the migrations. In this there is nothing remarkable, since it provides merely another illustration of the general difficulty of tracing the movements of peoples from archaeological evidence. (From such evidence, it has been pointed out, it is likewise impossible to establish when the Semites became dominant in Mesopotamia, or the Hittites in Asia Minor, or to follow the course of the Roman conquest of Europe.) A mingling of intrusive Andronovo elements has, however, been traced in the material cultures of various Central Asian lands. Broadly speaking, these elements are identified as dwelling-houses partly sunk in the ground; cemeteries away from settlements, with pit-graves; coarser, hand-made pottery; the (rare) appearance of the swastika and solar emblems; bronze arrowheads of distinct type and sickle-shaped knives; the remains (though few) of horses.

All these elements have been identified, from the beginning of the second millennium, in the Tazabagyab culture of the Oxus (Amu Darya) delta, in ancient Khwarezmia (modern Uzbekistan).[94] Here the old local economy was based both on stock-keeping and on a fairly intensive farming with irrigation, while the Andronovo elements may, it is suggested, have been brought in by proto-Indo-Aryans, moving south early off the steppes.[95] Some archaeologists are reluctant to correlate material developments with ethnic intrusions, pointing rather to the possibilities of influence through trade or merely cultural contacts;[96] but since linguistic and other evidence establishes the eventual Iranianization of Central Asia, and since southward movements by the Iranians' predecessors, the proto-Indo-Aryans, have been attested from the eighteenth century B.C., the hypothesis of actual immigration seems eminently reasonable for this particular area - perhaps the more so since the discovery also of surface finds of Andronovo pottery suggests the presence there as well of pastoralists from the north on merely seasonal migrations.[97] Cultures with strongly Andronovo elements have been identified in other northern parts of Central Asia. One is in Kayrak Kum in ancient Ferghana (the northern part of modern Tajikistan), its settlements being strung out on hillside sites along the valley of the Jaxartes (Sir Darya).[98] Another is in the Semerechensk ("Seven Rivers") region of Kirghizia.[99]

From around 1500 B.C. Andronovo elements occur in a number of more southerly regions of Central Asia, and their mixture there with older local ones shows, some scholars hold, sufficient homogeneity for the result to be identified as a distinctive culture. This has been given by Soviet archaeologists the general name of the "Early Iron Age" culture of Central Asia (even though little iron is in fact found at its sites), in order to distinguish it from the indigenous Bronze Age ones which preceded it there. It is also called regionally after various type sites. In general it has only thin occupation layers, and its attestation so far is patchy and uneven, with in some places only settlements known, in others only cemeteries, and with materials here fairly abundant, there few and controversial, with details of chronology debated. The area where it is so far best attested is the most recently explored, namely around the lower Murghab in ancient Margiana (modern Turkmenistan). Here its excavators named it "Yaz I" after the local type-site, Yaz Depe.[100] It is also represented along the northern skirts of the Kopet Dagh (likewise in Turkmenistan, formerly part of Parthia), where it is known as "Namazga VI".[101] In southwest Tajikistan (ancient Sogdia) sites which some attribute to this culture have been excavated in the valleys of the Bishkent (hence its local name), Vakhš and Kafirnigan.[102] This "Bishkent" culture is known only from its cemeteries, of which the chief is Tulkhar. Another group of Tajikistani sites, also once in ancient Sogdia, belonging to what is termed the "Zamanbaba" culture, has been discovered in the valley of the Zarafshan.[103]

Since the preceding cultures of southern Central Asia are held to be indigenous, this "Early Iron Age" one, appearing at what philologists would regard as approximately the right time, is the only candidate for a material attestation of the presence there of intruders from the steppes, presumably "Vedic" Indo-Aryans. There follows a most curious blank in the archaeology of this whole great region, in that so far not a single grave, let alone a cemetery, has been discovered from the centuries intervening between this culture and the coming of the Hellenes in the late fourth century B.C. Whether the explanation for this is to be sought in the dominance gained there in time by Zoroastrianism, with its funerary rite of exposure,[104] remains an open question.

To find an approximate date for the arrival of Iranians in this region it is necessary therefore to look to Iran itself. In western Iran, near Kashan, at the ancient site of Tepe Sialk, a graveyard has been excavated (cemetery B) which, it is generally accepted, belonged to a mixed community dominated by a group of evident newcomers. These newcomers, it is estimated, arrived around 1000 B.C., and in the light of the subsequent history of the region it is natural to identify them as Iranians, come down from the northern steppes by way of Central Asia.[105]   From this it has been deduced that "western" Iranians - the ancestors of the Medes and Persians - were probably moving into Central Asia itself, following the proto-Indo-Aryans, from at least a century earlier, around 1100; and this means that the "eastern" Iranian tribes, among them the Old Avestan people, were then still living on the steppes. These deductions fit with the fact that the *Gathas* reflect the dominantly pastoral life of the steppes, and not that of lands south of the Jaxartes, where farming was generally at least as important as stock-breeding, and where, in places, man had begun to make his mark on the natural world with irrigation canals and large villages which were almost towns;[106] and with the estimate, based on the internal evidence of Young Avestan texts, that c.1100 B.C. was "the lowest possible date for the founding of the Zoroastrian religion".[107]   The coincidence of these deductions is all the more telling because those made by the excavator of Tepe Sialk were free of any thought of their having a bearing on the date of Zoroaster.

Pastoralism on the Inner Asian steppes is generally, indeed almost automatically, associated with nomadism; but, as we have seen, this was a later development, the Andronovo peoples themselves being sedentary. The great alteration to life on the steppes in this respect was brought about by the change from driving horses to riding them - the former activity, because of its costliness, having been reserved for the few, the latter becoming general practice, so that whole tribes became mobile and wandered, at least during the summer.   This development took place, it seems, later on the Kazakhstan steppes than further west, and it is everywhere impossible, so far, to date closely. As has been observed, "domestication and herding of a fast animal like the horse would inevitably entail some kind of primitive and casual riding",[108] and this seems attested already in the fourth millennium, in the sedentary Stone Age "Sredni Stog" culture of the westernmost steppes. This culture, named from the type-site, was located mainly along the middle and lower Dnieper and Don. The horse was the chief domesticated animal, kept perhaps for meat, milk and hides; and in one grave a bone object has been found "resembling later ones positively identified as cheek-pieces of bits".[109]

Early bits themselves were presumably of perishable leather or wood, and it is such cheek-pieces (often referred to as *psalia*) which alone survive to bear witness to the practice of riding. A bone cheek-piece has been discovered in the Karasuk culture of southern Siberia (a local development of Andronovo), dated to the thirteenth to tenth centuries.[110] To the south, at Pirak in Pakistan, near the Bolan Pass, there have been unearthed terracotta figurines of odd, armless riders with beaked faces, identified as supernatural beings. These occurred in two distinct occupation layers, dated to c.1800-1300 and c.1300-1100. They provide the earliest evidence for the horse in the Indian sub-continent; and since they were found with camel figurines very like ones of the Yaz-I culture of Margiana, they have been attributed to intruders from the north, presumably Indo-Aryans of other than the "Vedic" groups.[111] The saddleless, bridleless steeds with their strange riders yield little information, however, about the actual practice of horse-riding.[112]

On the Iranian plateau representations of men with horses have been found on cylinder seals from cemetery B at Tepe Sialk. On one "a man stands in a chariot drawn by two horses and shoots an arrow at the animal he is hunting".[113] On another are shown, between fantastic animals, horsemen armed with bows.[114] The horses have bridles but no visible saddles, and their riders wear plumed helmets, short jackets and turned-up shoes - the same costume as that of a man shown on another seal fighting on foot,[115] and not one well adapted for riding. It seems probable that by the tenth century B.C. two independent, parallel developments were going on. One, in Assyria and its neighbouring lands, was of "military riding ... growing out of the use of the war chariot", with at first two horses being ridden side by side, one by the warrior, the other by a man who, like the charioteer, controlled the animals.[116] The other was among the Iranian tribes on the steppes. Clearly two inventions were needed for comfortable everyday riding: those of a saddle (since a horse sweats a good deal), and suitable clothing for the rider; and the latter - of trousers, boots, long-sleeved jacket and close-fitting headgear - first appears worn by an Iranian people, namely the Cimmerians. They occupied the steppes north of the Black Sea in the ninth century, and may have been the "milkers of mares - milk consumers" of the *Iliad*.[117] From the archaeological data they are indistinguishable from their close cousins, the Scythians, known in the same area from the seventh century; and elements in their common material culture go back to the older Abachevo-Srubnaya culture of this region.[118] Since horses had already been casually ridden for so long, it seems reasonable to look for some special reason for these developments among Iranians at this particular period; and the one which suggests itself was the need to control the ever larger herds of horses being kept to meet the steadily growing demand for war-horses, and, linked with this, the necessity of keeping such herds on the move in search of sufficient grazing. The resulting nomadism is seen as a gradual development, with probably at first a trickle of the wealthier tribesmen driving their herds further and further out over the steppes in search of fresh grazing, and staying away longer from the fixed settlements;[119] and so it may have been a matter of several generations before a whole tribe became mounted and semi-nomadic, and before this development, first traceable on the Black Sea steppes, spread to the Iranian tribes living east of the river Ural.

What is certain is that not only did the "Vedic" Indo-Aryans enter the Indian sub-continent led by chariot-warriors, but that thereafter their descendants associated horse-riding and the horseman's garb of trousers and boots with the Iranians. The Old Persians too, leaving the steppes after them, used the chariot in war, and continued to do so for centuries. Darius praised Ahuramazda for bestowing on him "good horses and good chariots"[120], and it was from the Medes living to the north of them that his people adopted riding and the horseman's dress. The Medes in their turn had most probably acquired these from their enemies and allies, the Scythians. Since before this, for more than half a millennium (from c.1600) chariot-riding had been the privileged activity of men of wealth and power, the priest-poets of both the Indo-Aryans and Iranians had come to envisage their gods also as driving in chariots, first with two horses and occasionally later with four (which involved sometimes a clumsy modification of Avestan verses).[121] The four-horsed chariot is not attested in use before the eighth century. Later still at least one of the Yazatas, great Mithra, was conceived as riding a horse,[122] but this was too radical and too late a change to be introduced into his *Yašt*.[123] Horse-riding is, however, referred to in the Young Avesta, where the distance which a well-mounted man could ride in a day is used as a land measure[124] - an indication, it would seem, of a regular practice of riding by individuals before this became, on the steppes, the usage of all. There this usage (to judge from Scythian custom) led to the abandonment of the chariot, only the heavy, solid-wheeled cart being kept for transport, which could lumber, laden, over most terrains. Thus by the time the Iranians of the steppes emerge into history their way of life had come to differ in such respects from that of the Iranians who lived there in Zoroaster's day.

As to when that day was, the number of broad indicators is thus slightly increased. An upper date is set approximately by the fact that the light chariot was evidently a familiar element in the lives of his people, providing him himself with poetic imagery, and being the cause presumably of "horse" names being given in his tribe. These developments can hardly be put much before 1500 B.C. As for a lower date, his people were plainly pastoralists among whom farming was little regarded, although their settlements appear to have been fixed ones. These facts, together with the essentially classless nature of their society, indicate that they lived on the steppes during the pre-nomadic period there. This sets them at somewhere before 1000-900 B.C., and harmonizes with the approximate date, c.1100, at which the "eastern" Iranians are held to have begun their major migrations south. Zoroaster himself evidently lived before his own people took part in these migrations, so this accords with the internal evidence of the Avesta, which suggests a date for him before, and possibly well before, 1100. The possible chronological limits thus appear to be c.1500-c.1200; and a date at the lower limit, i.e. around 1200, seems the most reasonable one to postulate, since it is reconcilable with all the known data and does not assume too huge a temporal gap between the Old and the Young Avesta.

NOTES

1   E.W. West, *SBE* XLVII, xlii.

2   This is accordingly the basic aim of Gnoli's large and in many ways admirable *ZTH*, see his introduction.

3   The idiosyncratic supposition of Kellens-Pirart, *TVA*, 17-20, that the *Gathas* were composed by a group of ritual priests, among whom Zoroaster may have been no more than "an obscure individual, working under instructions and supervision,but more skilful than the others at arranging syllables", was based largely on the odd premise that a poet cannot address himself in the vocative, or speak of himself in the third person.

4   There appears no reason to doubt the Zoroastrian tradition in this matter, recorded in *DkM*, p.412.5 f. (*Sources*, 114); and this invalidates the theory put forward by Hoffmann-Narten, *Sas. Archetypus*, 81 ff., that a fixed Avestan canon existed already in the 6th century B.C. See further *HZ* III 121-4.

5   For recent advocacy of this interpretation of the faith's history see Gnoli, *De Z. à M.*, 53 ff., esp. at p.69; Boyce, "The religion of Cyrus the Great", in *Achaemenid History* III, ed. A. Kuhrt and H. Sancisi-Weerdenburg, Leiden 1988, 15-31 (partly revising an earlier treatment in *HZ* II 49 ff.); Kellens-Pirart, o.c., pp.40-1. On the weakness of the theory that Cyrus worshipped Mithra as supreme god see *HZ* III 471 ff.

6   Against the hypothesis that Seistani priests played an equal part in their conversion (Hoffmann-Narten, o.c., pp.80-1, 86-7) see *HZ* III 122-3.

7   See E. Yarshater, *A grammar of Southern Tati dialects*, The Hague/Paris, 1969.

8   So T. Burrow, "The Proto-Indoaryans", *JRAS* 1973, 123-40, at p.138.

9   So, among others, Burrow, *loc.cit.*

10   See ib., with n.31.

11   Cf. above, pp.4-5.

12   Burrow, art. cit., pp.138-9.

13   Ib., p.139, who envisaged that it "could be a good deal earlier".

14   Kellens-Pirart, *TVA*, 12-13. Kellens considers that the best proof that a long period separates Old from Young Avestan is the striking difference between their verbal systems, with the aorist becoming neglected and all verbal categories being regrouped within the framework of the present system. For this, he holds, several centuries would have been needed - at his reasoned guess, some 400 years. See his "Quatres siècles

obscurs", in *Transition Periods in Iranian History, St. Ir.,* Cahier 5, 1987, 135-9 at pp.135-6; and cf. (with special reference to studies by F.B.J. Kuiper) his *Zoroastre,* 15-16.

15   Haug, *Essays,* 136.

16   This was stressed by G. Erdosy, "Ethnicity in the Rigveda and its bearing on the question of Indo-European origins", *SAS* 5, 1989, 40-1, as supporting his argument that the "Aryas" were Indian indigenes, not incomers - an argument which, he admits (p.44), the close affinities between Avestan and Vedic make it hard to sustain.

17   *Yt* 19:68, 18:2. See further Gnoli, *Idea of Iran,* 56.

18   This was stressed by Kellens-Pirart, o.c., pp.23, 25, 30.

19   See E. Benveniste, "Les classes sociales dans la tradition avestique", *JA* 1932, 121-30.

20   *Y.* 46:1.

21   *Y.* 48:5, 10.

22   Nowhere, *pace* Kellens-Pirart, o.c., p.23, is there mention of a particular ruler of a *dahyu,* as postulated by them for the supposed enemy of their hypothetical circle of "Gathic" priests.

23   *Y.* 32:11.

24   *Cf.* E.C. Polomé, "Indo-European culture with special attention to religion", in Polomé (ed.), *The Indo-Europeans in the Fourth and Third Millennia,* Ann Arbor, Michigan, 1982, 170. Against the attempt by Benveniste, *art.cit.,* p.122, to see Old Av. terms for three social groups in *Y.* 40:3 see Boyce, "The bipartite society of the ancient Iranians", in *Societies and Languages of the Ancient Near East, Studies in honour of I.M. Diakonoff,* ed. M.A. Dandamayev and others, Warminster 1982, 34; Narten, *YHapt.,* 276-9.

25   V.N. Basilov in Basilov (ed.), *Nomads of Eurasia,* 5-6. That of the settlement lost its importance with the development of nomadism in the first millennium B.C., on which see further below.

26   *Y.* 53:6.

27   *Y.* 53:4.

28   Bartholomae, *Air.Wb.* 1453; Benveniste, "Sur quelques dvandvas avestiques", *BSOAS* VIII, 1935-1937, 405-7.

29   In discussing these names Kellens-Pirart, o.c., p.7 ff., adopted the linguistically satisfying etymology of *Zarathuštra* as "he who possesses old camels", which had been strongly advocated previously by B. Schlerath, "Noch einmal Zarathustra", *Die Sprache* 23, 1977, 127-35. This is considered to be one of a group of Av. "deprecatory names", a type which, Schlerath points out (art.cit., pp.132-3), has many parallels in other societies. I. Steblin-Kamenskiy (in a personal communication) compares in particular the *nam-i past* "low name" sometimes given protectively by Pamiri peoples to their children when ill luck (as with prevailing sickness, bringing high infant mortality) seems to threaten.

30   E. E. Kuzmina, "Etapi razvitiya kolesnogo transporta Sredney Azii v épokhu éneolita i bronzy", *VDI,* 1980, 11-35 (with English summary).

31   Littauer-Crouwel, *Wheeled vehicles and ridden animals,* 50 ff.

32   V.F. Gening, "The cemetery at Sintashta and the early Indo-Iranian peoples", *J. of Indo-European Studies* 7, 1979, 1-29 (tr. from *Sovetskaya Arkheologiya,* 1977, 53-73, by W. A. Brewer). On the dating see further below, and for additional references A. Parpola, "The coming of the Aryans to Iran and India and the cultural and ethnic identity of the

Dāsas", *Studia Orientalia* 64, 1988, 234.

33   Pahlavi works derived from the *zand* (see Jackson, *Zoroaster*, 19) preserve a genealogy of the prophet giving his forbears back to Spitama in the 9th generation. In this the first "horse" name appears in the 6th generation before him, and in the following five generations there are four "horse" names. Since only two of these names (that of Spitama himself, in Zoroaster's patronymic, and Haechat-aspa) appear in the *Gathas*, at unknown removes from the prophet, it is unfortunately impossible to verify this genealogy, whose reliability seems unlikely (even though in ancient times genealogies were cultivated when history was not). - Kellens-Pirart, *TVA*, 8, consistent in their disregard of the tradition, argued for Haechat-aspa being Zoroaster's father, and, because no etymology suggests itself for Spitama, declined to see this as a personal name. (On Haechat-aspa see further Kellens, *Zoroastre*, 68.)

34   See Henning, "An astronomical chapter of the Bundahishn", *JRAS* 1942, 236 (= *Collected Papers* II 102).

35   *Yt* 5:49, 19:77.

36   *Y.* 30:10.

37   *Y.* 44:4.

38   *Y.* 50:6. On *raithī*- see Humbach, *Gathas*, II 85.

39   This fact is sometimes obscured in translation (e.g. Insler's "cultivator" for *fšānghyō*, *Y.* 49:9). The one allusion found by Kellens-Pirart, o.c., in *Y.* 49:1, depends on a highly dubious rendering of *yavā* as "grain" instead of as the adv. "always".

40   Kellens-Pirart, o.c., p.23 (on *Y.* 53:8).

41   See D. Sinor, intro., *CH Early Inner Asia, 7.*

42   A. P. Okladnikov, "Inner Asia at the dawn of history", in ib., p.87; Basilov, o.c. in n.25, p.3.

43   See I. Gershevitch, "An Iranianist's view of the Soma controversy", *Mémorial J. de Menasce,* ed. Ph. Gignoux et A. Tafazzoli, Louvain 1974, 60-2, commenting on *Yt* 15:31-2.

44   *Y.* 39:1-2 (fully discussed by Narten, *YHapt.,* 248-53).

45   Thus a Zoroastrian, Mrs. Tahmina Mehta, touching on this aspect of ancient Iranian society at a conference in the U.S.A., found her statements about it paralleled with remarkable closeness by those of the next speaker concerning North American Indians.

46   *Y.* 40:3.

47   *Y.* 40:4; cf. Narten, o.c., pp.276-81.

48   See ib., pp.281-5.

49   *Y.* 35:6; 41:2; 37:3; 39:2.

50   *Y.* 46:10.

51   Frumkin, *Archaeology in Soviet Central Asia,* 11.

52   Gnoli, *De Z. à M.,* 16.

53   For surveys see Mongait, *Archaeology in the USSR,* 146 ff; Frumkin, o.c., p.14 ff.; E. Tchernykh in V. Yanine and others, *Fouilles et recherches archéologiques en URSS,* 30 ff.

54   Tchernykh, o.c., pp.82 ff., 87. Further on the problems of the chronology and sub-divisions of this culture see E. E. Kuzmina, "Kul'turnaya i étnicheskaya atributsiya pastusheskikh plemen Kazakhstana i Sredney Azii épokhi bronzy", *VDI,* 1988, 35-59, with

Eng. summary (cited by Parpola, art.cit., p.231).

55 But on the enormous physical variations within any one group, and the difficulties accordingly of using skeletal evidence to identify any particular people with certainty, see the detailed exposition by J. L. Heim, lucidly summarized by G. Fussman in his survey of the work of a seminar on "L'entrée des Aryans en Inde", *Annuaire du Collège de France* 1988-1989, 517-18.

56 S. I. Rudenko, *Frozen tombs of Siberia,* 81.

57 Tchernykh, o.c., p.87.

58 Ib., p.42.

59 Ib., pp.43-6.

60 Ib., pp.83-4.

61 Gening, art.cit. in n.32.

62 Ib., p.16.

63 The chariots themselves had turned to dust, but with exemplary patience and skill the excavator was able to trace the imprint of their ten-spoked wheels in the tombs' earthen floors.

64 Tchernykh, o.c., p.93.

65 Gening, art.cit., p.21.

66 See J. Henninger, "Bones", *The Encyclopaedia of Religion* II, 284-5.

67 Gening, art.cit., p.20.

68 See Grenet in *HZ* III 168-71.

69 Gening, art.cit., p.29.

70 *Pace* Parpola (art.cit. in n.32), Erdosy (art.cit. in n.16), and other archaeologists, this still seems the hypothesis which best explains the linguistic, literary, religious and (broadly) archaeological facts, despite some perplexing problems in the last-named field.

71 In its early stages, it has been said, "the light chariot served a number of roles ... among which service in war was only one and quite possibly the least common", P.R.S. Moorey, "The emergence of the light, horse-drawn chariot in the Near East c.2000-1500 B.C.", *World Archaeology* 18, 1986, 196-215, at p.205.

72 Kellens-Pirart, *TVA,* 4.

73 *Y.* 49:4, 31:10.

74 *Y.* 32:11, 31:15.

75 *Y.* 32:10.

76 Cf. the destroying of grassland by the Scythians to halt Darius' pursuit (Herodotus IV 120, 140). On the varied succession of steppeland grasses from May to autumn see R. Taaffe in *CH Inner Asia,* 34-5.

77 *Y.* 32:10; 46:5; 53:8.

78 *Y.* 32:11, 12.

79 B. Lincoln, *Priests, warriors and cattle,* 149 ff.; Boyce, "Priests, cattle and men", *BSOAS* L, 1987, 525-6.

80 For a collection of references see Lincoln, o.c., p.131 n.132.

81 H.-P. Francfort, *Fouilles de Shortugaï,* 452, infers from the fact that the Vedic words for a warrior (*kṣatriya, rājanya*) contain no allusion to a chariot that "India thus did not know the chariot-warrior"; but the literature and mythology abundantly attest that

Vedic India did. There is no reason why the chariot should necessarily appear in terms for "warrior". W.W. Malandra, *EIr*. V 377, argues that, because the word *ratha-* "chariot" exists in Avestan and Vedic, this "shows that chariots were used by both groups in the time of the Indo-Iranian unity". This is, however, chronologically impossible. Etymologically the word derives from one for "wheel", and it was presumably first used for the block-wheeled cart.

82   *Yt* 10:85-6. (The *Fravarane* [*Y*. 12] belongs essentially to the Old Avestan world, and [*pace* Lincoln, o.c., p.131] the simile in *Vd* 13:45 is obscure.)

83   *Yt* 13:67.

84   G. Fussman's idiosyncratic case for seeing the Dasa as Iranians (o.c. in n.55, p.517) has marked weaknesses.

85   M. Mayrhofer, *Die Indo-Arier im alten Vorderasien*, Wiesbaden 1966; T. Burrow, art.cit. in n.8; Parpola, art.cit. in n.32.

86   There is debate among specialists as to whether the light chariot evolved in Near Eastern lands as the result of long, slow development, with the spoked wheel a modification of the cross-bar one (Littauer-Crouwel, o.c. in n.31, pp.68-72), or whether it was an invention of the steppe peoples, an independent modification, in the interests of speed, of the block-wheeled cart (S. Piggott, *The earliest wheeled transport: from the Atlantic Coast to the Caspian Sea*, London 1983). The arguments are summarized by Moorey, art.cit. in n.71, pp.199-203, whose own conclusion (p.211) is that "no single ethnic or linguistic group seems to have been the master innovator in the history of horse-drawn light chariotry in the Near Eastern Middle Bronze Age". There is no question, however, but that knowledge of metals was acquired, belatedly, by steppe-dwellers from southern peoples.

87   On the contrasted uses of the term *mairya/marya* in Avestan and Vedic see Boyce, art.cit. in n.79, pp.511-13. Whether this Indo-Iranian word is the source of Hurrian *maryannu* "chariot-warrior", widely attested in Near Eastern lands in the 15th-12th centuries B.C., is debated. For the literature see *ib.*; and on the *maryannu* add A.F. Rainey, "The military personnel at Ugarit", *JNES* 24, 1965, 17-27.

88   Boyce, art.cit., p.515.

89   See, with wealth of illustration, H.M. Chadwick, *The Heroic Age*, esp. Chs.16, 19; H.M. and N.K. Chadwick, *The Growth of Literature, passim* in connection with heroic literatures.

90   K. Jettmar, *Art of the Steppes*, 214-15.

91   See in detail I.M. Diakonoff, *CHIr*. 2, 48-53.

92   See with bibliography F.R. Allchin, "Archaeological and language historical evidence for the movement of Indo-Aryan-speaking peoples into India and Pakistan", *JCOI* 48, 1980, 68-102; and add Fussman, art.cit. in n.55.

93   See Diakonoff, o.c., p.53 with n.1; Burrow, art.cit. in n.8, who, pp.132-3, makes a striking case for some of the *daevic* words in Avestan being taken from the Proto-Indo-Aryan of eastern Iran.

94   So named by its discoverer, S.P. Tolstov. This culture was at first dated to around 1500-1000, but subsequent excavations have led to its origin being set half a millennium earlier, see H.-P. Francfort, *Fouilles de Shortugaï*, 424-5, quoting extensively from the Russian publications of M.A. Itina. See also P.L. Kohl, *Central Asia*, 183-4; Frumkin, *Archaeology in Soviet Central Asia*, 85 with map 14; Masson-Sarianidi, *Central Asia*, 147-9; S.P. Gupta, *Archaeology of Soviet Central Asia*, II, 189-91.

95   B.A. Litvinskiy, "Problemy etnicheskoy istorii Sredney Azii vo II tysyacheletii do n.e." in M.S. Asimov and others (eds.), *Ethnic problems of the history of Central Asia in the early period,* Moscow 1981, 154-66, cited by Francfort, o.c., p.153.

96   Such possibilities are exhaustively weighed by Francfort, o.c., p.422 ff. The most thorough attempts at linking material remains in Central Asia with known societies are those of P.L. Kohl (o.c., with references to his own earlier works) and M. Tosi (for a bibliography of whose articles see Francfort, o.c., pp.503-4).

97   Francfort, o.c., p.425, citing the conclusions of M.A. Itina.

98   See Francfort, o.c., p.426 (with reference chiefly to the works of B.A. Litvinskiy); Kohl, o.c., p.183; Frumkin, o.c., p.70 with map 10; Masson-Sarianidi, o.c., p.151; Gupta, o.c., pp.189, 190-1, 233.

99   First excavated by A.N. Bernstham.   See Frumkin, o.c., p.30 with map 6; Masson-Sarianidi, o.c., p.150; Gupta, o.c., pp.188-9; Francfort, l.c.

100   Largely excavated by V.I. Sarianidi (for whose publications see Francfort, o.c., pp.498-9). See Kohl, o.c., pp.143-50; Frumkin, o.c., pp.139-40 with map 18; Masson-Sarianidi, o.c., pp.158, 159-61; Gupta, o.c., pp.227-9. - Negatively, clay seals and figurines of the older local culture are not found at "Yaz I" sites. Nevertheless, Sarianidi made an ingenious attempt to see Avestan themes in some of their designs ("Seal-amulets of the Murghab style" in P.L.Kohl (ed.), *The Bronze Age Civilization of Central Asia,* New York 1981, 221-55, esp. at pp.245-7). He also sought to identify a large complex (T 21) at the important "Yaz I" site of Togoluk as centred on a temple of the *haoma*-cult, belonging to "Proto-Zoroastrians" ("South-west Asia: migrations, the Aryans and Zoroastrians", *International Association for the Study of the Cultures of Central Asia, Information Bulletin* 13, Moscow 1987, 44-56, at p.48 ff.). Both these interpretations were based on the theory that "Zoroastrianism took its roots from local religious and mythological beliefs of ethnoses living in the region" (p.48). His interpretation of T 21 has been comprehensively dismissed by V.A. Livshits and I.M. Steblin-Kamenskiy, "Protozoroastrizm?" *VDI,* 1990, 174-6, who think it possible that the five sunken "altars" were cooking pits, and the cells for the religious, storage rooms. The only established fact to link the complex with Zoroastrianism is that traces of ephedra leaves were found with other matter at the bottom of big jars in building no.34; but there is no reason, they point out, to regard the use of ephedra (in whatever form) as specific to the ancient Iranians.

101   Kohl, *Central Asia,* pp.135, 253; Francfort apud Kohl, o.c., p.262; Frumkin, o.c., p.139; Masson-Sarianidi, o.c., pp.137, 140-1; Gupta, o.c., pp.226-7.

102   Kohl, o.c., pp.174-8 with map 19; Frumkin, o.c., pp.68-9; Masson-Sarianidi, o.c., pp.151-2; Gupta, o.c., pp.191-4. (Francfort, "The late periods of Shortugai and the problem of the Bishkent culture", *SAA* 1971, ed. H. Härtel, Berlin 1981, 191-202, argued for the Bishkent, like that of the late Shortugaï, culture being of essentially indigenous growth.)

103   Kohl, o.c., pp.179-82 with map 20a; Masson-Sarianidi, o.c., pp.125-8; Gupta, o.c., pp.171-2, 191.

104   On this see Francfort, *Fouilles de Shortugaï,* 437.

105   See R. Ghirshman, *Iran,* 70-1, 76 ff.

106   This despite a marked decline from the early part of the 2nd millennium, over wide areas of Central Asia, Iran, and the Indian borderlands and sub-continent, from a previous partly urban state of civilization. This decline, archaeologists have established, preceded the presumably fairly large-scale incursions of Indo-Iranian tribes, and was not

occasioned by them.

107 Cf. above, p.29 with n.12.

108 Littauer-Crouwel, *Wheeled Vehicles*, 137 n.133.

109 Ib., p.25. Similarly, indirect textual evidence suggests that the inhabitants of the Syrian deserts and steppelands bred and rode horses before horse-riding was developed for warfare in the Near East, see I.J. Gelb, "The early history of the West Semitic peoples", *J. of Cuneiform Studies*, 15, 1961, 25-47 at pp.37 n.31, 41 n.45 (cited by Moorey, art.cit. in n.71, p.198).

110 Okladnikov in *CH Early Inner Asia*, 85.

111 Parpola, art.cit. in n.32, p.239 with P1.25a (citing J.F. Jarrige et M.Santoni, *Fouilles de Pirak*, Paris 1979, I 361, 365 f.).

112 V.I. Sarianidi, "Mesopotamiya i Baktriya v II tys. do n.e.", *Sovetskaya Arkheologiya* 2, 1986, fig.3.2 (cited by Francfort, o.c., p.452).

113 Ghirshman, *Iran*, 80.

114 Ib., fig.31; Jettmar, *Art of the Steppes*, 212 with fig.134.

115 Ghirshman, o.c., p.80 with fig.33. (This man's legs are, however, missing.)

116 Littauer-Crouwel, o.c., pp.134-6. On the military development of riding cf. Rudenko, *The culture of the population of the Central Altai in Scythian times*, Moscow-Leningrad 1960, 95-201, 223 (in Russian; summarized by the translator of his *Frozen Tombs*, q.v., pp.xxv-vi).

117 A.I. Melyukova, "The Scythians and Sarmatians", in *CH Early Inner Asia*, 98.

118 Ib., p.99.

119 Rudenko, loc.cit.

120 *Susa S* 5-6.

121 See Boyce, *BSOAS* L, 1987, 522 with nn.110, 111.

122 The main data are gathered by H.-P. Schmidt, "Mithras the Horseman and Revanta the Lord of Horses", in *Some Aspects of Indo-Iranian literary and cultural traditions*, ed. S.K. Chatterji and others, Delhi 1977, 132-58. See further *HZ* III, index s. "Mithra". The earliest attestation of this concept is in 333 B.C., when before the Persian army as it marched out to the battle of Issus were led an empty chariot for "Jupiter", i.e. Ahura Mazda, and a riderless horse "of remarkable size" for the Sun, i.e. Mithra (Quintus Curtius III.8).

123 In it (v.11) Mithra is addressed as one "whom chariot-standers worship at the manes of their horses, asking swiftness for their teams (*hitaēibyō*)." Some scholars have inferred from the phrase "at their manes" that *rathaēštārō* was here already being used as a generic term for "warriors", in this instance mounted men praying in their saddles; but others have seen rather a reference to "chariot-standers" praying by their horses' heads, and this seems borne out by the use of the term *hitaēibyō* (literally "tied [that is, harnessed] ones"). On the lines see Gershevitch, *AHM*, 168-9, and to his references add Marcelle Duchesne-Guillemin, "Une statuette équestre de Mithra", in *Etudes mithriaques, Acta Ir.* 17, 1978, 201-4 (where the libation poured by Mithra as horseman most probably mirrored the libations earlier poured to him by chariot-warriors).

124 *Yt* 5:14.

CHAPTER THREE

The Ancient Roots
of Zoroastrianism

Zoroaster thus belongs to a remote antiquity, and is the earliest by far of the founders of a credal faith. Indeed it is the fact that he founded such a faith which has made some scholars uneasy about accepting a date for him in the second millennium, which they regard as improbably early for the first manifestation of this major development in man's religious history. There are, however, three factors which help to explain how it then came about. One is the strength of the ethnic religion which nurtured the prophet. The ancient Iranians were a religiously minded people, given to worship; and their priests were evidently accustomed to thinking strenuously about the gods and the nature of the world, about man's duties here and the fate which awaited him hereafter. The second factor is the violent unrest which troubled the Iranian tribes in Zoroaster's own day, and which are likely to have driven others also to question traditional beliefs in a ruling justice and the goodness and power of the gods. The third factor is Zoroaster himself. His extant words show him to have been richly endowed with intellectual and visionary gifts, and to have united eloquence of speech with passionate moral convictions - a great prophet who was born at a time which challenged and brought out his powers, and which created listeners for his new teachings.

It is with the first of these three factors that the present chapter is concerned, namely the strength of the old Iranian religion, a strength which it shared with Vedic Hinduism. Since the Iranians and proto-Indo-Aryans are held to have been drifting apart around 2000 B.C., the elements which Zoroastrianism and the Brahmanic religion retained in common must have been firmly fixed before then, and so have existed already far back in the third, possibly even in the fourth millennium. Indeed a few, such as the veneration of gods of sky and earth, ancestor-worship with certain beliefs about the hereafter, and the cult of the hearth fire, have been traced to a proto-Indo-European religion of perhaps the fifth millennium. The survival of these ancient elements in Zoroastrianism meant that Zoroaster's new teachings were grafted on to a very deep-rooted stock, from which they drew additional strength and vitality.

These ancient elements had evolved in purely Stone Age cultures. There is, as is widely attested, no necessary correlation between levels of material culture and those of intellectual and spiritual capacity; but certain distinctive ways of apprehending the world occur very generally in archaic and "primitive" societies, and these are to be found among the Indo-Iranians. The most fundamental of them is animatism - the reasoning by which man, conscious himself of being alive, attributes conscious life to all other things, whether static or like him capable of motion.[1] This attitude of mind has been characterized as regarding each natural phenomenon not as "it" but as "thou", as a fellow living entity. The supposed cognitive force in each entity was called by the proto-Indo-Iranians its *manyu, a word derived from the root man- "think". The developed sense of Vedic manyu has been rendered in English as "force, impulse", whereas the cognate Avestan mainyu is most often translated as "spirit".[2] A Mainyu was attributed by the Avestan people to all phenomena, even in their smallest manifestations. So a clod of earth was felt to be filled with the Mainyu of earth, the Mainyu of water was believed to be present in the libation bowl as well as in the broadest lake, and a link was acknowledged between the Mainyus of humble hearth fires and the fiery sun on high. Mainyus were attributed also to intangible things, so that there were Mainyus of peace and prosperity, of strife and famine. There were also Mainyus of qualities and emotions, such as courage and joy, jealousy, greed and the like. These were perceived, that is, neither as abstractions nor as parts of man's own psychological make-up, but as active independent forces, which could be entreated or placated by him, and which, if he permitted them, would enter his being and affect him for better or worse.

This ancient way of apprehending the world and man's own nature changed very slowly for the Iranians. A material development which is held to have modified it eventually for all mankind was the knowledge and use of metal-working. Through this man was able for the first time by his own processes to transform inert nature. Initially, in the working of copper, he turned a fragile green stone into a heavy red substance which he could beat into whatever shapes he chose. Then, by mixing tin with copper, he evolved a new substance, bronze. He thus became dominant over this area of the natural world, a creator rather than a fellow being.[3] Yet for the ancient Iranians the impact of these great technical discoveries was evidently still too slight in Zoroaster's own day to provoke rethinking about the nature of inanimate objects. Most people would have acquired the new artifacts as finished products, and these they apparently regarded as no different in kind from their familiar stone counterparts, for, as Zoroastrian tradition shows[4], the man-wrought metal came to be accepted simply as another natural thing, possessing therefore its own Mainyu, both collectively and present in each individual metal object.

Among intangible things one to which great power was attributed was the formal spoken word, the deliberately shaped utterance. Eloquence, which could convince or persuade, stir up or pacify emotions, was highly prized, and public contests were held in which men jousted with each other with words for weapons.[5] More solemnly a priest, meditating, could hope to conceive "in his heart" a divinely inspired thought, and by giving it fitting verbal expression create a *manthra*, that is, a true thought clothed in right words. This was believed to have its own power and to be able to instruct and protect. *Manthra* (Sanskrit *mantra*) derives, like *mainyu*, from the verbal root *man* "think", but here thought attained its force through utterance.

Two forms of legalized utterance were held to be imbued with their own distinct Mainyus, whose workings were so vividly apprehended that in time they came to be revered as great gods.[6] One was the *mithra* (Sanskrit *mitra*, though this word does not occur in that language in this basic sense). This was a pact or covenant entered into by two parties - two persons, or tribes, or peoples. The other was the **varuna* (not attested as a common noun in Avestan or Vedic), apparently an oath taken by a single person, a solemn asseveration. The formal uttering of a *mithra* or **varuna* evoked, it was evidently believed, the Mainyu inherent in the words themselves; and this Mainyu was thought to watch thereafter, unsleeping, over those concerned, ready to punish any who broke faith. Humans too were naturally vigilant, at least those directly concerned in each case; and forms of trial existed for anyone accused of failing to keep his word. If the accused denied the charge, recourse could ultimately be had to the judicial ordeal. Essentially this again evoked the power of the spoken word. The accused was required solemnly to affirm his innocence, and was then made to undergo either a form of submersion in water (where a **varuna* was concerned) or exposure to fire (in the case of a *mithra*). The Mainyus Varuna and Mithra were then expected to intervene to save the faithful man, but to let water or fire kill the guilty one. So from proto-Indo-Iranian times water became the special helper and indeed element of Varuna, one of whose by-names was Apam Napat, "Son of the Waters", while fire belonged especially to Mithra.[7] There was thus a complexity here of apprehension, with fire and water having their own Mainyus, but being thought of as dwelt in also at will by these other two great Spirits.

It is not hard to imagine the terror of the ordeal, or the intensity with which an accused person, and his family and friends, would have prayed to the

Mainyu Mithra or Varuna, with life at stake; or the warmth of devotion to these beings among those who survived. Sometimes, moreover, a pact would have been entered into by two clans or tribes; and then the aggrieved one would have had to have recourse to fighting to enforce what was seen as right. Its members would then undoubtedly have called on Mithra to aid them in punishing the covenant-breakers, and this appears to be the genesis of the concept of him as a war-god, fighting always on the side of the just - a concept abundantly attested for this many-sided divinity in his Avestan *Yašt*.

This *Yašt* lists the many occasions for entering into a *mithra*, including such regularly recurrent ones as marriage contracts, pledges of friendship, and the binding of a pupil to a teacher.[8] Many other occasions doubtless called for a simple oath. The exalted positions attained by Mithra and Varuna in the proto-Indo-Iranian period suggest a society with complex social links and a strong respect for the law - but also one with a marked bent for litigation, for upholding justice and for identifying and punishing wrongdoers, if necessary with the utmost severity.

An especial title was accorded Mithra and Varuna, relatively "young" divinities, it seems, with no counterparts in other Indo-European pantheons. They were hailed as *ahura* (Sanskrit *asura*), meaning "lord" - a title of respect used also, like the English term, for men of high position. To judge from Avestan usage (more conservative, it appears, in this regard than Vedic), this title was originally given only to them and to one other divinity, who was venerated as greater still, their superior in a divine triad. This was Ahura Mazda (in Vedic called simply the Asura[9]), the Mainyu of wisdom, that power or spirit which should direct all thought and action. Some divine concepts were plainly linked with particular human occupations; and it seems likely that the concept of Ahura Mazda was originally that of the Mainyu of the wisdom which should enter most fully, and be most constantly dwelling in, the person of a high priest. The high priest was, or ought to be, the wisest and most learned of the learned group in society; and there are slight linguistic indications that he had a controlling voice in the deliberations of tribal councils, that it was he who was in a measure the leader or ruler of a proto-Indo-Iranian tribe.[10] If the concept of Mazda evolved as that of his celestial counterpart, Mithra and Varuna may well have come to be seen as having a divine affinity with the chief laymen of the tribe, powerful and upright elders who enforced decisions which owed much to the counsel of the high priest. Very possibly it was the members of the tribal council who were first addressed by the respectful title of *ahura* "lord", which then came to be used also in invocations of these three celestial beings, conceived as especially concerned with the wise and just conduct of human affairs.

Ideally these affairs were thought to be governed by *aša* (Sanskrit *ṛta*)the principle of order, that which ought to be. It was according to *aša* that law and justice prevailed, and that individuals acted well, bringing good Mainyus into their hearts. *Aša* was held to govern the world around them also: so it was by its rule that the sun rose daily, the seasons changed, rain came, and there was birth and growth. Threatening *aša* was the counter-principle of disorder, *drug* (Sanskrit *druh*), and people had to strive actively, together with the gods, to resist it. When they failed there came drought, famine and disease, lawlessness and strife, treachery and fear. This concept of order as the proper state of things, physically, socially and morally, with disorder breaking in irregularly, is again one which is found widely in the world.[11]   The ancient Iranians, believing the great Mainyus or gods to be generally benevolent, thought of each as maintaining some functioning of *aša* . In the physical sphere there were, for instance, the Mainyus of sun and moon and rain-bringing wind, while among the "social" Mainyus there was Indra. He was most probably conceived originally as hypostatizing the ideal qualities of the *mairyas*, the young men of the tribe who would have had as their duties tending the flocks and herds, driving off beasts of prey, hunting and if necessary fighting to defend the tribal lands. Their especial divinity was conceived accordingly as a being of strength and courage who delighted in daring activities, these being proper qualities (that is, ones in accord with *aša*) for *mairyas*, if used in the interest of the tribe. So Indra, if worshipped by them, would duly enter their hearts and strengthen them in these attributes.

The lesser Ahuras too, as we have seen, had their particular functions; but, presumably as their importance grew, they came to have attributed to them the all-embracing one of upholding *aša* generally, in its cosmic as well as social aspects, under the direction of Mazda. Their concepts were accordingly vastly enlarged, and these three appear, before the separation of the Indo-Iranian peoples, to have become their chief gods. The Iranian priests invoked them collectively by a cultic formula (still used by Zoroaster himself) as "Mazda-and-(the-other)-Ahuras";[12] and they put their *aša*-directed rituals, which were to promote the well-being of the world, under the especial guardianship of the lesser pair: Mithra (always set first, probably simply because his was the shorter name) was held to protect those solemnized between sunrise and noon, Varuna those between noon and sunset.[13]

The principle of *drug* seems to have been conceived by the mainly optimistic Indo-Iranians as much less powerful than *aša* (to judge from the only slight representations of *druh* in Vedic); and it was seen to be supported by lesser forces, malevolent terrestrial beings,[14] together with Mainyus of bad qualities or emotions. Prominent among the latter was Aešma, Mainyu of rage or fury, who was imagined as armed with a bloodstained club - a potent stirrer-up of quarrels and strife, and so an energetic helper of *drug*.[15] *Aša* and *drug* would, according to the general pattern of Indo-Iranian thinking, each have been conceived as possessing its own Mainyu; but the Vedic evidence suggests that in their case these concepts remained simple and undeveloped.

Linked with the priests' reflections on *aša* were their reflections on the nature and origins of the physical world which it should regulate. The proto-Indo-Iranian priests evidently achieved a schematic analysis which their Indo-Aryan and Iranian descendants developed in different ways. The ancestors of the "Avestan" people came to see the world as made up of seven distinct creations;[16] a "sky" of stone, conceived as a hard shell enclosing all the rest; water filling the bottom of this shell; earth lying like a flat dish upon the water; a single plant, animal and man at the centre of this earth; and fire, visible in the sun and in hearth fires, but also an unseen vital force within the whole cosmos.[17] Avestan and Vedic texts both suggest that the original materials for these creations were considered to be self-existent,[18] even, in Vedic thought at least, to some extent self-arranged. Thus there is a Vedic concept that at the birth of the world a small clod of earth rose to the surface of the primeval waters, floated and gradually spread to cover most of them.[19] How active a part in ancient Iranian thought was assigned to the gods in bringing such developments about, or in "arranging" or "shaping" the creations, cannot be fully discovered; but there are indications that there was no concept of a single "shaping" or "arranging" divinity, but that a considerable role was assigned to Varuna, presumably as Spirit of the solemnly spoken word. The Iranian priests imagined this world in its first state to have been static, with the sun standing still, as at noon. Then sacrifices were performed which gave it life and motion. The solitary plant was plucked and crushed, the bull who represented the animal creation was slain, together with the man, and from the seed of the three came all further life in its variety and abundance. The sun and the other celestial bodies began their movements, waters started to flow and rain to fall, and the cycle of the seasons, and of birth and death, followed. It has been suggested that the acts of creative sacrifice were attributed to Varuna's brother Ahura, Mithra,[20] and this, if so, would yield a familiar symmetry, with the two lesser Ahuras acting as usual in concert, and fulfilling presumably the command of Mazda. But the only positive evidence for it is late, just possibly from what may have been a stubborn local survival of a pre-Zoroastrian myth. In Zoroastrianism itself a new teaching obliterated this part of the older beliefs.

There is no evidence to suggest that the ancient Iranian priests sought a reason for the coming into being of the world - indeed, if this happening were seen as partly self-generating, it was not necessarily thought of as fully purposed. Thereafter, the expectation plainly was that it would continue to exist, governed by the rules of *aša* , if gods and men were both active in their proper tasks. For men an important part of these tasks, for laity and priests alike, was the regular performance of religious rituals in order to strengthen the beneficent Mainyus, and so help to maintain the vitality of all that was *spenta* -

that is, powerful, giving furtherance and increase, approximately "holy" in the original sense of that word.[21] The essential duties of lay people, to judge from common elements in the Hindu and Zoroastrian traditions, were to venerate the gods thrice daily in prayer (at sunrise, noon and sunset), and to care for their hearth fires and the springs or streams from which they drew water, making offerings to their Mainyus. It was also meritorious in them to provide for priests to perform rites for the common and cosmic good. Of these the main one was the *yasna* (Sanskrit *yajna*), "the" act of worship. This rite, solemnized (to judge from Zoroastrian usage) daily, re-enacted the cosmogonic myth of the three sacrifices, in so far as those of plant and animal were concerned (human sacrifice was probably also offered on rarer occasions), and one of its intentions was evidently to help keep the creations pure and *spenta*. All seven were represented there, so their Mainyus could be directly venerated and the physical creations strengthened through being consecrated anew. The ceremony was enacted in a very simple setting, that of the *pavi* - a small rectangle of clean ground enclosed by ritually drawn furrows. In this, which was itself consecrated, dwelt the Mainyu of the earth. The Mainyu of the sky was in the stone mortar, in which was crushed, with a stone pestle, the *haoma* (Sanskrit *soma*) that represented the plant creation. The animal creation was present through the sacrificial beast. There was water in the libation bowl and fire in a brazier to receive offerings, while the creation of mankind was represented by the officiating priest, who had put himself into a state of ritual purity in order that his purifying of the other six creations might be effective, and his worship acceptable to the gods.[22]

In all observances, both priestly and lay, there was a minimum of what was man-made. There was no temple or altar, statue or other artificial icon. The direct objects of veneration were natural things, and the major acts of worship thus fixed people's thoughts on the world about them, both its tangible forms and apprehended inner forces. The ancient Iranians evidently felt themselves very much a part of this world; but since man was the only self-conscious "creation", alone capable of considered action, his role within it was held to be vital: his life was to be lived with a sense of stewardship for the other creations and in alliance with the beneficent gods, so that *aša* might rule and the world continue from generation to generation.

Among the proto-Indo-Iranians there seems to have been natural joy in this life and unmitigated regret at departing it, with a general dread of the hereafter. Like other Indo-European peoples, they thought of the spirits of the dead as existing joylessly in a dark underworld, and they did what they could to help them with regular offerings of consecrated food and clothing, whose Mainyus would bring comfort to them. Great importance was therefore attached to the family, since only one's own descendants could be expected to perform these rites. But some time before the Iranians and Indo-Aryans evolved their separate identities a new hope became nurtured that some - probably the great men of the tribe and those offering the most sacrifices - might escape this dreary fate, their spirits ascending instead to the bright realm of the gods. The rite of burial was apparently linked with the old belief in a subterranean fate, those of cremation and exposure with the new hope of bliss on high. The Vedic evidence shows that with this hope went belief in resurrection of the body. This was to take place about a year after death (the period during which the most rituals were performed for the departed). Then the clean dry bones would be clothed again in flesh, so that the spirit, once more embodied, could enjoy to the full the tangible delights of heaven. As we have seen, all three ways of disposing of the dead were practised at Sintashta,[23] suggesting that in this small, presumably predominantly Iranian, community a diversity of expectations about the afterlife prevailed around the middle of the second millennium.

This diversity shows that the old Iranian religion into which Zoroaster was born was not static in its beliefs, and that some measure of innovation, and so almost certainly of controversy, existed well before his own day. The violent social changes traced in the preceding chapter probably then quickened divisive religious tendencies. The predatory *mairyas*, living by their daring and physical prowess, may be supposed to have offered worship more and more ardently to the god who was especially their own, namely Indra, invoking him for help before their raids, and thanking him with lavish sacrifices when these were successful. The same was evidently true of their counterparts, the Indo-Aryan *maryas* whose priests composed the Rigvedic hymns; and Indra gained so enormously in importance for them that he became "the favourite god of the Vedic people"[24]. In contrast the law-abiding pastoralists for whom Zoroaster spoke continued (to judge from his own works) to offer their chief worship to the Ahuras, the great upholders of *aša* . Yet there is no reason to suppose that, before Zoroaster gained a hearing, any of them went so far as to reject Indra. His Vedic worshippers, however ardent, continued to venerate with him the three great Asuras and the many other gods; and most probably the Iranian pastoralists likewise followed in the ways of their forefathers by worshipping all the gods, including Indra in his (presumed) traditional and beneficent role of especial god of the *aša*-abiding young men of the tribe. For despite developments, brought about, it seems, by the pressure of individual hopes and fears, as well as by social change, the old Iranian religion appears essentially profoundly conservative, faithful to beliefs and practices which went back for countless generations before Zoroaster's own day. It thus provided the prophet with a deep and solid bedrock on which to found his new religion.

NOTES

1   This term was coined by R. R. Marett, *The Threshold of Religion* (2nd ed., London 1914), to describe "non-personalized concepts of spirit" as against those of visualized supernatural beings usually implied in the word animism. Cf. Ruth Benedict, "Animism", *Encyclopaedia of the Social Sciences*, s.v., pp.65-7.

2   See H. Güntert, *Der arische Weltkönig und Heiland*, Halle 1923, 104 f. (cited by Duchesne-Guillemin, *Zoroastre*, 74); M. Schwartz, "The old Eastern Iranian world view according to the Avesta", *CHIr.* 2, 1985, 641. On OAv. *mainyu* see quite otherwise J. Kellens, "Un avis sur vieil-avestique *mainiiu-*," *MSS* 51, 1990, 97-123.

3   Cf. E. Tchernykh in V. Yanine and others, *Fouilles et recherches archéologiques en URSS*, 83-4.

4   See below, pp.117-18.

5   See F. B. J.Kuiper, "The ancient Aryan verbal contest", *IIJ* IV 1960, 217-81, esp. pp.243-52.

6   For references to some of the large literature on these two gods see *HZ* I 24 ff.

7   For simplicity's sake a proto-Indo-Iranian form, *Varuna, is used here throughout rather than the correctly postulated Av. *Vouruna. In Iranian tradition this divinity is known by cult names only, that is, Apam Napat, literally "Grandson of the Waters", Ahura Berezant "High Lord", and Baga, "the Dispenser" (that is, of good). His identification under these names was first proposed in *HZ* I 40 ff. See subsequently *HZ* II, index s.v. Baga, the findings there concerning Baga being modified in *HZ* III 112 n.235; "Varuna the Baga", *Monumentum G. Morgenstierne* I, *Acta Ir.* 21, 1981, 59-73; "Apąm Napāt", *EIr.* II 148-50; "Mithra Khšathrapati and his brother Ahura", *Papers in Honour of R. N. Frye, BAI* 4, 1992, in press. The identification is not accepted by those who still maintain a long-standing hypothesis that Skt. Varuṇa was to be equated with Ahura Mazda. There is no evidence, however, to support this, whereas the case for his identity with the Iranian Ahura known by these three cult names rests on a whole set of consistent and significant facts, drawn from the fields of ritual observance, iconography, and texts.

8   *Yt* 10:110-17.

9   For references to studies of the Vedic Asura by P. Thieme, identifying him with Ahura Mazda, see *HZ* I 37-40, 48.

10   See E. Benveniste, *Le vocabulaire des institutions indo-européennes*, Paris 1969, II 14-15.

11   For the closeness of parallels in, for example, Egyptian thought see *HZ* II 125-6.

12   *Y.* 30:9, 31:4. For a defence of the above understanding of the phrase (against "Ye Ahuras and Mazda") see I. Gershevitch in *Studia Grammatica Iranica, Festschrift H. Humbach*, ed. R. Schmitt and P. O. Skjaervø, Munich 1986, 85-101. That the phrase was a traditional one of the pre-Zoroastrian period is generally admitted, but those who seek to maintain that Zoroaster was a strict monotheist have to consider that he adapted it to mean something else.

13   This usage is attested in Avestan liturgies (with Varuna invoked as Apam Napat), and remains Zoroastrian ritual practice still today. That it is pre-Zoroastrian in origin cannot be more than a very strong probability.

14   See *HZ* I 85-8.

15   Cf. above, p.37. The Av. concept has no exact Vedic equivalent, and so cannot be traced back to the proto-Indo-Iranian period; but this demon with his primitive weapon can confidently be regarded as older than the time of Zoroaster.

16   Other cosmogonic schemes may have been developed by priests of other Iranian tribes, to remain unrecorded; but that which Kellens thought he had traced in the *Gathas* themselves ("La cosmogonie mazdéenne ancienne : huttes cosmiques en Iran", *Les Civilisations orientales, Cosmogonies*, Liège 1990, 1-15) rests on very slight bases - proposed special meanings for a pair of rare OAv. words, and some suggested Vedic analogies. The idea that the ancient Iranians conceived the world in the likeness of a nomad's tent, or that Zoroastrianism "inherited the old ideology of the nomads" (p.15) is in any case anachronistic, and contradicts the comment by Kellens -Pirart, *TVA*, 23, on *Y.* 53:8 (cf. above, p.32 with n.40, pp.43-4). Kellens nevertheless elaborates this theory in his *Zoroastre*, 41 ff.

17   See in detail *HZ* I 130 ff., with, p.141, a discussion of the creation of fire and, p.146, the reason for considering this cosmological scheme to be pre-Zoroastrian.

18   See *HZ* I 131; J. Kellens, "Ahura Mazdā n'est pas un dieu créateur", *Etudes irano-aryennes offertes à G. Lazard*, ed. C.-H. de Fouchécour et Ph. Gignoux, St. Ir., Cahier 7, Paris 1989, 217-28.

19   See F. B. J. Kuiper, "The basic concept of Vedic religion", *History of Religions* 15, 1975, 108.

20   See most recently P. Kreyenbroek, "Cosmology (Zoroastrian)", *EIr.* V (in press).

21   For references concerning this basic concept see *HZ* I 196-7. What follows here is deduced from the *Gathas* and other Zoroastrian texts, and from the Zoroastrian rituals (priestly and lay) and a comparison of them with Brahmanic ones. See in detail *HZ* I 147 ff.

22   For what follows see in detail *HZ* I 109 ff. That the seven creations are represented at the *yasna* is a tenet known from living Zoroastrianism, see below, pp.172-3 with n.74.

23   Above, p.35.

24   A. A. Macdonnell, *A Vedic Reader*, Oxford 1917 (2nd Indian repr. 1972), 41, 44. The development seems readily comprehensible as an internal Indian one, for if Indra was the divinity whom the Indo-Aryan warriors and their priests chiefly worshipped, it would be natural for them to have aggrandized him steadily, attributing to him qualities and activities transferred from other gods. So in the end Vedic Indra, destroyer of demons and releaser of life-giving waters, is hard to recognize as himself the Zoroastrian archdemon who is exorcised in *Vd* 10:9, chief agent of evil after Anra Mainyu (*Vd* 19:43), and opponent of great Aša (*GBd.* 5:1, 34:27). Similarly the link is far from immediately obvious between the divine *maryas*, that is, the Maruts who regularly accompany Indra, and the wolfish *mairyas* of Zoroastrian tradition. In this area of belief changing social conditions appear to have led Zoroaster to challenge and to change an old Indo-Iranian concept, namely that of Indra as the patron-god of the young men (*maryas*) of the tribe, so that from a mighty and kind helper he became a potent and wicked stirrer up of strife.

CHAPTER FOUR

Zoroaster's Teachings:
Inherited Beliefs
and New Doctrines

Zoroaster's is the first individual voice to be heard out of all the great family of Indo-European peoples,[1] and his community deserves both gratitude and respect for the faithful preservation of his words, without aid of writing, from so long ago. Yet because his voice is a solitary one, speaking from the remote past, and because his utterances are in an otherwise unknown stage of a long dead language, much obscurity invests them. Some of this is purely linguistic. There are numerous words whose sense is doubtful or quite unknown, and many problems of syntax. Since Old Avestan is highly inflected, much meaning can be packed into few words; but it is often uncertain just how those words should be construed, and so ambiguities arise. There are also, it appears, intended ambiguities, since the *Gathas* are composed in what has been identified as a very old esoteric tradition of mantic poetry, in which the poets deliberately invested their words with layers of meaning and subtle allusions, expecting full comprehension, it seems, only from those who had already attained a measure of spiritual experience and knowledge.[2] Zoroaster's verses constitute, moreover, only a very small body of literature and often give expression to his own inward dialogues with God. Where he does turn to address his hearers, urgently, it is not to teach them the elements of his beliefs, but to exhort them to act according to those beliefs,[3] which, the implication must be, they have already heard from him, expounded doubtless in good, plain, prose orations. Recognition of the *Yasna Haptanhaiti* as also his work has meant a most valuable extension of his transmitted utterances; but this devotional text, itself very short, presents its own problems, and cannot be expected to clarify all those of the *Gathas.*

The following assessment of the *Gathas,* made over a quarter of a century ago, may accordingly be held still to stand, namely that they "convey lofty ideas in noble verse, and, even through the lexical and syntactic haze which bedims them, a sense of deep sincerity, anxious inquiry for truth, and missionary urge. Whatever one may think of the numerous obscure verses, no sooner is the haze momentarily lifted than one meets with clear vision and clear presentation".[4] What is crucially important is that where there is this clarity, what is conveyed are beliefs which are alluded to in the Young Avesta and systematically expounded in the *zand* translations of lost Young Avestan texts. These are, moreover, beliefs which have shaped the lives and hopes of Zoroastrians throughout the known history of the faith. As one of the most learned and perceptive students of the Iranian religion long ago observed, once this continuity is recognized, a key becomes available for unlocking the complexities of the *Gathas.*[5] This key has in fact been used in varying degrees by all who have studied these ancient texts - even, perhaps sometimes unconsciously, by those who try to set aside the tradition and to interpret them as far as possible as a closed corpus, to be understood only on its own terms. The character of the texts makes any such attempt impractical; and since scholars of this school of thought tend to be comparative linguists, come to Old Avestan from Vedic studies, they appear at times unduly influenced instead by Vedic concepts. Such scholars have contributed enormously by their labours to the understanding of Old Avestan, for, as one of them has observed, "however innovative the religious doctrine [of the *Gathas*] ... the language, the rhetoric, the concepts which supply the images and metaphors, are astonishingly conservative and similar to those used by the Vedic *r̥ṣi*"[6] Nevertheless, a judgment made last century still seems sound, that their contribution to the actual comprehension of the *Gathas* themselves has remained "wholly disproportionate to their talents, because talent put to the service of a wrong method is nothing but a most potent instrument of error".[7]

The three major translations of the *Gathas* to appear in recent decades have all been by scholars whose main concerns have been linguistic, and whose interest in Zoroastrianism has been accordingly incidental and limited; and together they illustrate some of the weaknesses in this approach. An obvious one is a tendency to the negative. Where subtle allusions or ambiguities can yield meanings wholly consonant with known Zoroastrian beliefs or practices, the translator, either through ignorance or through a determined undervaluing of the Zoroastrian tradition, neglects this aid, resting in what appears unnecessary, even perverse, doubt. Linked with this is the fact that studying these very difficult texts in virtual isolation from the religion for which they are the fundamental holy works means that there is then nothing to act as a check on a scholar's imagination and so prevent him reading into them his own idiosyncratic ideas.[8]   As it happens, totally opposing ones informed the two earlier of these translations. The author of the first one identified a number of ritual allusions in the hymns, and since the rituals concerned belong to Zoroastrian as well as Brahmanic tradition, their identification was widely accepted as deepening understanding of the *Gathas*[9]. However, these elements dominated their discoverer's thoughts to the extent that he interpreted most of the hymns as being themselves ritual texts, even though they are arranged by metre and have no discernable liturgical pattern. The second translator thought that Zoroaster was too lofty a moralist to have had any use for rituals, and he explained these allusions as purely metaphoric, thereby losing almost all sense of the actuality of the ancient religion.[10] The authors of the third translation held to the interpretation of the hymns as ritual texts but developed it further, seeing them as dense with ritual references, mostly vaguely defined and supposed to be conveyed by general terms, whose ritual implications had to be divined from the context. This understanding of the *Gathas* was indicated by the frequent insertion in the translation, after a wide variety of words, of the adjective "ritual" in brackets.[11]   An entirely novel rendering of them was thus achieved, with almost all doctrinal and ethical matter eliminated. All these translations made very important contributions to the understanding of the texts; but for further progress in their interpretation it would seem desirable for such advances to be exploited by the use of what has been called "the more patient and humble historical method",[12]   which accords respect to the beliefs and practices of Zoroaster's followers (and hence to his own powers as a teacher of men), and so offers its practitioners some protection from speculative or anachronistic extremes.

Much of the strength and effectiveness of Zoroaster's teachings derives, it seems, from the fact that they were developed from an age-old tradition by a single ardent mind and spirit. That tradition was itself very strong, an ethnic religion which had already reached a point where it must have satisfied many emotional and imaginative needs; and from it Zoroaster evolved a clearly formulated and firmly based credal faith. The clarity and coherence of its doctrines undoubtedly owed much to his own intellectual powers, but something surely also to the fact that, alone among the founders of the world's great religions, he was a trained priest, steeped from a very early age in the professional study of religion. The Brahmanic and Zoroastrian traditions together show that the education of a priest among the ancient Iranians would have been rigorous, beginning in early boyhood. In that wholly non-literate culture it would necessarily have involved much learning by heart, essentially of sacred *manthras* and of the names and proper invocations of the gods. Exact knowledge would have had to be acquired of the rituals of worship, and when these were to be performed. There was much else to master besides, about the myths and functions of the divine beings, and traditional lore of all kinds, since it was the priests who were the guardians and transmitters of learning. There would have been teaching also in the different kinds of utterances through which worship was to be offered and wisdom enshrined; and the richly wrought verses of the *Gathas*, together with the formal cadences of the prose *Yasna Haptanhaiti*, bear witness to this aspect of the prophet's training. Like all oral compositions these texts contain fixed elements of speech, which can be shown by the occurrence of similar ones in the Rigveda to belong to an ancient heritage of elevated diction;[13] and these would have been acquired in the course of a priest's training, absorbed through learning by heart admired verses and the established forms of liturgical usage.

Most pupils were probably content to take their training to a level which allowed them to practise as family priests. Beyond that, there is likely to have been some specialization, with talented and inquiring youths going from sage to sage in search of further enlightenment, while for those with especial gifts (of whom Zoroaster was undoubtedly one) instruction was perhaps given in techniques of attaining mystical experience, of entering directly into communion with the divine. Various indications (including the material remains at Sintashta) suggest that divergences existed before his day in matters of belief and practice (notably over the goal of the departed spirit, the means of attaining bliss, and the associated problem of proper burial rites); and these must surely have stimulated reflection and caused disputes. It seems very possible, therefore, that in the prophet's own stirring and troubled times he was not the only *manthran*, that is, one with the gift of shaping *manthras* or inspired utterances, who used this medium to give expression to disturbingly new ideas.

Zoroaster was evidently justified in applying the term *manthran* to himself,[14] since he uttered brief, inspired words of power (such as the great *Yatha ahu vairyo* or *Ahunvar*). Yet a gulf separated him from the traditional *manthran* in that the latter (to judge from the evidence about his Indian counterpart, the *mantrakṛt*) simply spoke his *manthra* and left it to work its effect, whereas Zoroaster, proclaiming what he believed to be not only divine truths but divine commands, was urgent in pressing his hearers to listen, accept and act, so that they and the world might be saved. He was thus truly a prophet, and very possibly the first to arise among his people.

Of Zoroaster's extant works, the liturgical *Yasna Haptanhaiti* is likely to have been composed after he had founded his community under Vištaspa's protection, and so it will be considered in the next chapter. The *Gathas,* as internal evidence shows, cannot be assigned as a whole to any one period in his life, since he evidently continued to add fresh verses to them from time to time. Nevertheless, they give the strong impression that for the greater part they belong to that span (one would suppose his early manhood) during which he had his great visions - visions which perhaps were the basis for his intellectual formulation of doctrine, but which perhaps came to him as validation of beliefs which were already taking shape in his thoughts. It is impossible to determine which, because the verses which tell of his visions also convey his profoundest and most original teachings, thought and mystical experience being fused seemingly into one.

It is undisputed that Zoroaster offered his ardent personal devotion to the greatest of the Ahuras, Mazda. Since his own tribe was evidently one of *aša*-respecting pastoralists, he was most probably brought up from infancy to worship chiefly those divinities who were believed to guard *aša*, namely the three Ahuras; and of them, as we have seen,[15] Mazda was probably the most beloved by priests. On him, it seems, Zoroaster concentrated his thoughts and meditations, reaching thereby new apprehensions of his nature and his works. He conceived him in traditional fashion as a Mainyu - the Mainyu of wisdom - but identified him as the most bounteous or holiest of all Mainyus, Speništa Mainyu[16] (which was to be one of his regular invocations in the Young Avesta). He apprehended him further as a great cosmic divinity, wearing the sky as a garment, but also anthropomorphically, a being endowed with hand and eye and tongue, whom he had seen and with whom he had spoken face to face.[17] This very natural concept of God in the exalted likeness of man went, moreover, beyond mere outward seeming, for he attributed to Mazda in one very important respect a nature analogous to that of man. The ancient Iranians, as we have seen,[18] regarded man as simple in his psychic constitution, but able to open or bar the way to various Mainyus, some good, some bad, who might enter his heart and affect his thoughts, moods and actions. These Mainyus were independent powers whom an individual could, if he desired their presence within him, venerate and entreat, or whom he could seek to keep at bay. Zoroaster perceived Mazda, for all his greatness, somewhat similarly. He believed him to be wholly good as well as wise, and he thought that, in his entire goodness, he brought into his own being six lesser, but still very great, Mainyus, likewise *spenta* beings, who because of his unchanging goodness dwelt with him always. But as Mainyus they remained individual spirits who had their separate existence and so could enter also into mortals - whom, however, they left if they became unworthy, returning again if they reformed. Whether any other Iranian mystic had had similar apprehensions of the nature of a divine being before Zoroaster there is no means of knowing; but it seems probable that this was a wholly new concept, part of his all-embracing ethical interpretation of things, and of his especial vision of Mazda - for this complexity of being was apparently attributed by him to no other beneficent divinity.

There are six Mainyus who dwell with Mazda, and (as was already recognized a century ago[19]) their number was determined by there being seven "creations"[20] ; for these six, together with great Mazda (or his Holy Spirit) form a divine Heptad which is closely linked with this material world. The world is of huge importance in Zoroaster's theology, for, he believed, by creating or shaping it Mazda brought into existence not merely a stage for the battle between good and evil, but the means for this battle to be fought, since, as the *zand* translations plainly declare, each creation, in the beginning purely good, now longs ardently to free itself from the corruption which has come upon it, and to be pure and good again. This doctrine is profoundly animatistic,[21] and contributes very greatly to the uniqueness of the Zoroastrian outlook on the world.[22] Moreover, because Zoroaster (unlike, apparently, earlier Iranian thinkers[23]) perceived a purpose in the bringing into existence of this world, he necessarily saw Mazda, whose purpose it was, as the prime mover behind all acts of creation, and thus the ultimate "Creator of all things".[24] *Datar*, "Creator", is another of the regular terms of invocation of Mazda in the Young Avesta, and in its Middle Persian form, *Dadar*, it becomes almost his fixed attribute.[25]

The six Mainyus whom Zoroaster apprehended as dwelling with Mazda are very diverse in the forces or states which they hypostatize. They appear in verse after verse of his *Gathas*, and once he names them as a group[26]; but usually in his thoughts - which are faithfully reflected in the tradition - they join naturally in pairs; or they appear in groupings of two or three, or in company with other Mainyus whom he revered.[27] The number of times he names each of them has been taken to indicate the relative importance they had for him (and it duly accords with the degree of prominence given to each in the tradition). By this reckoning the two greatest were Aša Vahišta and Vohu Manah.[28] The former is the Spirit or Mainyu of *aša*, that order, cosmic and social, which the Ahuras tirelessly protect, while the latter is the Spirit of good intent or purpose, the *aša*-directed resolve which enables a man to entertain other good Mainyus and to achieve the good life. The second pair was formed by Khšathra Vairya and Spenta Armaiti, the Spirits respectively of desirable dominion (that is, of *aša*-directed authority) and of holy devotion or obedience. Lastly there were Haurvatat and Ameretat, the Spirits of wholeness or health and of long (or everlasting) life.

It is self-evident that these beings were not the only Mainyus which an *ašavan* could and should entertain within himself. Prominent among others whom the prophet actually names in the *Gathas* is Sraoša, the Mainyu of hearkening to God, a concept which merges into spiritual obedience.[29] This concept has spiritual connotations which are hardly present in those of the last members of the Heptad, Haurvatat and Ameretat, and as an individual divinity Sraoša came greatly to overshadow these two in the tradition. They have, however, immense importance as members of the Heptad, the key to whose somewhat puzzling and heterogeneous character is to be sought, it seems, in the focus of Zoroaster's meditations. To judge from the abundant Indian

testimony, and from the many ritual allusions in the *Gathas*,[30] it was general in
the Indo-Iranian tradition for priests to meditate on the rituals which they so
regularly performed, and to which they attributed the greatest importance,
believing them to help both to maintain the visible world and to strengthen the
invisible beings. It was natural that the objects present there before them
should provide a focus for their meditations, and that through these they should
be led to ponder on the nature of their worship and of the gods to whom it was
offered. In India the Brahmans evolved new beliefs about different aspects of
the divine beings, and new myths about their achievements, the most striking
developments in this way concerning Agni (ever-present in the ritual fire),
Soma, and Indra (the greatest *soma*-drinker among the gods[31]); while among
the Iranians it was probably through meditations on the *yasna* that priests
reached the concept of the seven "creations", which they saw as represented
there, and which they thus blessed, so purifying the world.[32]

It was this concept, it appears, which provided the basis for Zoroaster's
profounder meditations. It is virtually certain that as celebrating priest he would
himself, when there was choice, have dedicated the *yasna* most frequently to
Mazda; and very possibly the first stage in the development of his new
theology was a growing, intense awareness of Mazda's Spirit taking
possession of him as he solemnized the service in ritual purity. It was
presumably already established belief that at the *yasna* the priestly celebrant
stood for the whole creation of man; and it seems likely that it was the feeling
that he himself, thus representing one of the seven creations, was filled with the
Mainyu of Mazda which led him to believe that the representatives there of the
other six creations were likewise filled with powerful Mainyus distinct from
their own. Man was a complex being, with a material body but immaterial
parts.[33] The other six creations were simply material. Like all other things
each was believed to possess its own Mainyu, within it always; but traditional
thought allowed material things to be entered into also on occasion by the
Mainyus of immaterial ones. (We have met this already with Mithra and
Varuna, Mainyus of the oath and covenant, entering at the time of the ordeal
into water or fire.[34]) All Mainyus are immaterial, but by transference the
Iranian priests spoke of them according to what they informed as being
themselves either "material" or "immaterial". Thus (with use of the synonym
Yazata, "Being to be worshipped", for beneficent Mainyu) it is declared: "We
worship every immaterial Yazata and we worship every material Yazata".[35]
Zoroaster's thought was thus developed along traditional lines. Moreover,
several of the links which he apprehended between "immaterial" Mainyu and
material creation appear to have existed already in traditional belief, and this
must to some extent have directed his own thinking.[36] This is perhaps clearest
with the Mainyu of *aša* and fire; for the connections between *aša* and the fiery
sun, which regulated cosmic order, and between *aša* and the fire of the ordeal,

which helped to enforce social order and justice by testing truth, appear long-established. So too do the natural associations between Haurvatat and water, Ameretat and nurturing plants, while earth itself, bearing all, belonged almost as naturally to Armaiti, submissive devotion. Earth's natural partner is the sky, and it seems wholly fitting therefore that the "sky", strongest of all the creations in that it held all the others within itself, should be assigned to dominion, especially since the common noun *khšathra* meant not only "dominion, rule" but also the place where dominion was exercised, that is, "domain, kingdom", and in this sense was used (like Vedic *kṣatra*) for the kingdom of the gods on high.

There remains only one other association, that between the Mainyu of *vohu manah*, good purpose, and cattle. This has seemed forced and artificial to most modern scholars, who have sought to explain it in various ways, chiefly through recourse to Vedic myths and metaphors.[37] There is no reason, however, why it should not be understood in a manner similar to that of the other pairings of "immaterial" Mainyu with material creation, with which it forms an integrated system. In the theoretic analysis of the physical world the creation of animals was the one closest to man, and it merited therefore some great Mainyu to imbue and protect it. Mythologically it was represented by the "Uniquely created Bull"; and, as we have seen, cattle were of the greatest practical as well as symbolic importance to the ancient Iranians, forming with them a single community, the *pasu-vira* "cattle-(and)-men". Even today the highly-evolved "barnyard cow", which some Western scholars have found so humdrum a creature,[38] has its own character and will; and it cannot be doubted that the Iranian pastoralists of old knew their animals as individuals, caring for them almost as people and finding them in return responsive and benign. So for Zoroaster's fellow-tribesmen the concept of Vohu Manah dwelling in these nurturing, *spenta* creatures is not likely to have presented a challenge to either sympathy or comprehension. At the *yasna* the sacrifice which represented the animal creation was ideally that of a "bounteous cow" (*gav- spenta-*); and it would accordingly have been the sacrificial cow which was the focus for Zoroaster's meditations on this creation. The Indo-Iranians persuaded themselves that it was to the benefit of the animal itself, as well as to that of gods and men, that it should be offered as a sacrifice rather than die any other death, since the rituals were believed to release its soul to a happy state in the other world; and they thought it best if the creature came to the sacred precinct alert and unafraid,[39] thus by its seeming willingness freeing the sacrificer from blood-guilt. It is probable that among Zoroaster's own people this regularly happened, the animal being quietly handled by those familiar with it.[40] Hence to Zoroaster, meditating, it could well have seemed that it was indeed positively assenting, and so was filled with the Mainyu of good purpose - to him a virtue of the highest order, since without it sentient beings cannot pursue right paths nor entertain other virtuous Mainyus.

This association between Vohu Manah and cattle seems likely to have been a wholly new perception of the prophet's; and so surely was the remarkable concept of the six Mainyus dwelling always with Mazda, and also both with all righteous people and in the physical creations, so that through them all that is good is joined. The processes by which he arrived at this unique doctrine appear in part traditional, in part deeply innovative; in part rational, based on the then accepted analysis of the physical world, and in part mystical and intuitive, felt and imagined as well as reasoned.[41] The doctrine now seems immensely archaic, belonging fittingly to its own distant age[42] ; yet it yielded such a satisfying moral theology, and (with other elements in Zoroaster's teachings) provided so good a belief to live by, that it continued to inspire and guide his followers, with only minor modifications, over many centuries, and even partly survived the moment when they were at last brought suddenly and roughly into contact with modern scientific thought.[43]

Belief in the universal presence of Mainyus made early Zoroastrianism as polytheistic as Hinduism; but it is part of the richness and strength of the religion that Zoroaster combined this worship of many spirits, and hence a reverence for all "good" forms of life, with an exalted monotheism, in the sense of acknowledging one eternal self-existent Being, namely Mazda. How he reached this belief is necessarily a matter for reasoned surmise; but it seems that he could well have done so again through his meditations on the *yasna* rituals. These must have often led his thoughts to the cosmogonic myth of the one original plant, animal and man from which all the present diversity of being has come. Analogy played a large part in ancient thinking, and analogy with these mythic data may well have been an important ingredient in the processes, intellectual, imaginative and mystical, which brought him to apprehend one original divinity also, who had been the source of all lesser divinities, of every beneficent Mainyu.[44] The ground for identifying him as Mazda had evidently been prepared by Mazda's exaltation already as the greatest of the three great ethical Ahuras, but it nevertheless seems a gigantic leap in thought. The magnitude of the leap should not, however, be exaggerated. The *Gathas* themselves and the whole Zoroastrian tradition bear witness to the fact that the prophet's monotheism was a natural growth, fostered by his own genius, from the Old Iranian religion, and made no sharp break with it. He did not proceed, that is, from the postulate of one eternal divine Being to denying the existence of the many other beneficent divine beings of traditional worship, but saw these as come from Mazda - of his essence, and somehow evoked by him, or created by his thought.[45] Thus in the *Gathas* Zoroaster offers veneration not only to the lesser members of the Heptad and to Sraoša, but to other Mainyus of widely differing character - Aši, Mainyu of just recompense, Izha, that of the sacrifice and Tušnamaiti, that of silent thought. He also speaks of Geuš Tašan, "Shaper of the Cow", and twice, as we have seen,[46] invokes the three Ahuras with the traditional cultic formula: "Mazda-and-(the-other)-Ahuras". This formula, which must have been familiar to him from childhood, was in accord still with his new theology, since it clearly proclaimed the pre-eminence of Mazda. Finally in one verse he declares that he will worship by their names "those who were and are" - apparently a cultic expression equivalent to "all the gods";[47] and from these words his followers later evolved the *Yenhe hatam* prayer, which is recited at the end of all litanies of worship, so that no Yazata should lack veneration.

Yet although Zoroaster recognized the existence of lesser *spenta* divinities, and offered them his worship, he evidently concentrated his thoughts and devotion on Mazda himself, the mightiest of Beings, whose Holy Spirit yet enters into everyone who is worthy to receive it. The relationship of Mazda's spirit, Spenta Mainyu, to man is thus like that of the six lesser members of the Heptad to their creations, in which they are indwelling only when and where these are pure. It is a sin in Zoroastrianism to perform rites of consecration over anything impure, in which there will be no such indwelling spirit; and no priest who is physically impure, or not in an *ašavan* state - in whom, for instance,the Spirit of anger has entered, leaving no place for the Holy Spirit - should consider himself in a fit state to consecrate the *yasna*. In *Y.*47:1 Spenta Mainyu is named together with the whole Heptad, that is, the lesser Six and Mazda himself; but the Heptad does not thereby become an Octad, for Spenta Mainyu is virtually one with Mazda - his creative and active power, that extension of his being through which he can become immanent while remaining transcendent. In the *Gathas* the Holy Spirit is repeatedly called the Holiest Spirit, Speništa Mainyu, like Mazda himself,[48] while in the Young Avesta Mazda is named Spenta Mainyu as well as Speništa Mainyu,[49] so that the concepts of the two, though separate, are continually allowed to blend. For Christians a bridge to understanding this complexity is provided by their own doctrine of God the Father and his Holy Spirit. To adapt the words of the Athanasian Creed: "So the Father is God and the Holy Spirit is God, and yet there are not two gods but one god." Definition of doctrine has no place in the *Gathas*, but there Zoroaster's choice of expressions conveys the same belief, that there is no boundary of being between God and his Spirit.[50] Both are Mainyus, and, though distinct, essentially one, as a man and his spirit are one.

It cannot be divined in what order Zoroaster developed his thoughts, and so it is impossible to tell how his belief in one beneficent God and the good world created by him evolved in relation to his apprehension of a mighty force for evil which threatens the rule of Aša. Possibly the two concepts gained hold on his thinking more or less together, the one strengthening the other. The essentially hopeful character of his teachings, and the positive attitude to life with which he so powerfully imbued his followers, suggest that his formative years were happy ones, lived in a peaceful, well-ordered community; but the steppe-tribes were evidently not isolated from one another, and it seems highly likely that he would already as a boy have heard of roving war-bands, and have learnt to pray earnestly to the Ahuras for protection from them. *Yasna* 29 and verses scattered through other *Gathas* leave little doubt, moreover, that at some stage he himself experienced the terrors of a raid, with people killed, possessions looted, pastures perhaps burnt, and frightened cattle driven off, probably most of them to be slaughtered without ceremony. The use of chariots meant that such attacks could be swift, bringing a sudden change from peaceful prosperity to grief, poverty and desolation; and the contrast must have been sharp between the raiders themselves, fierce, greedy, and in the grip of battle-fury, and the people of the homesteads. There were therefore unquestionably materials here to feed a vision of the world in terms of opposites, of good assailed by evil, *aša* by *drug*. And if the men who carried out the raids were wicked, how could the gods whom they worshipped, and who seemingly granted them these cruel successes, be good? And, if not good, how could they have their being from Mazda, himself wholly good? By some such steps, it seems reasonable to suppose, Zoroaster was led to active denunciation of the "Daevas", with at their head, as the Young Avesta shows, the probably by then great Indra.[51]

The term *daeva* is one of ancient origin for divine beings generally, and no certain explanation has yet been found for the restriction of it in this way. It seems likely, however, that already before Zoroaster's own day there was a strong consciousness among the law-abiding "Avestan" people of being above all *ahura-tkaeša*, "adhering to the teaching of the Ahuras", while they may have looked on their more warlike fellows as indiscriminate "worshippers of the gods", *daevayasna*[52]; and that it was through this contrast that the meaning of the word *daeva* "god" came to stand particularly for those divinities whom warriors most venerated. It appears almost certain, however, that it was Zoroaster himself who took the immensely courageous step of actually repudiating these beings as supporters of Aešma, the Mainyu of fury, "with whom they have afflicted the world and mankind".[53] Further, operating with the intellectually satisfying premise of unity at the source of each category of being, he came to postulate a single origin for them also, namely another self-existent Mainyu, as ignorant and evil as Mazda is wise and good. No parallel for such a concept exists in Vedic thought, and with, it seems, no tradition of anything like such a being there was no traditional name to be used for him. Zoroaster accordingly speaks of him with epithets only, as the Mainyu which is hostile (*angra*) or bad (*aka*), the former term yielding his Young Avestan name, Anra Mainyu (Middle Persian Ahriman). This leaves open the question, of what quality or vice was he the Mainyu? Probably his concept went beyond simple definition, being apprehended not merely as ignorance in opposition to wisdom, but as ignorance with which dwelt aggressive malice and an active will to corrupt and destroy, hence evil itself, for which an all-embracing term was lacking.[54]

The apprehension of separate single sources for good and evil attained the character of revealed truth for Zoroaster through his great vision of the two Mainyus, Mazda and the Evil Spirit, alone together in the universe before either the invisible or the visible worlds were shaped - "twins" in their shared but otherwise unique quality of self-existence. In two of the best known *Gathas* he put this vision into words, from which it appears that he saw them as opposed innately and in all their purposing.[55] Yet he also declares that, at their coming together, the Deceitful One (Drugvant) chose achieving the worst things, while the Holiest Spirit, Speništa Mainyu, chose *aša* .[56] This would seem to imply that the two Spirits did not act simply according to their natures, but through the exercise of choice, as if the Evil Spirit could have willed to do good, Mazda evil, and moreover as if *aša* were not brought into being with the world of Mazda's shaping, but existed already in the void. Clearly it is useless to refine on such apparent anomalies. Although there appears a strong intellectual basis for Zoroaster's doctrines, he was a prophet, not a philosopher; and in his thoughts and through his mantic experiences he was evidently seeking not to apprehend the origins and causes of things for the sake of pure knowledge, but in order to understand how what was wrong in the present world had come to exist, and how it could be made right. Having attained such understanding, he had a prophet's burning urge to impart it and to inspire mankind to action, so that it and the world might be saved; and his vision shaped itself in a way that not only declared his perception of truth but also offered a divine example for human action: as the two Spirits had chosen, so every individual on earth has to choose, behaving thereafter accordingly.

Evidently no explanation was felt to be needed as to why Mazda himself should have been moved to choose and act. As the Spirit of wisdom he must "always" have known of the existence of the Evil Spirit, which, as long as only they two were, would appear to have been without consequences. But the myth is ethically fully satisfying: the two Spirits "came together", and the Holiest Spirit willed the destruction of the Evil One, so that only goodness should exist - something which moral man yearns for; and the means he took to accomplish this was to create this world, so that here their forces could encounter and the good ultimately triumph. Mankind and all the other creations were thus made in order to play their part in this great struggle, their existence having a noble common purpose from the very beginning.

Although the two Spirits appear equal before the moment of choice, the nature of that choice showed Mazda to be the "better"; for in the Indo-Iranian tradition *aša* , right order and right behaviour, was felt to be not only what ought to be but what generally was; and *drug*, the crooked and irregular, was no more than an erratic distortion of it. By choosing *aša* Mazda thus declared himself to be dominant and positive,while the Evil Spirit doomed himself to an essentially negative part, seeking only to corrupt and destroy what the Holy Spirit made. In the prophet's words, one created "life", the other "not-life" (*gaēmcā ajyāitīmcā*).[57] Nevertheless, Zoroaster clearly conceived the Evil Spirit to be very powerful, and he nowhere attributes absolute dominance over him to Mazda, in the past or present. In this again he remained within the tradition of his people, for, however magniloquent the praises which the Indo-Iranian priests offered to their gods, they did not in fact regard any one of them as omnipotent. All were felt to need men's worship and sacrifices to strengthen them in their divine activities, and it is clear from the *Gathas* that Zoroaster, although hugely exalting Mazda, still venerated him in this way. So one of the Gathic verses recited daily by his followers can be rendered as follows: "Arise for me, Lord! By Thy Most Holy Spirit, O Mazda, take to Thyself might through devotion, swiftness through good gift-offerings, potent force through truth, protection through good purpose".[58] Man's efforts, though individually puny, are thus needed by God in his battle against evil, and in their sum will help to bring about victory.

For Zoroaster the good life went far beyond offering worship and sacrifice, desirable as those activities were, and embraced being *ašavan* in the full sense of that word. His followers were "to accompany their knowledge [of the revealed truth] and sacrifices continually with words and acts of (good) purpose."[59] But though in this way man could help the divine plan, his own lifespan was short. What was then to become of his soul, when the Evil Spirit had destroyed his body by "not-life", that is, death? As we have seen, long before Zoroaster lived the Indo-Iranians had evolved the belief in a happy afterlife for some on high, in contrast to the shadowy joyless existence that awaited many in the underworld land of the dead.[60] Zoroaster developed this belief in two different fates into a purely ethical one: the souls of all who were *ašavan* would ascend to the kingdom (*khšathra*) of God on high, where Mazda is enthroned, and the souls of all who were *drugvant* would go down below the earth, to the dark realm which the prophet now assigned to the Evil Spirit. In the older belief the souls of the fortunate were probably thought to be saved through a treasure of merit stored up with the gods, it would seem through worship and generous sacrifices;[61] and this concept, of a treasure laid up in heaven during this life, persisted in Zoroaster's thought.[62] But a doctrine of the separation of all the righteous from all sinners demanded something more, an exact means of establishing the achievements of each. The ancient Iranians, as we have seen,[63] were evidently given to recourse to the law; and Zoroaster evolved a belief in a strictly impartial judgment for each soul at death, with the sum of its good thoughts, words and acts throughout adult life being weighed against the sum of its evil ones, and its fate decided accordingly. This was another enormously effective and challenging doctrine, for it gave significance to almost every waking moment, and offered hope of salvation to all through independent striving; for even those who had done great evil could hope, as long as life lasted, to outweigh their sins by new acts of counterbalancing merit.

Although it cannot be proved, it seems highly probable that it was Zoroaster himself, as a worshipper of the Ahuras, who saw Mithra as presiding over the judgment of souls; for the concept appears ancient of this lesser Ahura, in his role of guardian of the covenant, being the judge of mankind in this life[64], so that when a judge was needed also for the hereafter, he was the Yazata most obviously fitted for the role. It is also very possible that the prophet himself perceived Rašnu, the Mainyu of judgment, as actually holding the scales of justice while Mithra pronounced sentence, and that all that was added later was the presence of Sraoša, making up a characteristic Zoroastrian triad (for three is the pervasive auspicious number in the Iranian religion).[65]

Zoroaster modified established beliefs about the hereafter in yet other striking ways, coming to apprehend the fates of *ašavan* and *drugvant* as altogether contrasted. It had been believed (as the Indian tradition shows) that the souls who went up to the kingdom of the gods would there enjoy all conceivable delights, with delicious food, fragrant scents and sweet sights and sounds, while those in the underworld kingdom of the dead lacked all pleasures, existing merely as shades. Zoroaster, in his passionate anger against the wicked, now saw their sojourn in that realm as a time of retribution for their evil acts, during which they underwent not merely deprivation but "long torment", with "darkness, foul food, the crying of woe".[66] Thus he was able to sustain himself and his followers with the thought of those who were unjustly triumphant in this life suffering in their turn after death.

Fate at death was thus of immense importance to Zoroaster, as redressing the injustices of life on earth; and he partly based his concepts of what then took place on various traditional beliefs. One, going back possibly to Indo-European times, was that departed spirits, following downward paths to the kingdom of the dead, had to make a dangerous crossing - probably through or over an underground river - before they could reach that safe if cheerless abode. This belief had had to be modified for those for whom there was hope of ascending to heaven, in that their perilous crossing was to be of a bridge, one end of which rested on the peak of Hara, the mythical mountain at the centre of the world. Zoroaster combined these two beliefs with lasting effectiveness: he saw all spirits as ascending to Hara's peak at sunrise on the fourth day after death (the ancient tradition being that the soul lingered near its familiar haunts for three days before departing). There all were judged. Those who were worthy of heaven then crossed what the prophet called the "Chinvat Bridge" (the meaning of the name is disputed), which for them was broad and safe. The wicked tried to do the same; but for them it contracted to the width of a spear-blade, and they slipped and fell down into the mouth of hell, which gaped on the north side of the mountain peak.

Another myth had evidently evolved in connection with belief in the heavenly destination of privileged souls. It was that the fortunate spirit would be met at the Bridge by a beautiful young girl who became its companion, leading it on upward. This myth was plainly part of the hope in a heaven of all delights, including sexual love. In pagan times no woman, it seems safe to deduce, could expect bliss; and Zoroaster was presumably proclaiming a new teaching by his declaration that he would cross the Chinvat Bridge with all who followed his teachings, whether man or woman.[67] He nevertheless kept the myth of the girl, developing it with a remarkable moral refinement. He saw her, that is, as the Daena, a word whose exact meaning escapes translation, but is perhaps best reflected in English as Inner Self. The Daena was shaped by a person's thoughts, words and acts throughout life, and so, becoming beautiful or ugly, awoke in her possessor joy or revulsion when she showed herself at the Bridge. "He who makes better or worse his thought, O Mazda, he by act and word (makes better or worse) his Inner Self; she follows his leanings, wishes and likings. At Thy will the end shall be different (for each)".[68] "The Inner Self of the wicked man destroys for him the reality of the straight way. His soul shall surely vex him at the Chinvat Bridge".[69]

Abandoning the belief in a houri-like creature promising sexual delights, Zoroaster also abandoned the belief that souls in heaven received again their resurrected bodies within a year or so of death, so that they could once more taste all material pleasures. For him heaven was to be enjoyed in spirit only, just as hell was to be suffered in spirit only (though both intensely) until the end of time.

The phrase "end of time" has now both a solemn and a familiar ring; but Zoroaster, as far as is known, was the first man on earth to conceive of such a thing - of an end, that is, of historic time set within the frame of eternity; and with it an end of birth and death, destruction and renewal - a cessation of all change. This cessation is to come when the earth has been made "glorious", *fraša*, by the defeat of evil, and Mazda's kingdom is established upon it. Paradise, that is Mazda's domain, is to come down from above, with all its divine inhabitants, and be established on Mazda's originally perfect creation, earth, now made perfect once again. Life here will then take on the essentially static quality attributed to the other world, its joys and splendours unthreatened by blemish or alteration. This wholly original concept of time and history having an end was a necessary corollary of Zoroaster's other deeply original one of Mazda's great moral purpose in creating the world. Once that purpose has been achieved, activity and striving will be no more needed. The prophecy in many ways satisfies human instincts and longings, not least in that it makes this dear and familiar earth, which has been the arena of contest, the setting also for eternal bliss.

The events which Zoroaster foresaw as taking place before Frašo-kereti,the "Making glorious", are richly dramatic. Aša will by then have been made strong through the actions of the Yazatas and all just people, and Mazda will have absolute power. The forces of evil having been defeated, there will be a general resurrection of bodies, and the souls of the blessed and the damned will be brought from heaven and hell and incarnated again, so that with those still living they can undergo in the flesh a last judgment.[70] This judgment is to be achieved in a traditional way, through ordeal by fire, but in a Bronze Age form of that ordeal, with use of molten metal. As we have seen,[71] one attested way of administering this was to pour burning hot metal on the bared breast of the accused. If he survived he was judged innocent, saved by Mithra because he was *ašavan*; if he died he was plainly guilty, abandoned by the Yazata to his proper fate. Zoroaster foresaw such an ordeal taking place on a vast scale for all humanity, through immersion in a river of metal, melted by fire. All will have to pass through this river, and the *ašavan* will be saved by the divine beings, whereas the *drugvant* will perish, body and soul - an utter destruction which will be part of the total elimination of evil from the cosmos.[72]

The aim of a complete purging of evil, and the comprehensive, logical nature of Zoroaster's thought, makes it possible to attribute to him himself the belief that the fiery river will then pour down into hell, burning away its horrors and sealing its once dreaded entrance. Hell will thus cease to exist, with all its demonic inhabitants, including the Evil Spirit.[73] The earth will become one level verdant plain, blossoming as in springtime and ready for Mazda's kingdom to come upon it. The blessed will share a communal meal consecrated by a last *yasna*, at which Yazatas will act as priests; and through this their resurrected bodies will be made unblemished and as in their prime, and also immortal, so that they will be fit inhabitants, for ever, of Mazda's realm.

Zoroaster's vividly imagined and immensely powerful vision of the last things was thus, like all his other teachings, partly evolved from traditional elements (the expected dominance of *aša* over *drug*, justice established through a fiery ordeal, bodily resurrection for the few with corporeal life for them ever after in the paradise of the gods) and partly from what appear wholly original ones (an absolute end of time and history, the annihilation of evil, a general resurrection of the dead with a general Last Judgment, and God's kingdom to be established here on earth for ever). The adoption of the essential pattern of his eschatology by the three great Semitic monotheisms has made a number of his leading doctrines familiar to much of mankind,[74] and hence these particular teachings may seem both less original and less archaic than the unfamiliar ones concerning the Mainyus and the Heptad; but if such familiarity can be banished from the mind, all his doctrines can be seen in fact to belong properly to the world of ancient Iranian thought, and to mesh together in a fully integrated, profoundly imagined system.

NOTES

1 So H. H. Schaeder, "Zarathustras Botschaft von der rechten Ordnung", in *Zarathustra*, ed. Schlerath, 106.

2 Kellens ("Methodes pour une nouvelle interprétation des *Gāθā* : la question du *ślesa*", *Proceedings of the 1st European Conference of Iranian Studies*, ed. G. Gnoli and A. Panaino, Rome 1990, 207-16, at p.216) states that, because of the difficulty they felt at knowing whether or not ambiguity was intended, he and E. Pirart had decided always to postulate a single, unequivocal meaning and to take the text quite literally, so that for them, for example, a cow is always just a cow. This method of rigid literalism was long ago criticized by Darmesteter (*ZA* I xxxiv-v) as failing to elucidate the text, but when strictly applied it means that interpretation is deliberately left to the reader.

3 So Lommel, *Rel.*, 8. (Kellens' statement, *Zoroastre*, p.69, that the author of the *Gathas* never addresses ordinary people, but only the gods and his enemies, is at odds with the texts.)

4 I. Gershevitch, "Old Iranian literature", in *HdO* I.iv.i, 1968, 17. Cf., earlier, A. Meillet, *Trois conférences*, 53: "One should not let oneself be deceived by the difficulties and obscurities of the text: the Gāthās are dominated by a fixed theology ... whose coherence is perfect".

5 Darmesteter, *ZA* I cv. Cf. Lommel, *Rel.*, 9: "It is not a case of attributing later thoughts to an earlier time when it is shown that crucial parts of an edifice of thought, set out for us in detail in the later literature, are indissolubly and necessarily linked with others which are earlier attested. Rather it is often the case that shadowy indications of such systematic connections are actually present in the oldest texts, but cannot be recognized if the Gāthās are studied in isolation." This has recently been illustrated in the case of one Zoroastrian divinity by G. Kreyenbroek in his monograph, *Sraoša*, in which he observes (p.30): "The most important functions which are attributed to Sraoša in the later tradition appear to be subtly alluded to in the *Gāthās*: his link with the Sacred Word, his role as mediator between the world and the sphere of the divinities, his close connection with the battle between good and evil as it is fought on earth, his powers of discrimination between right and wrong, and his partnership with Aši, can all be found in the *Gāthās*."

6 Kellens, *Zoroastre*, 24-5.

7 Darmesteter, o.c., p.xxx.

8 Cf., e.g., Henning, *Zoroaster - politician or witch-doctor?*, 14-15 (with reference to J. Hertel, *Die arische Feuerlehre,* Leipzig 1925).

9 Humbach, *Die Gathas des Zarathustra*. The ritual terms studied by him were conveniently brought together by K. Rudolph ("Zarathuštra - Priester und Prophet", *Numen* VIII, 1961, 81-116, repr. in *Zarathustra*, ed. Schlerath, 270-313, at pp.290-2), and are impressive in their number and range.

10   S. Insler, *The Gāthās of Zarathustra*.

11   Kellens-Pirart, *TVA*. The insertion of the adjective "(rituel)" is in fact made by them 102 times, to qualify the substantives *actes, existence, envoi, emprise, succès, parole, annonce, place, mention* and *désastre*. The substantive "(rituels)" and the adverb "(rituellement)" are also occasionally supplied. This way of translating is all the more surprising from scholars who aim at pursuing an exact literalism, see n.2 above.

12   Darmesteter, *ZA* I xxx.

13   See most recently R. Schmitt, "Aryans", *EIr*. II 686.

14   *Y*. 32:13, 50:6.

15   Above, p.55.

16   *Y*. 30:5, and probably 47:2.

17   *Y*. 43:4, 31:13, 3, cf. 28:11.

18   Above, p.53.

19   Darmesteter, *ZA* III lvi.

20   Cf. above, p.57.

21   Cf. above, p.53.

22   On a curious echo of it in the words of St. Paul (*Romans* 8:19-23), which are perhaps an indirect testimony to the long presence of Zoroastrians in Tarsus, see *HZ* III 444-5.

23   Cf. above, p.57.

24   *Y*. 44:7.

25   In his article "Ahura Mazdā n'est pas un dieu créateur" (see above, p.61 n.18), Kellens demonstrated that the OAv. verb *dā* still had the sense of "to put in place, put in order" rather than "to create" (that is, from nothing). But giving order to shapeless mass is a form of creativity, and a mighty act; and to seek to render the distinction by translating OAv. *dātar-* as "establisher" instead of "creator", even if etymologically exact, may well not be truer to Zoroaster's own sense of the word, with the overtones it is likely to have acquired. - Kellens' further contention, that belief in Ahura Mazda as the prime "establisher" could not have contributed to Zoroaster's concept of him as God, is logically obscure.

26   *Y*. 47:1.

27   These facts led the distinguished comparative philologist Johanna Narten, whose Iranian studies have been concentrated on Old Avestan, to question, in her *Die Aməṣa Spəṇtas*, whether the Six were really apprehended by Zoroaster himself as a group having special links with Ahura Mazda and the creations. This is admittedly one of the essential Zoroastrian doctrines which it is impossible to establish in all its fullness from the devotional OAv. texts alone; but there is overwhelming attestation of it as a fundamental teaching of the faith in later dogmatic works and in the written and the living traditions generally. It can be traced quite substantially in the *Gathas*, and so to doubt its being part of Zoroaster's own beliefs seems all too good an illustration of the negative results to be obtained by studying the OAv. texts in isolation, and by treating them moreover out of character as systematic doctrinal works. See further the present writer's more detailed observations in *BSOAS* XLVII, 1984, 159-61.

28   The adjectives *Vahišta* "Best" and *Vohu* "Good" occur with the nouns Aša and Manah in the *Gathas*, but it is only in the tradition that they become their fixed epithets and finally a part of their names. The same is true of *Vairya* and *Spenta* for the following pair. It is often, and probably intentionally, impossible to tell in the *Gathas* whether, for instance, it is the Mainyu of *aša* which is meant, or the principle of *aša*, or both together, this being part of the hymns' complexity (first noted by Darmesteter, *ZA* I cviii, but with the Mainyu defined, as

has been standard usage, as an "abstraction"). The statistics of the occurrence in the *Gathas* of the names of these six beings and/or the thing or quality of which each is the spirit are: *Aša/aša*, 157 times; *Vohu Manah/vohu manah*, 136; *Khšathra/khšathra*, 56; *Armaiti/armaiti*, 40; *Ameretat/ameretat*, 14; *Haurvatat/haurvatat*, 11. See Schlerath, "Avestan aša", *EIr.* II 695.

29   See Kreyenbroek, *Sraoša*, esp. Ch.1.

30   See especially the studies by Humbach, above, n.11.

31   On the great promotion of Indra see also above, p.61 n.24.

32   Cf. above, p.58.

33   On these parts see Bailey, *Zor. Problems*, 98.

34   Above, p.54.

35   *Y.* 16:1-2 (*vīspəmca ... mainyaom yazatəm yazamaide ... vīspəmca ... gaēθīmca yazatəm yazamaide*). Cf. the reference to "immaterial Yazatas" in *Vd* 2:20, cited above, p.2. Since Avestan has grammatical gender, Mainyus take the gender of the substantives naming what they inform. Thus of the six lesser members of the Heptad three (Aša, Vohu Manah,Khšathra) are neuter, three feminine, while the word *mainyu* itself is masculine. This word is not used of the Six in the extant Avesta, but in Pahl. works they are designated by its Middle Persian form, *mēnōg* (cf., e.g. below, p.139). They are more often referred to as the Ameša Spentas/Amašaspands/Amahraspands, a term which first occurs in *YHapt.* (see below, pp. 91, 93), and which can be applied generally to any beneficent divinity.

36   Johanna Narten, through her fresh and close scrutiny of the OAv. texts, has established that only five of the seven links between the Heptad and the seven creations are indicated in them, namely Aša with fire, Vohu Manah with cattle, Armaiti with earth, Haurvatat and Ameretat with water and plants; but five out of seven seems ample attestation in these undogmatic works. On the one complexity, that of Khšathra with the stone sky and with metal, see below, pp. 117-18. In general on the traditional associations see in more detail *HZ* I 205 ff., with reference especially to the admirable studies of H. Lommel.

37   For example H. P. Schmidt, *Zarathustra's religion and his pastoral imagery*, Leiden 1975 (q.v. for further references).

38   The expression was used by G. G. Cameron, "Zoroaster the herdsman", *IIJ* X, 1968, 267, who undoubtedly spoke in this for others also.

39   *Nirangestan*, ed. Sanjana, fol. 128 V ff., tr. Bulsara, pp.323-7. Further on animal sacrifice in Zoroastrianism see *HZ* I 149-51, *HZ* III 428-9.

40   For similar observances in recent times see *Stronghold,* glossary s.v. "sacrifice", and especially pp.244-5, 260.

41   Cf. Lommel in *Zarathustra*, ed. Schlerath, 32: "I do not believe that speculation was solely or even predominantly a matter for theologians as distinct from the creative prophets, who were able to unite visionary perception with meditative speculation."

42   This fact is disregarded by those who, unwilling to attribute this basic but difficult doctrine to Zoroaster himself, assign it vaguely to unknown theologians of some unspecified later epoch, without seeking to explain either how it was evolved or how it should then have come to be an essential element in the fabric of Zoroastrian belief. In general the properly archaic character of Zoroaster's doctrines has been effectively masked by scholars through the description of his Mainyus as "abstractions".

43   See Boyce, *Zoroastrians*, 196-9.

44   Cf. *HZ* I 192. Monotheistic beliefs are held to have developed in other religions on the social analogy of absolute monarchy; but the *Gathas* suggest an Iranian society in Zoroaster's day of tribes and tribal chiefs, with probably even a high chief not much exalted above his fellows.

45   Cf. *Y.* 31:11. For images for Mazda's creative act in the tradition see *HZ* I 194-5.

46 Above, p.56.

47 *Y*.51:22, following the (unpublished) translation and interpretation of W.B. Henning, see *Sources,* 43.

48 *Y.* 33:12, 43:2, 16: 51:7.

49 *Yt* 13:76, 19:44, 46.

50 That Mazda and his Spirit are essentially one was accepted as self-evident by Darmester (*ZA* III lxiv, lxvi). A wholly artificial difficulty over this doctrine, and the interpretation of the relevant Gathic passages, was created by the "European heresy" (see *HZ* II 232 n.106 and below, n.54), first put forward by the German philologist Martin Haug in the mid 19th century. Against the full weight of orthodox Zoroastrian tradition, and of foreign testimonies from classical times onward, he interpreted *Y.* 30:3 (on which see pp.72-3, above) to mean that Spenta Mainyu was seen by Zoroaster as a "son" of Mazda, with an identity quite distinct from his.

51 See*Vd* 10:9, 19:43 (for him as mightiest of archdemons).

52 These two terms are first attested in early Young Avestan or artificial Old Avestan (i.e. the *Fravarane*).

53 *Y.* 30:6.

54 The fact that the Evil Spirit has no proper name helped the development of the "European heresy" (cf. above, n.50). According to this the twin spirits of *Y.* 30:3, spoken of there by Zoroaster as the Better and the Bad (*vahyō akəmcā*) are to be identified as Spenta Mainyu (seen as wholly distinct from Mazda) and Angra Mainyu; and they are then understood as "twins" in a genetic, not metaphoric, sense, their postulated "father" being Mazda. Ahura Mazda thus becomes the begetter of both good and evil, and the Iranian religion is afflicted with the same problem of theodicy which burdens the three Semitic monotheisms. No support for this interpretation is to be found anywhere in Zoroastrian tradition. On its adoption by 19th-century Parsi reformists, eager to rid themselves of what they felt to be the derogatory label of "dualists", see Boyce, *Zoroastrians,* 202-3.

55 *Y.* 45:2, 30:3.

56 *Y.* 30:4, 5.

57 *Y.* 30:4.

58 *Y.* 33:12 (which forms the beginning of the daily recited *Ataš Niyayeš,* cf. below, pp. 85-6).

59 *Y.* 53:2.

60 Above, pp.58-9.

61 Cf. *Yt* 10.32 (tr. *Sources,* p.28).

62 Cf. Zoroaster's own words in *Y.* 49:10 (on which see Humbach, *Gathas,* I 145).

63 Above, p.55.

64 Cf. *Yt* 10:94, with commentary by Gershevitch, *AHM,* 240-1.

65 Justification for this could be found in the *Gathas, Y.* 43:12.

66 *Y.* 30:11 with *Y.* 31:20.

67 *Y.* 46:10.

68 *Y.* 48:4, following the translation of Gershevitch, *JRAS,* 1952, 177.

69 *Y.* 51:13, cf. 46:11.

70 Belief in the "future body" (Pahl. *tan ī pasēn*), repeatedly affirmed in later Zoroastrian works, appears as an integral part of Zoroaster's eschatological teachings (cf. Darmesteter, *ZA* III lxvi), but is one of his doctrines not alluded to in the *Gathas.*

71 Cf. above, pp.34-5.

72 *Y.* 51:9. On the doctrine see Lommel, *Rel.,* 219 ff.; *HZ* I 242-3; *HZ* III 365-7, 393-4, 403-9. This teaching of Zoroaster's is obscured in some translations of his words,

which suggest that he foresaw the wicked as suffering in hell "for ever"; but in one of the passages concerned, *Y.* 46:11, *yavōi vīspāi* can be understood, without putting any constraint on the words, as "for all (their) lifetime," and in the other, *Y.* 31:20, *darəγəm āyū* is most naturally rendered as "for a long lifetime". In both verses, that is, the sufferings of the wicked are foreseen as lasting for all the remainder of their existence - that is, until the Last Judgment. That in Zoroastrian doctrine hell is not eternal is repeatedly affirmed in Pahl. texts (including *zand* translation), and is indirectly confirmed by early foreign sources. Subsequently it was recognized as one of the doctrinal differences between Zoroastrianism and Islam. On the modification by Zoroastrians themselves of the doctrine of the annihilation of sinners see below, p. 143, 169-70.

73   Cf. *HZ* III 394 n.150.

74   This is treated to some extent in *HZ* III, Chapter Eleven.

CHAPTER FIVE

The Founding of the Zoroastrian Community

Zoroastrianism is the only credal religion which established and maintained itself for hundreds of years without benefit of written texts - a matter for wonder already among the Greeks of old; and since a body of its prophet's exact words is preserved, it is evident that Zoroaster succeeded in founding a community which flourished in unbroken continuity from his day onwards; for where there is only an oral tradition, a break of a single generation is enough to extinguish the knowledge of texts: they perish with those who knew them.

According to tradition, Zoroaster lived long,[1] and this would have enabled him to instruct his first followers thoroughly. From his own words it is known that he, like other prophets, failed to win a hearing from his own people;[2] and success for his mission apparently began when he found acceptance in another "Avestan" - speaking clan or tribe, and there converted Hutaosa, one of the few women honoured in the Avesta. She is praised in one of the *Yašts* because she "believed devotedly in and understood the Mazda-worshipping religion".[3] Conceivably it was the hope which Zoroaster gave to women as well as men of a blessed hereafter which inclined her to listen to him; but whether this was so or not, her husband, Kavi Vištaspa, was also converted "and came forward as the arm and help of this religion".[4] Their whole clan was apparently brought to follow suit, and so the first Zoroastrian community was established. It must have thriven, and appears to have sent out teachers to carry the religion to neighbouring tribes, in keeping with Zoroaster's conviction that Mazda had given him a message for all humanity.

These teachers were plainly not everywhere well received, and the chief of one neighbouring tribe, the execrated Arejat-aspa[5], is said to have tried to suppress the new religion by force. The *Yašts* name others who were hostile to it, and the old confession of faith, the *Fravarane*, gives indications of the persecution of believers, with homes destroyed, property stolen, and lives sometimes forfeited.[6]

For those who whole-heartedly embraced the faith (as the history of other credal religions shows) such persecution is likely to have made them more resolute, and bound them more closely together. It cannot be doubted that there was an intense life of devotion and study among the first believers; and in the absence of books or sculptures or paintings, their understanding of their prophet's spoken words, and still more their ability to transmit this understanding to following generations, must have owed much to his expounding his teachings in association with significant rituals and recurrent observances, which by repetition helped to imprint them deeply in their minds.

One of the most important of these essential observances was the five daily acts of prayer, obligatory for every admitted member of the community. Traditionally, it seems, worship had been offered three times in the twenty-four hours, at sunrise, noon and sunset; and there is no reason to doubt that it was Zoroaster himself who extended it to five times, seeking from his followers a more strenuous devotional life.[7]   The additional times were midnight and dawn; and always the prayers were to be said in the presence of some manifestation of fire, which, since it belongs to Aša, is the icon of truth and justice. This manifestation might be the hearth fire, or the ritual fire, or the sun by day and moon by night. The symbolism of fire as an icon is very powerful, for it not only "shows forth" *aša* but also gives light. The concept of light being linked with goodness, darkness with evil, is not expressed directly in the *Gathas* - indeed in one verse Zoroaster seems to imply that when Mazda created the world he made both light and darkness; but it is hardly special pleading to see in this verse simply the use of a traditional antithesis, traditionally expressed, since in other Gathic passages light is implicitly associated with Mazda, enthroned on high in bright heaven, and darkness with the Evil Spirit, in whose underworld realm sinners suffer. Hence light is a positive, *spenta*, good, and by praying before it the worshipper was helped to fix his thoughts on Mazda himself and his goodness, as well as on truth and justice.

Prayers were said standing; and while praying the worshipper performed what appears to have been a new ritual with the sacred cord, which was always worn. The custom that youths should be invested with such a cord on attaining manhood is one which, being shared by Hindus and Zoroastrians, goes back, it seems, to proto-Indo-Iranian times. Hindus wear the cord over one shoulder, and each cord is knotted by a priest once and for all, the wearer simply slipping it aside when necessary. It is very possible that these were the usages of the ancient Iranians also, and that Zoroaster, in order to create a distinctive badge and ritual for his followers, required them instead to wear the cord round the waist, and moreover to untie and retie it whenever they prayed, as a tangible reminder of their commitment to the faith. It is also almost certain that it was he who introduced the custom of its being worn by women as well as men. The cord was fastened with two reef-knots (a knot widely used in sacred rites, because of its strength and perfect symmetry), and was made of sheep's wool or goat's or camel's hair. Since it was thus from a beneficent animal, belonging to the creation of Vohu Manah, worshippers, holding the untied cord in both hands while praying and gazing at fire, had the visible prompting to think of both Vohu Manah and Aša, the two greatest of the lesser members of the Heptad.[8]

As to the words to be spoken, these are the same at each of the five times of prayer. The prayers said today, although still quite brief, contain both Young Avestan and Middle Persian utterances, but they begin with the *Kemna Mazda*, spoken while the worshipper is holding the untied cord, and this consists largely of the following verses from the *Gathas*: "Whom, Mazda, hast Thou appointed as protector for me, when the Deceitful One seeks to make me do wrong, other than Thy Fire and Thy (Good) Purpose, by whose acts, Lord, Thou dost nourish Truth? Proclaim this teaching to my Inner Self!...Then let Hearkening come to him with Good Purpose, O Mazda - to him whomsoever Thou dost wish. ... (Let there be) reverence with which there is devotion and sacrifice."[9] It is evident that Zoroaster set immense store by the *Gathas*, verses composed by him over the years in the light of his visions and intuitions; and it is highly probable that he himself chose these particular verses and instructed his followers to use them as their daily prayers, for much doctrine and spiritual longing is compressed in them: the opposition of Mazda and the Evil Spirit (here called the Deceitful One); the trust in Aša, with the symbolism of fire, and in Vohu Manah; the need for enlightenment of one's Inner Self, the Daena, and the yearning for Sraoša, Mainyu of hearkening or obedience to God. For the first generations of believers, speaking the same language as the prophet, and taught by him or by those close to him, the words would have had full meaning and instructive as well as devotional force.

Another observance at which Gathic verses were recited was the ritual tending of the hearth fire. This was not a general obligation, like the sacred-cord prayers, but devolved on one member of a household, being a service to the fire itself. For practical reasons the ancient Iranians kept the hearth fire always burning, and they made regular offerings to its Mainyu, in gratitude for warmth and light and the cooking of food. Because of fire's importance for Zoroastrians as an icon, its tending became for them an act of wider religious significance; and it was practical that it should regularly be done just before the time for the sacred-cord prayers, so that the fire should be burning brightly then. Hence this ritual too was generally performed five times a day, with the "Prayer to Fire", the *Ataš Niyayeš*, being recited meanwhile. This now has 17 verses, mostly in Young Avestan; but the first three and the last are from the

Gathas, and again it seems very probable that these were taught by the prophet to his followers, to recite during this domestic rite. In one rendering they are as follows: "Arise for me, Lord! By the Most Holy Spirit, O Mazda, take to Thyself might through devotion, swiftness through good gift-offerings, potent force through truth, protection through good purpose. Thou who seest afar, reveal to me for support, Lord, the incomparable things of Your kingdom, which are the recompense for good purpose. Instruct, O Holy Devotion, our Inner Selves through truth. For as a gift Zarathuštra gives the breath even of his body, so that for Mazda there should be predominance of good purpose, of act and word in accord with truth, so that there should be both hearkening and dominion. ... Then we wish Thy fire, Lord, strong though truth, very swift, mighty, to be of manifest help to Thy supporter, but of visible harm, O Mazda, with the forces in his hands, to Thy enemy."[10] Through these verses the worshipper is taught that the self must be offered as well as material gifts; and the words, which have the characteristic Gathic wealth of overlaid meanings, of allusions at once both to a quality and to its Mainyu, bring awareness of all the greatest members of the Heptad - Mazda with his Most Holy Spirit, Aša, Vohu Manah, Spenta Armaiti, Khšathra (the Avestan word is rendered here perforce as both "kingdom" and "dominion"), and with them great Sraoša, and Aši, Mainyu of recompense. The verses have moreover another highly significant Gathic feature, that of addressing Mazda as "Thou" and yet following this with the plural "Your" as in "Your kingdom" - a simple linguistic means, it seems, of expressing the complex doctrine that Mazda is God alone, and yet, since the lesser Six dwell with him, has also a plurality of being. In addition, the first verse has been cited earlier as illustrating the belief that Mazda, although the mighty Creator, still has need of the devotion, worship and other good acts of the *ašavan*, so that these words prompted those who spoke them with understanding to an actively good life. The last verse contributes a vivid reminder of the continuous struggle with evil, and the hope of victory for the good.

The symbolism of fire for this struggle was very potent, especially at midnight, when, "awakened" from under its bed of ashes, it leapt up in flames and drove back the "evil" darkness. Then the *ašavan*, tending it, and those saying their prayers in its presence, could feel they were strengthening it to do so. So too at dawn, as they prayed before the again brightly burning fire, they could think that they were thereby helping the growing light, and with it all the creation of Aša. For the modern Zoroastrian this is pure symbolism; but in Zoroaster's own distant day there would have been no clear distinction made between physical and moral darkness, and the power of prayer was thought to affect both the material and immaterial worlds, the *gaethya* and the *mainyava*. Thus it is said in the *Khoršed Niyayeš*, the Young Avestan prayer to the sun: "When the sun with his light brings warmth .... the immaterial Yazatas ...

gather up his glory, they distribute it over the Ahura-created earth, to prosper the world of Aša. .... He who worships the Shining Sun, life-giving, bountiful ... in order to resist darkness, in order to resist demons born of darkness ... he rejoices all the immaterial and material Yazatas."[11]

The sacred-cord prayers and the prayer to Fire would have been said daily in every Zoroastrian household, priest and lay. Further, at some point in his life Zoroaster taught the complete text of all the seventeen *Gathas* to priests among his followers, and thereafter these were recited every day with the liturgy of the *yasna*. The *yasna* service itself, as we have seen,[12] was very ancient, having its origins with the main act of priestly worship of the proto-Indo-Iranians. Its rituals consisted essentially of the blood sacrifice and preparation of the *parahaoma*, a fluid containing the expressed sap of the *haoma* plant (Sanskrit *soma*). From the sacrifice and the *parahaoma*, offerings were made to the Mainyus of fire and water, the fragrance of the sacrifice, together with words of praise and worship, being enough, it was held, to gratify the other divinities invoked to be present. The offering to Fire was made to the ritual fire, that to Water to a source of pure water nearby, being carried to it (to judge from known usage) when the service was over. During the service (which in ancient times was evidently quite short) the celebrant priests ritually consumed a portion of the consecrated offerings, and afterwards others present might also partake of them, and so share in the holiness they conferred.[13] These ancient rites were maintained in Zoroastrianism[14], but there has been debate over whether Zoroaster himself celebrated them, or whether they were revived after his death. By now the identification of allusions in the *Gathas* to animal sacrifice and the libation to water,[15] together with the abundant and consistent testimony of actual Zoroastrian observance,[16] appears to have decided this matter.

It is, however, very likely that the prophet introduced some minor changes in the celebration of the *yasna*; and one was probably that, whereas the Hindu *yajna* (and hence presumably the Old Iranian *yasna*) might be celebrated at any time of day, the Zoroastrian *yasna* may be solemnized only between sunrise and noon. This can be seen as having doctrinal significance, since this is the one period in the twenty-four hours when the light and heat of the sun, Aša's fiery orb, is steadily increasing, a symbol of what should be the steady daily increase of righteousness, furthered by the service itself.

A far greater change, and one which can also be attributed with all reasonable certainty to the prophet himself, was the composing of a fixed liturgy for the service, that known as the *Yasna Haptanhaiti* "Worship of the seven sections".[17] Creating such a liturgy appears to have been a complete innovation, and one which set no immediate precedent. The ancient tradition of Indo-Iranian worship, in which Zoroaster himself would have been trained,was one of extemporized utterances. At each service, that is, the celebrant priest would, while performing the rituals, have spontaneously composed accompanying words of praise and supplication, weaving into them customary phrases and fixed forms of invocation. The persistence of this tradition for centuries after the prophet lived (as the Young Avesta attests) shows how strong it was, and how natural the priests found it. The only parts of the Avesta which were fully memorized from the early days of the faith, and so survive in the Old Avestan dialect, are the *Gathas* and *Yasna Haptanhaiti* together with the two brief manthras, the *Yatha ahu vairyo* and *Airyema išyo*. The *Gathas* were recited in two groups, one before and one after the *Yasna Haptanhaiti*, so that they framed and protected its rituals with their sacred power; and the *manthras* were set one before and one after the *Gathas*. Together these texts formed the original *Staota yesnya* "(Words of) praise and worship"[18]; and they were a single solid rock within the otherwise continually evolving stream of Avestan religious literature. It seems wholly improbable that that rock should not have been of a unified substance - that the words of some unknown author or authors should have been set between Zoroaster's own utterances in this way, and equally reverently preserved. Like the *Gathas*, the *Yasna Haptanhaiti* is much cited and imitated in the Young Avesta;[19] and, given their difference in character, the two sets of texts are essentially harmonious both in content and style.[20]   There are moreover passages in *Yasna Haptanhaiti* which have a remarkable ring of authority, fitting in the founder of the faith; and it seems entirely reasonable that Zoroaster, with his intense concern, evinced in the *Gathas*, for the acceptance of his message, should have composed a fixed form of service for his followers' use, so that they would always worship, day by day, in strict accordance with his teachings.

Yet although Zoroaster's authorship of *Yasna Haptanhaiti*, once seriously considered, can seem self-evident, there are a number of reasons why it was not even envisaged until recently. The simplest is that, whereas the prophet refers to himself repeatedly in the *Gathas*, his name does not occur in the liturgy. This is, as it were, not signed. The difference is readily comprehensible, however, in that the *Gathas* are profoundly personal utterances, whereas the *Yasna Haptanhaiti* is intended for use at a regular act of formal worship. Nevertheless, had it been composed after the death of the faith's revered founder, the likelihood is that he would in fact have been honoured in it by name,[21] or his *fravaši* venerated, as is the case, repeatedly, in Young Avestan parts of the extended *yasna* liturgy.[22]

Another reason has been that *Yasna Haptanhaiti* is in prose - an elevated, poetic prose suitable for solemn chanting,[23] but nevertheless contrasting strongly with the intricate versification of the *Gathas*. A parallel Indian use of liturgical prose shows that this was a formal tradition going back to proto-Indo-Iranian times[24]; and the art of composing such prose presumably formed part accordingly of a priest's basic training. It would in any case be absurd to suppose that the author of the *Gathas*, a master-craftsman, was capable of only one type of literary composition, and that he could not readily fit words and style to any purpose he chose.[25]

A more compelling reason for not attributing *Yasna Haptanhaiti* to Zoroaster was that certain Western preconceptions had become widely accepted academic dogma, namely that Zoroaster's own teachings represented an "enlightened", almost solely rational, faith with virtually no rituals other than prayer in the presence of fire. There were accordingly elements in *Yasna Haptanhaiti* which were not only identified - undoubtedly correctly - as being older than Zoroaster's own day, but which were regarded as referring to rituals which he would not himself have been prepared to solemnize. As long as such prejudices prevailed, and Zoroaster's own beliefs and practices were held to be separated by a great gulf from those of his immediate followers (despite their being the sole transmitters of his faith) there could be no thought of considering him to be the author of the liturgy. Once, however, this supposition - both anachronistic and more than a little irrational - is abandoned, the liturgy can be seen as a devotional text which in spirit and doctrine not only harmonizes with but complements the lyrical *Gathas*; and brief though it is - its seven sections contain only 40 "verses" - it furnishes invaluable materials for a fuller understanding both of the devotional aspect of Zoroaster's teachings and of him himself as priest as well as prophet.

Although clearer and simpler than the *Gathas*, the *Yasna Haptanhaiti* presents numerous difficulties. As an Old Avestan text it is liberally sprinkled with otherwise unknown words (forty-three in all, or almost an average of one to each verse). In one passage it expresses what seem to be mystical apprehensions, in others the words have that complexity of meaning which is characteristic of the *Gathas*. The sense of a number of lines remains accordingly debated or obscure.[26] In general the liturgist uses the first person plural, so that the priestly celebrant speaks for himself, his fellow-priests, and others present. Thrice, however, an "I" occurs, as might be expected from the religion's founder; but even then it sounds like a single voice speaking on behalf of a group, the tone remaining wholly different from the deeply personal one of the *Gathas*.[27] The liturgy is carefully structured, with the three central sections (*Y.* 37-39), which appear to have accompanied ritual acts, being characterized by expressions of direct worship and invocation,while the "outer" ones (*Y.* 35 and 36, *Y.* 41 and 42) contain more general affirmations of belief and devotion. These "outer" sections are expressly offered to Mazda (here addressed as either Ahura Mazda or Mazda Ahura);[28] but, like the *Gathas*, the whole liturgy is imbued with veneration of him, and his name occurs in every part. Deep reverence is offered also to Aša, and only a little less to Vohu Manah, to Khšathra, and to Armaiti. This is broadly the pattern of the

Gathas,[29] with Haurvatat and Ameretat, the two members of the Heptad least often mentioned in the hymns, not being named at all in the liturgy. Other "immaterial" Mainyus are, however, invoked there who do not appear in the *Gathas*. This is another reason why Zoroaster's authorship of *Yasna Haptanhaiti* has not been considered, since the more numerous the lesser divinities he is seen to revere, the more difficult this is to reconcile with the frail theory of his strict monotheism.

A more striking difference between the two works is that evil is only once alluded to in *Yasna Haptanhaiti*, and there is no mention there of Angra Mainyu, the Daevas or the Drug, or of struggles against the wicked. The liturgy is filled instead with the positive spirit which is as characteristic of Zoroastrianism as its dualism, expressed here in worship of the divine beings, reverence for the natural world, moral resolve, and delight in joy and goodness. *Vohu* "good" is a word which constantly recurs; and, whereas evil is virtually absent, two other distinctive Gathic themes are well in evidence, namely those of fire and the cow.[30]

The liturgy begins with a declaration that the worshippers are those who embrace "good thoughts, good words, good acts" (*humata- hukhta- huvaršta*).[31] This, the basic Zoroastrian ethical formulation, is expressed repeatedly with subtle variations in the *Gathas*, but is here enunciated with a simple clarity that brings it within the understanding of all.[32] The affirmation comes at the beginning of the liturgy because, it is suggested,[33] this all-embracing ethic applies also to the solemnization of the service itself, which requires right intention, right words and rightly performed rituals if it is to be "good", and hence effective. The worshippers further declare that it is through "beautiful Aša" that they have chosen (a strong Gathic emphasis) to think, speak and act as shall be best for "the two existences". (This is an expression which recurs in the liturgy, and which seems used with a complexity of meaning, both for the co-existing material and immaterial states, *gaethya* and *mainyava*, and also for this life and that to come[34].) They then urge all by such conduct to provide "peace and pasturage" for the cow. This appears to be both a literal injunction (appropriate in a pastoral society beset by violence), and a metaphor, caring for the cow representing a tranquil, productive way of life directed by Good Purpose, Vohu Manah.[35]

The worshippers then say, by what has been seen as the stately use of a solemn legal formula:[36] "We give, convey and assign dominion (*khšathra*), as far as is in our power, to Mazda Ahura and to Aša Vahišta, truly the best of rulers"; and they urge all, men and women, to realise the good for themselves and others. They ask Ahura Mazda to accept their words and to be their teacher, and they declare that their praise and worship will be unending, through truth, good purpose and good dominion (*aša, vohu manah, vohu khšathra*). The first section of the liturgy, *Y*. 35, is thus filled by a spirit of devotion and moral commitment, and strengthens the faithful through the affirmation of essential beliefs.

Throughout the next section, *Y.* 36, the celebrant concentrates his thoughts and those of his fellow-worshippers upon fire and the Mainyu of fire, Atar, beginning with these words: "In community with this fire here we first approach Thee, Mazda Ahura, Thee with Thy Most Holy Spirit, who is harm for him whom thou dost destine for harm". This is the one allusion in *Yasna Haptanhaiti* to punishment and (implicitly) wickedness, contemplation of the ritual fire awaking, it seems, thoughts of the fire of the ordeal and of Mazda's mighty judgment to come, when through his Holy Spirit he will separate the just from sinners. The words have their close parallels in the *Gathas*.[37] Naming the Most Holy Spirit, Mazda's immanent power, then leads the liturgist, it appears, into a mystical apprehension. He has the worshippers entreat the Mainyu of fire, as "the most joyful one", to approach them, while they will themselves draw near him "with good purpose, good truth, with acts and words of good insight"; and they address him thus: "Thou art truly the Fire of Ahura Mazda. Thou art truly his Most Holy Spirit", distinction of being between the two Mainyus apparently dissolving in this moment of adoration. Further, the worshippers proclaim to Mazda Ahura that "this light here", that is, the glowing fire, is his own "most beautiful form of forms", so that at this instant Zoroaster's God is perceived as himself manifest in the great icon of the faith, the "truth-strong" fire.[38]

The next section of the liturgy, *Y.* 37, is the first in which the verb *yazamaide*, "we worship", occurs, to be steadily repeated throughout it and the two following ones. Its first verse runs: "Thus we now worship Ahura Mazda, who created the cow and order (*aša*), created waters and good plants, created light and earth and all things good". Thereby are enumerated the creations other than man, with *aša* representing fire (the intermingling of *mainyava* and *gaethya* entities is characteristically Gathic), and light standing for the sun-lit sky.[39] The worshippers then venerate Mazda "by the Ahuric names" desired by him - an obscure, probably traditional expression.[40] They worship him, they declare, with their bodies and their lives. They worship also Aša Vahišta, a whole verse being devoted to him here as the guardian of fire - "the most beautiful, the Holy Immortal (*spəntəm aməšəm*), possessing light, bestowing all good"; and finally, in this section, they worship Vohu Manah, with Khšathra, Daena (here the Mainyu of the religion), Armaiti, and another, unknown, Mainyu, Fseratu, all qualified as "good".

There is also in this section, at the end of v.3, the declaration: "We worship him (that is, Ahura Mazda), the *fravašis* of the just, of men and women". This is not only grammatically awkward, with no conjunction between the two objects of *yazamaide*, but is not in harmony with the general tenor of the section. It would be the only mention of the *fravašis* in Old Avestan; and it has all the appearance of a clumsy later interpolation, made so that there might be explicit early authority for the immensely important *fravaši* cult.[41]

The next section, *Y*. 38, is devoted to worship of the Waters. Reverence for water is almost as strong in Zoroastrianism as that for fire; but, rather as Zoroaster's ardent devotion to Mazda caused most of his utterances to be directed to him, so, it seems, the intensity of his feeling for fire as the icon of Aša and the instrument of justice meant that it is fire-imagery and the veneration of fire which permeate the *Gathas*; and when in *Yasna Haptanhaiti* worship is offered to water, it is expressed in more traditional terms than that to fire, with less ethical and spiritual content. Thus *Y*. 38 begins with worship for "the earth which bears us, with the Ladies" (that is, the Waters), and continues: "We worship Thy Ladies, Ahura Mazda, who are excellent through *aša*". With them are worshipped a number of "immaterial" Mainyus, all female, all qualified as "good", and some named in the *Gathas*, others not.

The following three verses, which make up the rest of this section, appear even more strikingly traditional in content and expression. In part they run: "Then we worship the Waters, wives of the Ahura - you, easy to cross, flowing well, good to bathe in ... We invoke you as the Waters, as milch cows, as mother cows, you choice kine, caring for the needy (*drigu-*), having drink for all, you the best, the most beautiful". The waters are similarly addressed as "choice kine" (*aghniyā*) in a Vedic *mantra*,[42] while their appellation "wives of the Ahura" (*ahurānī-*), that is, of the Ahura Varuna[43], has its counterpart in their Vedic name, "wives of Varuna" (*varuṇānī*). It is in these verses that Zoroaster appears most clearly as a priest brought up in the old religion, keeping reverently elements from traditional worship which were in harmony with his own new teachings, and which he evidently did not feel called upon either to alter or greatly to intensify. Only the expression "caring for the needy" appears Gathic in spirit, *drigu* being used, it seems, by Zoroaster for the impoverished *ašavan* as distinct from the *drugvant* who enriched himself unjustly.[44]

The opening lines of the next section, *Y*. 39, are: "So we worship the Soul and the Maker of the Cow" - Geuš Urvan and Geuš Tašan, divine beings, Mainyus, of whom the latter figures also in the *Gathas*. These words have been identified as an appeasement formula,[45] uttered to assuage the spirit of the sacrificial animal (typified by the cow) which was thought after its consecrated death to be absorbed into that of Geuš Urvan.[46] They too are thus likely to be wholly traditional. There follows the declaration that "we worship our own souls and those of the domestic animals",[47] the two parts of steppe society, the *pasu-vira*, being thus drawn together at this solemn moment. The worshippers also venerate "the souls of wild animals which are not harmful", presumably because such animals too might be offered sacrificially.[48] They continue: "We worship the souls of the just (*ašavan-*) wherever they may have been born, of men and of women, whose good Inner Selves (*Daenas*) conquer or will wherever they may have been born, of men and of women, whose good Inner Selves (*Daenas*) conquer or will conquer or have conquered" - a remarkable utterance which takes the worshippers beyond the confines of their own small community, with reverence for virtue wherever it is to be found. Zoroaster's individual voice sounds here among the traditional elements, with the characteristic stress on the spiritual equality of women with men, and the reference to the Daena, the Inner Self, which, if good, will triumph at the Chinvat Bridge.

The last of the *yazamaide* formulas is devoted to all beneficent divine beings, with the declaration: "So then we worship the Good Ones, male and female, the Holy Immortals (*spənta- aməša-*), ever-living, ever-flourishing, who stand by Good Purpose (Vohu Manah)." The term *ameša*, with its Vedic counterpart *amṛta* "immortal", was evidently a traditional one for the gods; but the qualification *spenta* was presumably given to it by Zoroaster to distinguish the life-furthering divinities, whom he worshipped as emanating from Ahura Mazda, from the Daevas whom he saw as destroyers, "defrauding mankind of good life and immortality".[49]   In the tradition the term Ameša Spenta continued to be used generally, as here, for all the beings of Zoroastrian worship, but often also specifically for the six lesser members of the Heptad, because of their unique importance.[50]

Finally this central part of the liturgy ends with Mazda being addressed again directly: "As Thou, O Ahura Mazda, dost think and say and create and work that which is good ... so we therewith worship Thee, so we reverence Thee, so we strengthen Thee... With the kinship of a good kinsman of good Aša, ... of good Armaiti, we approach Thee."

The last two sections, *Y*. 40 and 41, devoted wholly to Ahura Mazda, contain, essentially, variations on the worshippers' earnest plea that he will accept their offerings and them themselves, as far as they are *ašavan*, and grant them companionship with him and with Aša in his kingdom (*khšathra*) for ever. "Here by these offerings, O Mazda Ahura" they pray, "show Thy wisdom (*mazda-*) and bounty". This is the only place in the whole Avesta where *mazda* is used, not as the divine name, but for the quality of which, by origin, the great Ahura was the Mainyu - something which, it seems, was still apprehended in "Old Avestan" times. Another verse runs: "We declare Thee to be of wondrous power (*humaya-*), deserving of offerings, a Being worthy of worship (*yazata-*), accompanied by Aša". The word *humaya-* has an archaic ring, for the Indian Asuras too are possessed of good *maya*; but it is possible that Avestan *yazata* and the occasional Vedic *yajata* were independent coinages,[51] with "Yazata" being evolved by Zoroaster himself for a beneficent divine being in contra-distinction to the Daevas, whom he so passionately affirmed were *not* to be worshipped. The term, like "Ameša Spenta," is a

The liturgy ends with a prayer which expresses the hope for salvation that is at the heart of Zoroaster's message: "We call ourselves Thy praisers and *manthrans*, Ahura Mazda ... What Thou hast established as reward for one like me, for our Daenas, that give to us, for this existence and that of the mind, that thereby we may attain it - community with Thee and with Aša, for ever".[52] The "existence of the mind", *ahu- manahya-*, is yet another expression for the other-worldly existence of the spirit, as distinct from this one on earth. The usage is Gathic.[53]

The *Yasna Haptanhaiti* thus shows Zoroaster developing a traditional act of worship into a service for his own faith. During it he evidently made the customary offerings according to age-old rituals, and spoke words which were in part themselves traditional, but which he infused with his own devotion and ardour, and enriched by affirmations of his own beliefs, spiritual and ethical. He thereby developed a rite of deep significance for his followers, which was thenceforth their vehicle for daily priestly worship. Formerly, the extemporized words of praise and supplication had probably varied according to the dedication of the service; but in Zoroastrianism, though the *yasna* might still be dedicated at will to any of the Yazatas, the words of *Yasna Haptanhaiti* remained unchanged, and so the service was always essentially Mazda-worship, devoted to the fountain-head of all beneficent divinity.

Just as verses from the *Gathas* were appointed for use as sacred-cord prayers and for tending the fire, so, it seems, a verse from *Yasna Haptanhaiti* was appointed to be said before the nearly sacramental act of eating and drinking. This is the *Itha aat yazamaide*, that is, *Y.* 37:1, which offers worship to Ahura Mazda as Creator of the six creations other than man, and of "all things good".[54] It is very possible that in the original order of the service these words preceded the ritual tasting of the offerings by the priest, and were therefore chosen by the prophet as appropriate also for this more general use. Eating with reverence, Zoroastrians were taught, was especially an act of respect for Haurvatat and Ameretat, the Mainyus of wholeness or health and long life or immortality. Haurvatat is the guardian of water, and it was of course recognized that all life depends on water, while Ameretat's creation, that of water-fed plants, in its turn nourishes all animal life. So all that is eaten and drunk comes ultimately from the creations of these two members of the Heptad, and consuming food and drink with gratitude and conscious pleasure, not casually, is a form of care for them, and a reminder of their immanence in the natural world.

This care, as the tradition shows, could be shown in other ways also, notably by guarding the purity of water in springs and streams, and by the careful tending of plants, crops and trees. It has been one of the enormous strengths of Zoroastrianism that, because all the world was thought to be imbued with the presence of the six great Ameša Spentas, a believer could show reverence for them by caring for their physical creations as well as by cultivating the virtues and qualities they represent. His daily life, that is, was lived with a sense of the two states of *gaethya* and *mainyava* being wholly interfused. Zoroaster's subtle doctrines thus became assimilable, through regular, repetitive, significant acts, by the simplest of his followers, and the satisfaction of carrying out his precepts, and of serving the world of Aša, could be constant.

One of the most important ways, for the Zoroastrian, of caring for the physical world was by striving to maintain its purity generally, impurity in all its forms being regarded as the work of Angra Mainyu. Here again there was an ancient heritage of observance to draw on, for the Indo-Iranians evidently had a number of purity laws which could be maintained in Zoroastrianism with new doctrinal justification. For Zoroastrians, these laws affected chiefly fire, water, earth, and man himself. One of the ways of guarding the good earth from impurity was by never burying impure things in it; and since a decaying corpse was clearly a great impurity, of the three funerary rites practised on the steppes in the second millenium - burial, cremation and exposure[55] - the last was chosen, presumably by Zoroaster himself, for the community. A corpse was laid in some barren place for the flesh to be quickly devoured by birds and dogs,[56] and the bones to be bleached clean by sun and wind and so to be made fit for resurrection.

Earth's traditional partner, the sky of stone, was alone among the creations in not being vulnerable to man's abuse; but it was still possible to show respect for Khšathra by keeping scrupulously clean and scoured tools and vessels of stone - such as, for instance, the pestle and mortar used both in the *yasna* service and in domestic tasks. The care of Aša's creation, fire, was largely traditional, but Zoroastrians learnt to be especially scrupulous in avoiding sullying their hearth fires, while as a pastoral people the prophet's early followers clearly had no lack of opportunity for serving Vohu Manah, Good Purpose, through his creation, beneficent animals. But it was naturally with humanity itself that Zoroaster's moral theology was most profoundly concerned. Caring for the other six creations, and bringing their Mainyus into his own self was part of the duty of the *ašavan*; and he should also strive earnestly to be fit for Mazda's Holy Spirit to dwell with him, caring thus for his own moral and spiritual being. Zoroastrian ethics are in many respects like those of other great ethical religions and philosophies, but they have their special emphases and particularities. Much stress is laid on the Ahuric virtues, hypostatized in Mithra and Varuna, of being just and honest, and telling the truth. Great importance is also attached to self-reliance, to responsibility for one's own thoughts, words and acts; but there is emphasis also on caring for one's fellow men, who are likewise Mazda's creatures. Linked with this is the value put on honest work and the honest acquisition thereby of possessions;[57]

for a poor man tends to be less able to help himself or others than a rich one.[58] Moreover, possessions thus gained should be positively enjoyed. Thus the cow in calf, with its promise of increase to the herds, was "joy-bringing" to the pastoralist.[59] Zoroastrianism is opposed to asceticism in any form, partly because this involves a rejection of good things created by Mazda, which it is rational and grateful to take pleasure in, partly because it tends to weaken the body and make it less able to receive Haurvatat and Ameretat, and to pursue the active way of life proper to an *ašavan*. Fasting was accordingly a sin, as was any self-inflicted form of suffering; and to be joyful was a virtue, since Mazda created joy, and sorrow has no place in his perfect world, which every *ašavan* should be striving to help recreate, pushing back evil, bit by bit. The breadth and vigour of Zoroastrian ethic, embracing spiritual, moral and physical health, is part of the religion's strength; and a vital element in it is that the aim of all just endeavour is not only to please God and to save one's own soul, but also to strive together with God to save the whole world. The faith is not man-centred, but perceives all the creations as seeking, consciously or unconsciously, to reach the one glorious goal of Frašo-kereti. For individuals to see themselves as part of this huge common endeavour, allies, however humble, of Mazda, meant that they could feel their lives to be significant; and this was in itself an aid to happiness, an incentive to purposeful living.

Zoroaster also gave his followers the two *manthras* which "frame" the *Gathas*, and which thus begin and end the original *Staota yesnya*. The first of these, the *Yatha ahu vairyo* (*Ahunvar*) is so highly regarded that at need its repetition may replace any other act of devotion. This *manthra* is recited daily - often many times - by all observant Zoroastrians; but it has long since become, in its Old Avestan complexities, an utterance of mystical power that is not literally understood. It has in a high degree the Gathic characteristics of allusiveness and density of meaning, and although the declaration can be discerned in it of grand elements of Zoroaster's teachings, it has so far defied satisfactory rendering into any modern tongue. [60]

The other *manthra* is the *Airyema išyo*. Airyaman is the Mainyu of friendship and healing. In the Young Avesta (as known through *zand* translation)[61] he has a part at the Last Day, which accords with the tenor of the *manthra*. This seems simpler and more direct than the *Ahunvar*, one English rendering being as follows: "May longed-for Airyaman come to the support of the men and women of Zoroaster, to the support of good purpose. The Inner Self (Daena) which earns the reward to be chosen, for it I ask for the longed-for recompense of truth (*aša*), which Ahura Mazda will hold in mind."[62] Perhaps because this *manthra* follows directly after the "Wedding *Gatha*", *Y.* 53, with its references to the marriage of the prophet's daughter Pouruchista, perhaps because Zoroaster was in fact inspired to utter it on that occasion, priests have traditionally recited it at marriage services, directing the couple thereby on a shared path to future bliss. With its yearning for salvation, justly earned, the *manthra* also made a fitting conclusion to the *Yasna Haptanhaiti*.[63]

It is evident that comprehension of Zoroaster's doctrines would have been at different levels even among his first followers, ranging from a full understanding attained by other mystics and thinkers to a simple acceptance by many of his hearers of what could be plainly formulated and put into practice in daily life. This acceptance must have been helped by the fact that so much of the old religion survived into the new in both beliefs and practices. Nevertheless, there was enough in it that was radically different to demand informed assent, a deliberate act of choice for its adoption. This choice having been made, it was clearly the possibility of living life in all its aspects, trivial as well as solemn, in the light of the new beliefs which enabled these to be fully assimilated by the first community. Zoroastrian tradition knows the names of two of Vištaspa's sons, celebrated as having also upheld the faith; but neither is said to have succeeded him as ruler of his tribe, and nothing more that is reliable is known of the family.[64]   The survival of the religion suggests, however, that at the least a second generation of the "Old Avestan" people continued to live reasonably secure lives, growing up within the faith and being taught its doctrines and observances from childhood, so that a stable community of convinced and instructed believers was able to establish itself.

NOTES

1   Cf. above, pp.13-14.

2   *Y.* 46:1.

3   *Yt* 9:26, on which see Jackson, *Zoroaster,* 68.

4   *Yt* 13:99-100.

5   Cf. above, pp. 11, 12-13, 15.

6   *Y.* 12:2-3 (on which see further p.103 and *HZ* I 263-5).

7   It could perhaps be argued from *Y.* 44:5 (where Zoroaster refers to the three times of daily prayer) that the five times were established after his lifetime; but it is very likely that, like Muhammad (who is widely held by scholars to have finally fixed on five times of daily prayer on the model of Zoroastrian observance), he evolved the devotional practices of his new faith gradually, so that he may have composed this Gathic verse years before he came to require the two additional times of prayer from his growing community.

8   Cf. below, p.172. On the permitted materials for the sacred cord see *Nirangestan* and *Shayest ne-shayest,* cited together by Dhabhar, *Pers.Riv.,* 26 n.2. Sheep's wool is not in fact mentioned in these texts, plainly because it was the material most commonly (nowadays exclusively) used, and so no question arose as to its ritual acceptability.

9 *Y.* 46:7 (following mainly the translation of Kellens-Pirart), 44:16 (only partially rendered here), and the 3rd line of 49:10. (In current usage *Vd* 8:21 is recited before this last line.)

10 *Y.* 33:12-14, 34:4 (= *Ataš Niyayeš* 1-3, 17) (following essentially Insler's translation).

11 *Khorshed Niyayeš* 11-13. On immaterial and material Yazatas cf. above, p.68.

12 Above, p.58.

13 Cf. the archaic-sounding *Yašt* passages which specify certain groups of people who might not partake of the offerings, *Yt* 5:92, 17:54; with Zoroastrian modifications, *Yt* 10:122, 14:51-2.

14 Animal sacrifice at the *yasna* was continued in traditional Zoroastrian centres in Iran down to the mid 20th century; a vestigial meat-offering at this service was made among the Parsis until the late 19th century. The rite is well attested in Pahlavi texts. See *HZ* I 214-16 with nn.90-97. The offering of the *parahaoma* continues to this day.

15 See *HZ* I 164, 214.

16 The strength of this testimony is admitted even by Kellens-Pirart, *TVA*, 32.

17 Gershevitch ("Old Iranian literature", 18) proposed assigning parts of the liturgy to the prophet. Its attribution entirely to him was suggested, cautiously but with an admirable marshalling of the evidence, by Johanna Narten, *YHapt.* 35-7. Kellens subsequently proposed, on the grounds of small differences in terms, idioms and grammar, to identify rather a "Gathic" and a "Haptahaitic" school (*Zoroastre*, 66-7, cf. pp.17-8); but these differences appear readily explicable in that one set of texts represents mantic poetry, the other formal but relatively plain liturgical prose.

18 This name came to be applied later to a longer section of the extended *yasna* liturgy; but in the Pahl. translation of *Y.* 55:3 it is explained as meaning "these five" (that is, the five groups of *Gathas*, which have just been named) "and those seven" (i.e. the seven sections of *YHapt.*), see Darmesteter, *ZA* I 353 n.7; Dhabhar, *Pahl. Yasna*, 237. The two *manthras* were regarded as belonging with the *Gathas*.

19 Kellens (*Zoroastre*, 67) stated that *YHapt.* (and hence its putative "school") was even more influential than the *Gathas*. Doctrinally this has little meaning, since the two do not diverge. Formally it is of course true, since as a liturgical text it provided a model for later liturgies.

20 See Narten, o.c., pp.28-35.

21 Cf. Narten, pp.36, 37. Kellens-Pirart, o.c., p.39, found themselves in a contradiction over this matter, for they argued (see above, p.45 n.3) that because Zoroaster's name occurs in the *Gathas*, these hymns cannot be by him, yet because it does *not* occur in the liturgy, this cannot be by him either. Subsequently (in his *Zoroastre*, 20) Kellens sought to reverse this argument against Narten, but ineffectively, since she had offered a reasoned justification for this difference.

22 *Y.* 16:2; 68:22; 3:2 etc.

23 Narten, o.c., pp.18-20, 21, 35, 184.

24 Cf. Kellens-Pirart, o.c., p.36; Kellens, *Zoroastre*, 19.

25 Cf. Narten, o.c., p.36.

26 All such difficulties are fully discussed by Narten in her excellent and exhaustive commentary.

27 Narten, o.c., p.25.

28   The variation is assumed to be caused by the demands of the prose-rhythms of the text, see Kellens-Pirart, *TVA* 38.

29   Cf. above, p.79 n.28.

30   There are some 25 single references to the cow in the *Gathas*, and five in the briefer *YHapt.* (Narten, o.c., p.99).

31   These words come at the beginning of *Y.* 35:2, which is in fact the first "verse" of the OAv. liturgy, see Darmesteter, *ZA* I 256 n.1, 482 n.2; Narten, o.c., p.17.

32   Cf. above, pp. 74, 76, and see Narten, o.c., pp.86-7, with reference to the studies by Humbach and Schlerath. P. Gignoux has since written an article on this ethical concept ("Thought, word and deed: a topic of comparative religion", *K.R. Cama Oriental Institute, International Congress Proceedings 1989*, Bombay 1991, 41-51). There he conceded that "we can consider that Zoroaster knew it", and referred (citing Schlerath) to this *YHapt.* passage and to the abundant attestations in the YAv.; he further argued for its being of I.E. origin, and admitted that it is "in the centre of the Mazdiasn moral code". Yet his conclusion - astonishing in its total illogicality - was that "it has been probably inherited [by Zoroastrianism] from the Judeo-Christian world". This was a contribution to this scholar's recent attempts to understand Zoroastrianism as in the main a construct of the Sasanian period, modelled largely on Judaism and Christianity.

33   Narten, loc. cit., cf. *HZ* I 241.

34   Narten, o.c., pp.290-5.

35   Ib., pp.103-4.

36   Narten, o.c., pp.183-4. This accords with the occurrence of legal terms in the *Gathas*.

37   Notably *Y.* 43:4, 47:6. On the passage see Narten's admirable commentary, o.c., pp.142-5.

38   Understood differently by Kellens, *Zoroastre*, 46-7, with a rendering of *imā raocå* which appears somewhat forced.

39   This verse is known from its opening words as the *Itha at yazamaide*. On it see further, p.94.

40   Narten, o.c., p.178. Otherwise Kellens-Pirart, *TVA*, 136.

41   See further below, pp.106-7. Otherwise Narten, o.c., pp.180-1, who seeks to explain the lines as genuine on the basis of her own interpretation of OAv. *fravaši* as meaning "preference, choice". In this (which rests on an etymological conjecture only and is wholly at odds with Zoroastrian tradition) she is followed by Kellens-Pirart, o.c., p.136. On the passage in question see also Kellens, "Les fravaši", in *Anges et Démons*, Actes du Colloque de Liège et de Louvain-la-Neuve 14, 1987 (Louvain-la-Neuve 1989), 101-4.

42   Narten, o.c, p.237.

43   On "the Ahura" as an Iranian cult-name for Varuna see above, p.60 n.7. Narten, who keeps to the theory that Zoroaster rejected the lesser Ahuras as well as the Daevas - in fact all the old gods - is driven to producing an elaborate explanation for this expression, o.c., pp.215-16. Comparably, in their translation, Kellens-Pirart, o.c., p.137.

44   On the expression see, with references, Narten, o.c., pp.238-41.

45   Narten, o.c., p.249.

46   Cf. above, p.69, and *HZ* I 150.

47   Cf. above, p.31.

48   Cf. the statement in a Parsi treatise, that the sacrificial rites may be performed "over a she-goat or sheep or deer or any *gosfand* (i.e. beneficent animal) which may be eaten", see J.J. Modi, "An old manuscript of the Kitāb-i Darūn Yasht", *JCOI* I, 1922, 25-6; Boyce, "Haoma, priest of the Sacrifice", *Henning Mem. Vol.*, 79.

49   *Y.* 32:5.

50   Cf. *HZ* I 197.   Ignoring this double usage of the term (which is clearly attested in YAv. and Pahl. texts) has caused a number of misunderstandings.

51   See the discussion by Narten, o.c., pp.287-90.

52   These words, from *Y*. 41:5-6, are partly a repetition of the end of *Y*. 40:1, which can be taken as a sign of the urgency of the wish expressed. See Narten, o.c., pp.297-302. Kellens-Pirart in their translation, o.c., p.140, omit v.6.

53   It occurs also in *Y*. 53:6.

54   Cf. above, p.91.

55   Cf. above, p.35.

56   References to the disposal of corpses in the YAv., and in records of Achaemenian and Sasanian times, invariably identify the carrion-eating animals as dogs, see Boyce, "Corpse, disposal of, in Zoroastrianism", *EIr.* V, in press. There is a striking parallel here with the usages of the nomadic cattle-keeping Turkana people of north-west Kenya, who have many dogs. These live as members of the family, and are gentle, obedient and attached to their owners. They have a useful role in giving warning if wild beasts threaten the herds, or hostile raiders from another tribe are approaching. Traditionally the Turkanas expose their dead for vultures to devour, but the dogs often get there first, and do this work also. (Report on the Turkanas by Malcolm Dean, entitled "Fight for life under the acacia", in *The Guardian* newspaper, London, June 1991.) The importance of this parallel for the understanding of ancient Zoroastrian usage is that it establishes that dogs can eat the flesh of human corpses without developing any sort of savagery towards living humans, or becoming repugnant to their human companions. Since the development of tower *dakhmas*, carrion-eating birds have alone performed this task in the Zoroastrian community.

57   Cf. Zoroaster's own words, *Y*. 44:18 (with, for references to discussions of them, *HZ* I 186-7), and also *Y*. 46:19.

58   Cf. Zoroaster's lamentation in *Y*. 46:2.

59   *Y*. 44:16.

60   There is a large scholarly literature on it. See, with references to earlier translations and discussions, Insler, "The Ahuna Vairya prayer", *Monumentum H.S. Nyberg, Acta Ir.* 4, 1975, 410-12, and for another translation Kellens-Pirart, o.c., p.101, with commentary, *TVA* III, 13-15.

61   *GBd.* 34:18-19.

62   This represents a fairly broadly agreed rendering, but, as with any OAv. text, there are differing translations. Kellens, against the tradition, argues for "airyaman" being merely a social grouping ("Un 'Ghost-God' dans la tradition zoroastrienne", *IIJ* 19, 1977, 89-95), and he and Pirart offer accordingly their own interpretation of the prayer, *TVA*, 195.

63   By an extraordinary piece of speculative fantasy, Kellens (*Zoroastre*, 69), having analysed the name Pouruchista as "She who is remarked by many", extends this to mean "She who is remarked by numerous (gods)"; and suggests that *Y*. 53 "corresponds to a ritual of hierogamy", with male divinities invited to have sexual union with girls of his hypothetical "Gathic circle", of whom Pouruchista is taken to be the prototype. It is hard to accept that any of this is seriously intended, but such is evidently the case.

64   In the epic tradition, as represented in the *Shahnama*, Spentodata (Isfandiyar) is provided with four warrior sons (cf. above, p.24 n.80).

CHAPTER SIX

The Spread and Development of Zoroastrianism in the "Young Avestan" Period[1]

Zoroastrian tradition knows no early patron of the faith other than Vištaspa, so the spread of the religion was presumably the work of numerous individuals - probably mainly missionaries going from one Iranian community to another, and succeeding in making converts despite the hostility of those who thought like Arejat-aspa. In such circumstances it would seem that it was largely Zoroastrianism's own innate strength which enabled it to survive and become in course of time the dominant religion among the Iranian tribes who settled in eastern Iran and its borderlands.

Once a missionary had won a hearing in a new place, and had begun to instruct his converts more fully, it must have been his prime concern to find at least one among them to whom he could teach Zoroaster's own words as they were embodied in the *Staota yesnya*. Presumably in most cases those who learnt this painstakingly by heart, becoming word-perfect in it, would have been till then priests of the old religion, trained already in memorization and familiar with the basic rituals of the *yasna*. Since all the Old Avestan parts of the obligatory and customary prayers are contained in the *Staota yesnya*, once one convert had mastered this he could act as mentor for the whole new congregation; but it seems likely that a missionary would usually himself have taught all his converts the short texts concerned, since these were instructive as well as devotional, and an understanding of them would have been an important step in establishing and maintaining belief. There was also what was presumably the new sacred-cord ritual to be taught, to women as well as men,[2] and a stern ban to be imposed on all worship of the Daevas and on all propitiation of lesser evil powers, with a courageous defiance of wickedness in all its forms to be inculcated instead.

In the first days it seems likely that putting on the sacred cord in the way special to Zoroastrians, with recital of the *Kemna Mazda*, would have been all the avowal of faith that a convert was required to make; but there exists what appears to be in essence a very early formulary,[3] which was probably evolved subsequently for a convert to recite before an open assembly. This formulary, known from its first word as the *Fravarane*, "I profess", was incorporated eventually in the extended *yasna* liturgy as *Y.* 12. Like all religious utterances except Zoroaster's own words it evolved linguistically with the living Avestan language; but at some stage (in tribute presumably to its central importance) it was recast, not wholly consistently or accurately, in Old Avestan, and it was perhaps then that it was enriched with brief citations from the *Gathas* and embellished in other ways.

The *Fravarane* begins with a set of affirmations of religious loyalty which show how the early believers felt themselves to be distinguished from those who kept to the old religion. These affirmations run: "I profess myself a worshipper of Mazda (*mazdayasna-*), a Zoroastrian (*zarathuštri-*), opposed to the Daevas (*vidaeva-*), upholding the Ahuric doctrine (*ahura-tkaeša-*), one who praises the Holy Immortals, worships the Holy Immortals (*staotar-, yaštar-amašanam spantanam*)". The order of these terms was clearly carefully weighed. Putting the worship of Mazda foremost lays full stress on the belief which is at the heart of Zoroaster's teachings, namely his particular form of monotheism, in which the divinity who had been to his ancestors no more than the greatest of the Ahuras was seen as God himself. Since Zoroaster was Mazda's prophet, and founder of the community of his worshippers, the believer next declares his loyalty to him. The most formidable consequence of his doctrines for early converts was doubtless the need to reject the powerful Daevas, who were well able, many must have thought, to smite those who chose to spurn them. The explicit repudiation of this group of gods is accordingly required next, and is followed by a positive declaration of adherence to the "Ahuric doctrine". This was presumably the law of upholding *aša*, which (to judge from Vedic and Young Avestan texts) was traditionally the task of the two lesser Ahuras, Mithra and Varuna, with Mazda in his wisdom directing their activities.[4]   It was for this reason, it would seem, that the doctrine was defined as "Ahuric", having been associated already in the old religion with this great triad of ethical divinities; and adherence to it was explicitly required because the "Zarathuštri" was to follow *only* this doctrine, instead of acknowledging also the validity of the amoral law of the Daevas. The set of affirmations concludes with the avowal of veneration for all beneficent divinities - those, that is, whom Zoroaster believed Ahura Mazda had called into being to aid him in his battle against evil, and whom it was therefore meritorious for the *ašavan* to strengthen by his worship.[5]

In the *Fravarane* as it exists today there is a second set of affirmations which repeat the two essential ones from the beginning of the first set, but add to them a formulation of the basic Zoroastrian ethic. The lines run: "I profess myself a Mazda-worshipper, a Zoroastrian, having pledged myself to and avowed the faith. I pledge myself to the well-thought thought, I pledge myself to the well-spoken word, I pledge myself to the well-acted act. I pledge myself to the Mazda-worshipping religion, which throws off attacks, which causes weapons to be laid down ..., which is just, which of all faiths which are and shall be is the best, the fairest, which is Ahuric, Zoroastrian".[6]   These lines were made part also of the sacred-cord prayers, so that thereafter all the faithful repeatedly declared themselves, day by day, to be Mazda-worshippers and Zoroastrians, and committed themselves to a moral way of life. This steady, regular avowal of faith, accompanied by a simple, exact ritual, was undoubtedly one of the strengths of Zoroastrianism, and later, when Young Avestan in its turn had become a dead church language, not understood by most believers, this was compensated for by the addition to the sacred-cord prayers of the brief but significant *Ohrmazd Khoday*, in the then current vernacular.[7]

Between the two affirmations of faith the *Fravarane* contains other matter which seems genuinely old, suggesting as it does that in the early days of the religion's spread there were some who played the part of Paul towards Christianity, first persecuting and then embracing the faith. This part of the text, slightly abbreviated, is as follows: "To Ahura Mazda, the good, rich in treasures, I ascribe all things good ... to the Just One, splendid, glorious ... whose is the cow, whose is truth, whose is the light ... Spenta Armaiti, the good, I choose for myself. Let her be mine! I renounce the theft and raiding of cattle, and harm and destruction for Mazda-worshipping homes. To those who are worthy I shall grant movement at will and lodging at will, those who are upon this earth with their cattle. With reverence for Aša, with offerings lifted up, that I avow: henceforth I shall not, in caring for either life or limb, bring harm or destruction on Mazda-worshipping homes. I forswear the company of the wicked Daevas ... and the followers of Daevas, ... of those who do harm to any being by thoughts, words, acts or outward signs. Truly I forswear the company of all this as belonging to the Drug, as defiant (of the good), even as Ahura Mazda taught Zoroaster in each instance, at all deliberations, at all encounterings at which Mazda and Zoroaster spoke together ... By the choice of the Waters, the choice of the Plants, the choice of the beneficent Cow, the choice of Ahura Mazda who created the Cow, who created the Just Man, by the choice of Zoroaster, the choice of Kavi Vištaspa ... - by that choice and doctrine am I a Mazda-worshipper."[8]   There appears here a blending of plain statements with others in which Gathic layers of meaning - physical and metaphysical - are attached to the concept of the cow. The emphasis, through reiteration, on *choosing* what is good seems intended to confirm the convert in his decision to adhere to Mazda-worship by making him aware that he is choosing, not only as his prophet had chosen, but also as the creations had chosen, so that in making this choice he has put himself in harmony with all the *spenta* world.

The allusions to persecution lost their significance as Zoroastrianism became established; but the deep conservatism which the faith developed - a trait it inherited from the old religion - brought it about that the *Fravarane* continued in transmission with these unaltered, and, being preserved by its incorporation in the extended *yasna* liturgy, it is still recited daily in its entirety by celebrant priests.

This old profession of faith contains no definitions of doctrine, and the allusions in it to the creations are not systematic.   At no stage has Zoroastrianism possessed anything like the Christian creeds, with their carefully formulated statements of beliefs. These creeds were hammered out by convocations of clerics who were generally familiar with Greek, or at least Hellenistic, philosophy, with its habits of orderly exposition, and whose aim was to achieve exact definitions in order to confound heresy. In contrast Judaism, which evolved slowly and with difficulty from an ethnic to a partly credal religion, took a long time to formulate any widely accepted articles of faith. Among the Iranians it was Zoroaster himself who made the huge transition from the ethnic religion of his forefathers to his own credal one, to which he demanded adherence by conscious choice; and essentially the *Fravarane* is a public declaration of having made that choice. It affirms very positively, but the extent to which it defines is limited.

To set against the lack of brief, comprehensive definitions of their faith the Zoroastrians were provided with more varied and extensive opportunities for putting their beliefs into practice than the adherents of any other credal religion. This was because the doctrine of the Heptad taught that every part of the physical world about them is potentially imbued with sanctity, that is, by an indwelling, "immaterial", divinity. This doctrine, as well as being absorbed as an integral part of a believer's daily life, was celebrated annually by a chain of festivals.   Through successive epochs the Zoroastrian community has been noted as a convivial one, whose members readily come together to celebrate holy days first with worship and then with feasting, music and merrymaking - thus putting to rout, for a time at least, the gloomy forces of darkness. Like other major religions Zoroastrianism evidently took over existing festivals and gave them a new significance of its own; and it seems highly probable that this process was initiated by Zoroaster himself with regard to the greatest holy day of his faith, the "New Day" feast, best known by its Middle Persian name, No Roz. This feast was in all likelihood by origin a new year's day festival of the

"Old Avestan" people, which Zoroaster endowed with greater meaning for his own community as an annual prefiguration of the "New Day" of eternal life which will dawn at Frašo-kereti, with evil overthrown and all things glorious. The Zoroastrian feast is celebrated accordingly with the utmost joyfulness, and with a number of richly symbolic rites and charming observances, which have undoubtedly been added to over the years.

Since there was good doctrinal justification for Zoroastrians to seek occasions for merry-making, it was natural that holy days should multiply among them; and a calendar of generally kept feasts was probably created fairly soon in the faith's history. For developments in observance to have been generally adopted after the prophet's own lifetime there must have been communication and accord between the various congregations, and it is reasonable to suppose that leading priests from different regions met from time to time to discuss community matters and to consider ways in which the religion could best be lived and taught and further propagated. The founding of feast days is likely to have been one matter of pressing early concern, in order to prevent converts being attracted back to celebrations of the old religion; and clearly the most effective way of forestalling any such backsliding was to take over some of those celebrations, already beloved, and consecrate them to Zoroastrianism. Their Young Avestan names suggest that in fact six festivals of the pastoral and farming year (later known collectively as the *gahambars*) were thus annexed, to make with No Roz a chain of seven feasts in honour of the Heptad and the seven creations.[9] The importance of these feasts, instilling as they did essential doctrine, is marked by the fact that they were to remain the only Zoroastrian holy days of obligation. Many other feast days came to be established, whose celebration was considered meritorious; but it was only failure to keep one of these seven which was a sin, and as such "went to the Bridge", that is, was weighed among the soul's sins of omission when it was judged after death at the Chinvat Bridge.

These seven holy days have probably been second only to the sacred-cord prayers in sustaining the religious life of the community. Like those prayers, they laid on every member of it a recurrent duty, but in their case this duty was a shared social one. All had the obligation to take part then in the acts of worship and in the celebrations, with only a bare minimum of necessary work being permitted. Everyone who could was expected to contribute something, however small, to the banquets which were held, and which rich and poor alike attended; and these were occasions for forgiving wrongs, healing enmities and renewing ties of fellowship, as well as for making charitable gifts - for living the life of the faith, that is, at a high level of intensity with regard to one's fellow man.[10]

No Roz was the greatest of these seven feasts, and was seen as the last one, even as the "New Day" of Frašo-kereti will be the last day of measurable time.

So it was allotted to the celebration of the seventh creation, fire, and devoted to its great guardian, Aša. The first festival of the new year was assigned to the first creation, the all-protecting sky, and to Khšathra Vairya, and so on at irregular intervals through the year up to the sixth feast, dedicated to mankind and to Ahura Mazda himself. This was celebrated on the last day of the old year, and so merged, as the sun set, with a festival of All Souls, known among the"Avestan" people as Hamaspathmaedaya (a name still to be satisfactorily explained). This festival is likely to be very ancient, a heritage from the old Iranian religion, for similar ones have been widely celebrated among the Indo-European peoples on the last night of the old year; and the founding just before it of the sixth great feast (which took its name) was presumably a deliberate measure to sanctify it by creating a continuous Zoroastrian observance in honour of all humanity, the living by day, the dead by night. The rites of the night-time festival (to judge by parallels from among other Indo-European cultures) remained virtually unchanged: the souls of the dead were welcomed back after sunset to their old homes with religious rites and with offerings of consecrated food and clothing, from whose Mainyus, it was believed, they would derive comfort. They were thought to remain throughout the hours of darkness; and at dawn the next day they were bidden a formal farewell, before the sun rose on the new year.

By a confusing double terminology the souls of the dead are referred to in the Young Avesta both as *urvan* and *fravaši*; and in the *Farvardin Yašt* the festival of Hamaspathmaedaya is described as devoted to them under the latter name. As we have seen,[11] there appears to be no authentic reference in Old Avestan to the *fravašis*, and, although this may not be significant (there being no comprehensive coverage of doctrine in Zoroaster's surviving utterances), it is possible that the prophet was mildly opposed on doctrinal grounds to their cult, or at least indifferent to it. (Had he been strongly opposed to it, one would expect his rejection to have been stern and explicit.) By origin, and essentially, the festival of Hamaspathmaedaya is associated with the ancient belief in a shadowy, joyless hereafter for all souls in the underworld kingdom of the dead, from where they are released on this one occasion in the year to be comforted by the veneration and gifts of their descendants. The observance could logically be maintained even after the belief had developed that some souls ascended to Paradise to live there joyfully with the gods, all desires satisfied;[12] for the majority were evidently still thought to take the downward path to a cheerless existence below, and there was no certainty as to any individual's fate. Any departed soul might be in need of his or her descendants' care. With Zoroaster, all this was changed. According to his teachings, all just souls have gone up to heaven, and need nothing to add to their felicity there, while all the wicked have descended to hell, where in their deserved torment they are beyond human help; and those whose sins and virtues exactly matched are in a limbo, and merit no assuaging joys before the coming of Frašo-kereti. Since the prophet appears to have been exceptionally logical and clear-sighted, and had evidently pondered such matters deeply, these beliefs were presumably not only lucidly apprehended by him but ever present in his thoughts; but most people are less consequent in their ideas, and are capable of entertaining, simultaneously and vaguely, totally opposed concepts about the fate of the dead, as well as being intensely conservative over rituals regarding them. Thus many Christians have believed, as they have been taught to, that departed souls are in heaven, hell or purgatory; but they have also thought of them at times as resting in their bodies' graves, or haunting churchyards or their old dwelling-places. Ancient beliefs in the yearly return of all souls have moreover persisted in many Christian countries, with graves being annually decked at the appropriate time with offerings of flowers and candles, with in a few communities food offerings still being made; and in some places (such as, for example, rural Ireland) the festival of All Souls is still observed in ways not unlike those of Hamaspathmaedaya, with the difference of an overlay of Christianity instead of Zoroastrianism.

Given what was clearly an immense hold by this ancient feast on popular imagination and on family affection and piety, it is natural that many Iranians should have been reluctant to abandon it on converting to Zoroastrianism; so that the leaders of the community yielded to popular persistence, according it recognition and Zoroastrianizing it by association with one of their holy days of obligation. (Christian authorities dealt in much the same way with the pagan festival of All Souls when they followed it directly with a newly founded Christian one of All Saints.) Zoroastrians were required, moreover, to invoke only the *fravašis* of the just, the *ašavans*; and at some stage, it seems, the cult was still further legitimized by the interpolation of the reference to worship of the *fravašis* in the venerated *Yasna Haptanhaiti.*

Recognition of the *fravaši* cult was to have considerable consequences for later stages of the religion's development; but it appears to be the only real deviation (if such it was) from Zoroaster's teachings which can be identified in Young Avestan times. Plainly all the great prophets would be startled, could they return to earth, by what succeeding generations have made of the religions ascribed to them; but Zoroaster would have perhaps the least cause, since his was a faith founded by an Iranian prophet which spread almost exclusively among Iranian peoples, and so was not required to make any great adjustments to the beliefs and practices of peoples of other races and cultures. In particular, its growth during the important Young Avestan period seems to have taken place entirely among the eastern Iranian tribes, and any additional elements which were extraneous to Zoroaster's own teachings could readily be harmonized with them in that they came, like the *fravaši* cult, from the old

Iranian religion which had provided the substratum for his beliefs, being brought in by converts as the faith spread more widely.

The seven great holy days, with the night-time feast of the *fravašis* thus fenced in between the sixth *gahambar* and No Roz, would, as old seasonal festivals, have had their fixed places in the "Avestan" calendar. This was, it seems, a 360-day one, divided into 12 months of 30 days each, and kept in harmony with the natural year by a thirteenth month being added every six years or so; and at some stage, it appears, in the Young Avestan period[13] the Zoroastrians developed from it their own distinctive calendar by piously devoting each of the thirty days by name, as "the day of So-and-so", to one of the Yazatas. This divinity was thereafter invoked at all acts of priestly worship solemnized on that day, and was looked to then generally for especial concern and protection. The thirty dedications were enumerated in a ritual chant, doubtless originally for mnemonic purposes, which is incorporated in the extended *yasna* liturgy (as *Y.* 16:3-6). There is no similar enumeration of the dedications to Yazatas of the twelve months, and this is one of the reasons for thinking that these were given later.

There is also reason to suppose that at first each day was accorded a separate dedication, and that it was only later that three additional days were devoutly put under the protection of Ahura Mazda, thus giving him four dedications in all, and reducing the number of "calendar" Yazatas to twenty-seven. Even when thirty dedications were available, some selection was necessary from among the divinities of the pantheon, and this selection, together with the order of the dedications, sheds interesting light on the Zoroastrianism of this period. The first day, naturally, was devoted to Ahura Mazda, and the next six to the other members of the Heptad, who follow him in what was to be their accepted order: Vohu Manah, Aša Vahišta, Khšathra Vairya, Spenta Armaiti, Haurvatat and Ameretat. (This order, in keeping with the strongly ethical character of Zoroastrianism, corresponded not with that of their creations, but with their relative importance to man as he strives to live the good life, to be *ašavan*.) Then in the original form of the Zoroastrian calendar the eighth day, it seems, was dedicated to Varuna under his cult invocation of "kingly, shining Apam Napat". Among the Vedic Indo-Aryans Varuṇa appears to have been even more deeply venerated than Mitra, and profound reverence for him also among the Iranians seems indicated by their other invocations of him as "the Dispenser", "the High Lord".[14]   Thereafter, possibly as the chief creator-god of the old Iranian religion, he gradually ceded more than did Mithra to Zoroaster's Mazda; but at this relatively early period in the faith's history it was apparently still felt to be fitting that he should take precedence over all the lesser Yazatas after the Six. He was then followed - perhaps because of his ancient associations with creativity, perhaps also because of the close associations of the two lesser Ahuras with water and fire - by a group of "material" Yazatas, those of fire and water, sun and moon and the rain-star Tištrya. Then came the cult-god Geuš Urvan,[15] and with him, it seems, the other chief cultic divinity, Haoma, who thus received the dedication of the fifteenth day. Then Mithra was given the sixteenth, Varuna's brother-Ahura thus being set at the head of the Yazatas of the second part of the month. This structure of the dedications undoubtedly suggests that the creators of the calendar, no less than the composers of the *Fravarane*, felt themselves indeed to be both *mazdayasna* and *ahura-tkaeša*, honouring accordingly, like their prophet, Mazda chiefly, but also the other Ahuras. Moreover Mazda, now elevated to be God, stood not only high above the other two, but a little apart from them, in company with the six great Mainyus whom Zoroaster had perceived as dwelling always with him, and forming with him an indivisible group. It is also significant that, although Spenta Mainyu appears in a *Yašt* verse as a member of the Heptad,[16] he received no calendar dedication, his virtual identity with Ahura Mazda being evidently accepted.

It is of considerable interest that the two days which follow Mithra's were given to Sraoša and to Rašnu. As we have seen, Rašnu, Mainyu of the act of judging, had his place beside Mithra at the Chinvat Bridge; and there was a basis in the *Gathas* for seeing Sraoša as joined with them there.[17] In the Pahlavi and later literature these three divinities are regularly named together in this connection, and always in the same order as in these calendar-dedications. It is therefore reasonable to deduce that already in the Young Avestan period the concept of the divine tribunal had received its familiar form - if indeed it had not already taken this shape in Zoroaster's own thoughts, for his references to the Chinvat Bridge and the Daena there show that he visualized the moment of individual judgment very vividly. The dedications of these three days are further significant in that they suggest that Mithra was venerated chiefly in his aspect of Judge. This accords both with his original concept (as Mainyu of the covenant) and with his essential role in Zoroastrianism, a religion in which divine judgment has so important a part.

After the dedications to these three divinities, associated through thoughts of judgment with death, it seems natural that a day should be devoted to the *fravašis*; and this was followed by a dedication to Verethraghna, Yazata of the victory which all hope at life's end to achieve. Then came Raman, presumably representing, here as elsewhere, the greater but ambiguous Vayu, with his associations with both life and death; and he brought after him his brother wind-god, the simpler Vata.

The twenty-third day was then, it seems, devoted to Dahma Vanhvi Afriti, Yazata of the "pious (or instructed) good blessing." This benediction, incorporated in the *yasna* liturgy as Y. 60:2-7, was regarded as one of the most powerful of utterances; and in known observance its Mainyu is especially invoked at the funerary service held at dawn on the fourth day, when the soul is believed to be departing to be judged by Mithra. Dahma Afriti, who is female, appears accordingly admirably chosen to stand between the divinities just discussed and those of the final group, several of whom are likewise female. Thus she is immediately and appropriately followed by Daena, Yazata of the religion. Then come Gathic Aši, and Arštat, Yazata of justice. They are followed by the Yazatas of sky and the female earth; and finally, in pious conclusion, there are dedications to the Yazatas of the holy word (*manthra spenta*) and the endless light (*anagra raochå*), that is, of Paradise.

When, presumably under the Achaemenians, three new dedications were made to "Ahura Mazda the Creator (*Daδvah*)", the days chosen were the 8th, 15th and 23rd, whereby the month was divided into four roughly equal parts.[18] Apam Napat, Haoma and Dahma Afriti were accordingly displaced. They do not therefore appear in the (presumably revised) mnemonic list of *Y.* 16; but on the 30th day of every month they are invoked together, a disparate group, after Anagra Raochå.[19]   Further, in the ceremony now known as the *Ferešte*[20] , in which an *Afrinagan* and a *Baj* service are solemnized for every calendar Yazata individually (the three "Creators" being honoured as three distinct beings), an *Afrinagan* and a *Baj* are devoted to each of these three "extra-calendary" divinities also, so that thirty-three, not thirty, services are performed. In this way, it seems, the priests managed to venerate them faithfully still with the other calendar divinities, even after they had lost their own day-dedications.[21] This appears as the earliest example of the tenacity in observance which was later to create cumulative problems in connection with calendar reforms,[22] the effects of a change made hardly later than the early fourth century B.C. being thus still traceable in observance in the late twentieth century A.C. When their fidelity is demonstrable in such relatively small matters, there seems little reason to question the Zoroastrians' capacity for faithfulness in great ones.

The thirty beings of the calendar-dedications remained the chief Zoroastrian divinities, with only a few of those not thus honoured being or becoming prominent at various times and places (such as Airyaman, Nairyosanha, Druvaspa, Aredvi Sura Anahita in her partial transformation into "Anahit"). But worship of all beneficent divinities, great or less, was meritorious and therefore encouraged. For this lay people needed the services of a priest, who knew the right rituals and invocations; but it was open to each individual to choose, according to his means and inclination, the rite which he wished to have performed. He was thus the *nar mainya*, the "man in authority", that is, the authorizer of the ceremony[23] (in Pahlavi idiom the *framadar,* "one giving the command"); and whatever rite was chosen, when it was concluded the priest would always recite the *Ahmai raesca*. This, which is almost certainly in essence an inheritance from the old religion, consists of a short benediction calling down multifarious blessings on the *nar mainya*, such as health and strength, wealth, noble progeny, long life and bliss hereafter.[24]

By tradition (to judge from the Indian evidence) the *yasna* itself could be devoted to any divine being whom the *nar mainya* chose to name; and this did not change with Zoroaster's creation of a fixed liturgy for this service as it was to be solemnized in his own community (except of course for the utter exclusion of the Daevas). Before each celebration of it a formula was recited known as the *khšnumaine* (literally "for the satisfaction"), which contained the chosen Yazata's name and ritual invocation; and it was vividly apprehended that he or she would respond, coming before all other divinities to receive the first share of the worship and offerings. (It is presumably simply the desire for such dedications which is meant by the much-discussed longing attributed to individual Yazatas to be worshipped "with worship in which (my) name is spoken", *aoxtō.nāmana yasna.*[25]) In the *Yašts* (the hymns to individual Yazatas) there is a recurrent verse which, variously adapted, refers to the dedication of a *yasna* in this way. It runs: "We worship such-and-such a being with *haoma* mixed with milk, with *barəsman*, with skill of tongue, ... with offerings and rightly spoken words."[26] This verse is regularly followed by the *Yenhe hatam,* the prayer adapted from Zoroaster's own words which piously extends the intention of any act of worship to be for the benefit, secondarily, of all *spenta* beings.[27]

The preparation of the *haoma* offering, indicated in this verse, involved an elaborate ritual which is attested only as part of the *yasna* service and its extensions; and this service was always celebrated within a ritually enclosed space, the *pavi*, which had first to be consecrated. It was possible, however, for the *nar mainya* to have a simpler - and hence less costly - rite performed in any "clean" place, often (to judge from the *Yašts* and other sources) on a hilltop or beside water.[28] This involved animal sacrifice, offered by a priest, who called down the Yazata with the same fixed invocation that he would have used for the dedication of a *yasna*, and then chanted verses of praise for the divinity with supplications on behalf of the *nar mainya*. It was such verses which were eventually gathered into the fixed forms of the existing *Yašts*. These Zoroastrian works, though composed and transmitted by generations of pious Mazda-worshipping priests, contain a considerable proportion of pre-Zoroastrian material. This is readily understandable, since the prophet's teachings altered the concepts of individual Yazatas only in so far as they were no longer to be venerated as independent divinities, but were to be seen instead as evocations and agents of Ahura Mazda. The tasks which the supreme Deity was believed to have called them into being to fulfil were not different from their functions according to the old religion, for these were the gods whose activities Zoroaster saw as beneficent. So Mithra and Apam Napat continued to support *aša*, Tištrya and Vata to bring rain, Aredvi Sura fertility and Aši good fortune; Verethraghna granted victory in a just cause, Hvar made the sun appear again each day, and so on. There was no reason, therefore, when invoking and praising these beings to abandon traditional descriptions of them and their attributes and activities, or to neglect their ancient myths. Priests of the old religion would have acquired knowledge of all such things in their apprentice days (as Zoroaster himself must have done), and, bringing it with them on conversion, would have been able to pass it on to succeeding generations of priests brought up in Mazda-worship.

In the *Yašts* these traditional elements, although proportionately large, are naturally subordinated to Zoroastrian beliefs, and a frequently recurring verse line, "Said Ahura Mazda to Spitaman Zarathuštra", sustains the dogma that these hymns, like all other Avestan works, were ultimately inspired by the prophet's own teachings, which were themselves based on revelation granted him by Ahura Mazda. The same dogma was conveyed more tersely simply by using the vocative "O Zarathuštra" or "O Spitaman", with the implication that the words uttered had been spoken by Mazda to his prophet. In other passages Zoroaster himself questions Mazda (as in the *Gathas*), sometimes with a fixed form of address: "O Ahura Mazda, Holiest Spirit (*Mainyō Spəništa*), Creator of the corporeal world, just!" The Yazatas too address their Maker in this way;[29] and he duly responds to them, or makes declarations on their behalf to mankind. A considerable part of the *Yašts* is thus in the dramatic form of direct speech or dialogue, and these devices bring the divine and human worlds close together, as in the *Gathas*.

A good deal of doctrinal matter is moreover touched on in the *Yašts*. The essential doctrine of the Heptad is celebrated in diverse ways, and with the customary small variations in concept and terminology so exasperating to those seeking precise and consistent formulations. Thus in *Yt* 10:92 it is declared that Ahura Mazda himself professed the religion (an extension of his having made choice of *aša*), as did the six lesser members of the Heptad (who are all named), and the (other) Ameša Spentas. Here the term "Ameša Spenta" is used in its general sense of any divinity other than a Daeva[30]; but in another passage, *Yt* 19:16-18, the term is restricted, as often, to members of the Heptad. There (as in the Gathic verse *Y.* 47:1) Spenta Mainyu is considered as a separate entity making up the number seven, for it is said that the Ameša Spentas are seven beings "whose mind is one, whose voice is one, whose act is one, whose father and ruler is one, the Creator, Ahura Mazda; of whom one beholds the soul of the other, thinking upon good thoughts, good words, good deeds ...; who are the creators and fashioners and makers and observers and protectors and guardians of the creations of Ahura Mazda."[31] The physical creations guarded by the Heptad are alluded to repeatedly in the *Farvardin Yašt*; and there (v.28) Spenta Mainyu is said to support sky and water, earth, the cow, the plant, and sons in the womb (that is, mankind). Here all the creations are named or alluded to except the all-pervading seventh creation of fire, with are named or alluded to except the all-pervading seventh creation of fire, with the plant - perhaps because of the requirements of the verse-stress - being misplaced, from third to fifth position.

The theme of the struggle between good and evil runs all through the *Yašts*, and is repeatedly expressed as the opposition of Spenta Mainyu and Anra Mainyu, it not being possible always to tell when Ahura Mazda himself is meant by the former term, and when his active power, his agent Mainyu. The former is clearly the case in the story of the fabulous monster Snaviδka, who rashly boasted that when he reached his full strength he would "lead down Spenta Mainyu from bright Paradise, and bring up Anra Mainyu from horrid Hell", and yoke them to his chariot; but, with the help of Khvarenah, the hero Keresaspa was able to slay him (*Yt* 19:43-44). This illustrates how myths and legends were used to convey Zoroastrian doctrine, the Yazatas being shown as furthering goodness, with famous heroes as their agents. In another instance of an old legend being Zoroastrianized the culture-hero Takhma Urupi is granted by Vayu the power to subdue Anra Mainyu and ride him as his steed around the earth (*Yt* 15:12). The Yazatas also take direct part in the conflict between good and evil, both through performing their regular tasks and in other ways. Thus Mithra not only guards all just Mazda-worshippers (*Yt* 10:120), but crushes the heads of the Daevas, who with their master, Anra Mainyu, recoil from him in dread (ib., vv.97, 99), while Tištrya, as well as defeating each year the demon of Dearth by bringing rain, also subdues the Spirits of the shooting stars cast out by Anra Mainyu (*Yt* 8:39). There is a fixed formula which recurs celebrating the overcoming, by both Yazatas and righteous mortals, of "all hostilities of Daevas and (their) men [i.e. their worshippers], of wizards and witches, tyrants, *kavis* and *karapans*"[32] the two latter being categories of evildoers who are fiercely denounced by Zoroaster in the *Gathas*.

Another way in which Zoroaster's dualistic world-view finds expression in the *Yašts* is in their vocabulary. There was a whole series of common things for which the priest-poets used special nouns and verbs when speaking of creatures of the Evil Spirit. These "daevic" words sometimes had bestial connexions, or conveyed violent or noisy action. The beginnings of this convention have been traced to the *Gathas*,[33] where *hunu-* "(daevic) son" occurs beside the usual *puthra-*, and *həndvar-* "rush together" is used of daevic action; but its systematic development was clearly the work of scholar-priests thereafter, with its use being well drilled into their pupils, for the convention is maintained throughout Young Avestan and Pahlavi literature.

Zoroaster himself figures prominently in the *Yašts*, where he is regularly given his family name, "Spitaman", or the epithet *ašavan*, sober and factual attributes. Yet he is also drawn into the divine and mythic worlds, and thereby piously transformed from the recognizably real figure of the *Gathas* into a revered, semi-legendary one. Khvarenah, the divine Glory, is said to have religion (*Yt* 19:79). Aredvi Sura tells him that Ahura Mazda has made him the judge (*ratu-*) of the material world; and he himself, invoking Aši, identifies himself to her as the first man to have worshipped Ahura Mazda and the Ameša Spentas (*Yt* 17:18). In the *Farvardin Yašt* he is hailed as the first priest, warrior and pastoralist, and praised as the first to turn from the Daevas and their worshippers, the first to praise *aša* and to choose to worship Mazda. At his birth and growth, it is declared, the plants and waters recovered (that is, from Anra Mainyu's attacks), and beneficent creatures flourished; and all the Ameša Spentas rejoiced, saying "According to our wish a priest has been born, Spitaman Zarathuštra. Zarathuštra will worship us with offerings, with strewn *barəsman*. Henceforth the good Mazda-worshipping religion will spread out over the seven climes" (*Yt* 13:89-94).

It is probably significant that most is said about the prophet and about doctrine in the *Farvardin Yašt*, as if to Zoroastrianize the *fravaši* cult as thoroughly as possible. The *Yašt* begins very strongly on this note, with Ahura Mazda proclaiming to Zoroaster the power of the "mighty Fravašis of the just", and relating how they had helped him in the work of creation (*Yt* 13:1 ff.); and how if they had not done so "there would not now have been cattle and men (*pasu-vira*) ... To the Druj would have been power, to the Druj dominion (*khšathra*) ... Thereafter the conqueror would not yield to the conquered, Anra Mainyu to Spenta Mainyu" (*Yt* 13:12-13). It is inconceivable that Zoroaster would himself have countenanced this vaunting claim on behalf of the Fravašis. Yet since he taught that Mazda evoked the lesser benign beings in order that they might help him, this assertion of his dependence on the Fravašis, startling though it is in its extravagance, is not utterly at odds with the spirit of his theology, and the authors of these verses were evidently able to have it accepted in the context of the *Yašt*. It has always to be borne in mind that the *Yašts* were composed by priests who depended for their livelihoods on what they were paid for individual services by lay clients. It was therefore very much in their own interest to exalt the dignity and power of whatever divine beings they were asked to invoke, for thereby they confirmed the client's confidence in the capacity of those beings to answer his prayers, and so increased his readiness to employ the priests as intermediaries and to reward them well. Among the Brahmans this professional concern led to kathenotheism, that is, a theism which attributed to each of the major divinities "in turn" (*kathenos*), as they were invoked, "the totality of cosmic and divine functions".[34] Zoroaster's doctrine that Ahura Mazda alone is God prevented this development among his priests, but evidently could not wholly check minor tendencies evolving sporadically along something of the same lines.[35]

The desire to encourage the laity to be generous patrons manifests itself also in a recurrent theme in the *Yašts*, that of a prince or renowned hero who when petitioning a Yazata for a boon makes lavish sacrifices to gain his or her favour.

There is again a set formula for this situation, which regularly recurs: "For him (that is, the Yazata) So-and-so sacrificed a hundred stallions, a thousand cattle, ten thousand sheep."[36] There is a fine exaggeration here which may well owe something to ancient Iranian epic poetry, for it cannot be doubted that priests, enjoying conviviality as good Zoroastrians should, listened on feast days to minstrel lays in which the deeds of these same heroes were celebrated. The theme of a great man sacrificing plainly belongs to a pre-Zoroastrian tradition; but the composers of *Yašt* verses piously added to the names of legendary and mythical heroes those of Vištaspa, Zoroaster's princely patron, and of others of his circle. In one verse Vištaspa asks Aredvi Sura for the boon that he may overcome "Tanthryavant of bad religion, and Pešana the Daeva-worshipper, and the wicked Arejat-aspa" (*Yt* 5:108), and this boon is granted him; but when Arejat-aspa sacrifices to the same divinity and asks for the boon that he may overcome Vištaspa, this is refused. This forms the regular *Yašt* pattern: defenders of the faith, and heroes who, generally speaking, support *aša*, have their prayers granted. The wicked, who range from enemies of the religion to ravening monsters, have theirs rejected. Material offerings alone are thus not enough. *Vohu manah*, good purpose, must always be present in the worshipper's mind. He is naturally almost always a layman, a pattern for those to whom the priests looked for their regular support; but Zoroaster himself, as the most impressive of all possible mortal exemplars, is also shown petitioning individual Yazatas, for instance Aredvi Sura Anahita, whom he asks that he may convert Vištaspa (*Yt* 5:104); but what he as a priest offers is a *yasna* (the regular formula being used of "*haoma* mixed with milk" etc.).

Despite so many overtly Zoroastrian elements and so much generally sound doctrine, the *Yašts* have been regarded as virtually a pagan literature by those who have argued that Zoroaster himself was a strict monotheist. Once that theory has been abandoned, they can be accepted without difficulty as Zoroastrian works composed by Zoroastrian priests for Zoroastrian patrons. Nevertheless, it cannot be denied that many of their verses represent a coarsening and clouding of Zoroaster's teachings, with rather too much of old beliefs and old polytheistic ways of thought being allowed to seep back into his religion, with occasional allusions even to magic and the use of spells.[37] A great gap is thus apparent in spiritual perceptions (though not in basic doctrines) between the Old Avestan texts and the *Yašts* in general. This was, however, an inevitable development as the religion spread and gained ever more adherents, many, no doubt, simply yielding to the tide of a majority movement and having no particular spiritual gifts or aspirations. As far as the surviving Avestan literature is concerned, the *Yašts* have in fact an especial importance in that they represent forms of the popular devotion which was to be another strong strand in the fabric of developed Zoroastrianism - for this is an element which no great religion, commanding the fidelity of whole populations, has ever lacked.

Veneration of the lesser Yazatas has indeed had a great part in the devotional life of the community at all known stages of its existence. Thus it has been accepted practice for each believer, on first putting on the sacred cord, to take one of them as his or her guardian divinity; and this custom may well go back, unrecorded, to the Avestan period. Moreover, it has been general usage to pray to particular Yazatas for communal or private needs - to Tištrya, for instance, for rain, to Haoma for gifted sons, or to Aši for good luck. As well as celebrating great men seeking heroic boons, the *Yašts* contain many references to ordinary people praying to the Yazatas for ordinary wants, such as health and strength and long life, wealth in cattle and horses, good crops and ample food.[38]   Priests ask for knowledge, girls for good husbands, and wives for fine children. Belief in a host of beneficent beings, acting under Ahura Mazda and accessible to humble prayers, has been a strong support to many of the devout, and has manifested itself in a rich devotional life of worship, offerings and rites, all in addition to the regular observance of the obligatory religious duties.

Since performing, or having performed, supererogatory rites was meritorious, this helped the *ašavan* to lay up treasure in heaven;[39] and plainly such treasure could more readily be accumulated by the rich than by the poor. This can be seen as one of the reasons why Zoroastrianism approves of wealth, if rightly acquired and used. There was clearly scope in this for abuse, such as is attested in later times when an over-numerous priesthood tended to press the laity to have rites performed to excess; but Zoroaster's basic teaching continued to be faithfully transmitted and understood, namely that all that was essential for the individual to obtain personal salvation was that his own good thoughts, words and acts should at the end of his life outweigh his bad ones. To attain future blessedness was thus within the grasp of every man; and if the poor lacked the means to perform so many meritorious rites as the rich, they perhaps also escaped certain of their worldly temptations to sin, and so were as well able to keep their spiritual accounts in credit.[40] This doctrine of the absolute responsibility of each person for his or her own fate hereafter, linked with that of the duty to engage strenuously in the battle of good against evil, has instilled in Zoroastrians marked qualities of self-reliance and moral vigour. There was further the doctrine that in attaining his own salvation the individual added, however minutely, to the sum of goodness in the world, and so contributed to bringing about Frašo-kereti; and this gave a nobility to daily endeavour.

Such endeavour was not limited to spiritual and moral striving, but included the observance of purity laws, whereby the creations might be kept as free as possible from pollution, and so be fit for the indwelling of their guardian Ameša Spentas. Detailed injunctions about the application of these laws came to be gathered together in the compilation known as the *Videvdat* or *Vendidad*, "Law against *daevas*" (the term *daeva* being used in its debased sense of "demon, agent of evil"). Some of the prescriptions found there may reasonably be held to be of pre-Zoroastrian origin, since they are in accord with widespread usages concerning what was generally regarded in ancient times as unclean; but others, supporting Zoroaster's unique teachings about the creations, are themselves unique. These deal at length with how earth, water and fire should be kept clean from the contamination of *nasa*, that is, polluting dead matter, especially that of human corpses. The death penalty is demanded for anyone putting *nasa* on to a fire, and there are instructions for the ninefold purification of any fire that has been thus polluted.[41]   There are also detailed directions for the cleansing of clothing and utensils which have become contaminated, the threefold cleansing agents being cattle urine, *gaomaeza* (once widely used as a disinfectant, because of its ammonia content), sand and only then (the pollution having thus almost been banished) the pure creation of water. The same three agents were used in the elaborate purification of a contaminated human being, which was followed by a period of strict seclusion for the last traces of pollution to disappear. This rite has no name in the *Vendidad*, but was known later as the *barašnom-i no šaba*, the "washing of the nine nights", from the length of the time of this final retreat.

Cleansing of cattle and plants was more difficult, and no prescriptions are made for this in the *Vendidad*. There are, however, repeated injunctions in the later Zoroastrian literature about their care, together with that of the other creations. In each case this care had naturally to be shown to their representative parts - a patch of tilled ground, a single fire or stream, an orchard or herd of cattle; but the need of each creation, as the sum of all its parts, for man's solicitude and active stewardship could be readily apprehended - with one exception. This was Khšathra Vairya's creation of the sky of stone, lofty, unchanging and far beyond man's reach. As a late Zoroastrian text acknowledged: "None can take hold of the sky, nor can anyone defile it."[42] Nevertheless, it was still possible to serve Khšathra by cleaning to perfection stone vessels and implements, with a sense of the guardian of the stone sky being immanent in these lowly objects also. Gradually, however, many of them were being replaced by ones of metal. In antiquity the concept of "stone" was sometimes extended to include any hard substance found within the earth. Thus one definition of the "stone" of the sky given in the Pahlavi books was "crystal"[43] - rock crystal being extracted (in Bactria, for instance) from veins in rock. But so too were metallic ores, and in a passage in the Young Avesta (a verse, as it happens, of the exceptionally dogmatic *Farvardin Yašt*) the substance of the sky is spoken of as "*shining metal", *ayah- kh^vaena- (ayah-* being a general word for "metal" which only latterly came to mean particularly "iron").[44]   This understanding of the sky's nature was presumably born of the cogitations of priestly thinkers, focussed as so often on the rituals of worship, and prompted by the substitution of metal ritual vessels for ones of stone.[45]

Changes in ritual utensils are likely to have been slow, but nevertheless there is a reference in the Young Avesta to the pestle and mortar of the *yasna* being either of stone or of metal (*asmanaca havana ayaŋhaēnaca havana*).[46]   Plainly caring for metal objects was much more obviously necessary, and much more satisfying, than caring for stone ones, since, if unpolished or undried, they might tarnish or rust - visible signs of pollution.   Hence (it appears) an influential school of priests came to define the traditional stone of the sky itself as metal, and so to see Khšathra, lord of the sky, as lord thereby of metals, who could be served by keeping all metal objects clean and bright.   This development underlines the fact that the doctrine of the Heptad was always given practical application, with the concept of serving the great Ameša Spentas through care of their creations being very important for the active life of the *ašavan*.

The authors of the purity chapters of the *Vendidad* occasionally and quite unsystematically (like Zoroaster himself in the *Gathas*) emphasized the link between a creation and its guardian Ameša Spenta by using the name of the "immaterial" divinity to represent the material creation. This is done clearly and without complexities in the case of earth and Spenta Armaiti (for example "a third ... of the waters, a third ... of the plants, a third ... of Spenta Armaiti"[47]). It also occurs in the case of Khšathra Vairya and his creation, with in two passages instruction being given that a furrow or furrows should be drawn "with a sharp Khšathra Vairya".[48]   This refers presumably to the knife used by a priest for various ritual purposes; but whether the original authors of these words had a stone or metal knife in mind cannot be known.   Naturally for uncounted generations Iranian priests had used knives of sharpened stone, and, like the priests of other ancient religions, they may well have been slow to give these up for more efficient but new-fangled metal ones.   In another passage instructions are given that a woman in her courses is to be provided with food in a vessel "of iron or lead - the two lowliest Khšathra Vairyas", *ayaŋhaēnəm vā srum vā - nitəma khšathra vairya*.[49]   The last three words have been held to be a gloss,[50] and it is very possible that they were added with the pedagogic purpose of instilling the new belief that Khšathra's lordship extended over metals. In yet another passage[51] Vohu Manah stands for polluted garments to be cleansed, for these, whether of wool or leather, belonged to his creation, being from beneficial creatures; but he there also represents the polluted wearer of these garments, perhaps because the *ašavan*, seeking at this moment to become wholly pure, is entertaining Vohu Manah within himself.

The purity laws which underline the *Vendidad* prescriptions were based on Zoroaster's dualistic conception of the world.   Achieving and maintaining purity was a victory for the good over the dark forces of corruption. Another positive way of attacking these was held to be by killing *khrafstra*, a general term for creatures harmful or disgusting to man, which were all regarded as belonging to Anra Mainyu. One of the priest's professional implements was a *khrafstraghna*, a "*khrafstra*-smiter", a stick with a leather flap at the end.[52] Only insects are explicitly named as *khrafstras* in the *Vendidad*, and then only clothes-moths and corn-stealing ants, but a long list of daevic creatures which it is a merit to kill is given elsewhere in that work[53].

There is a famous Zoroastrian work of unknown date whose intent is to strengthen acceptance of the whole Zoroastrian code of living, with regard to moral conduct and religious observances, not by dry precepts but by the recounting of a dramatic vision. This, known by its Middle Persian title as the "Book of the just Viraz" (*Arda Viraz Namag*) tells how its eponymous hero, to satisfy doubts, ventured while living to send his spirit into the other world, seeking confirmation of Zoroaster's teachings; and how he narrated thereafter all that he had seen of the righteous being rewarded in heaven for their just acts, and the wicked being punished in hell for each of their "sins" (some of which were moral transgressions, others breaches of the purity laws or neglect of religious duties). There is a genre of ancient oral literature, which has been termed "visions of the homes of the dead", that was widespread among the peoples of the world;[54] and it is very likely that this was cultivated among the Iranians long before Zoroaster lived, with mantically gifted individuals being believed to make such journeys into the underworld kingdom of the dead, for diverse reasons; and since this Zoroastrian version of such a journey would obviously have been powerfully effective for proselytizing, or for strengthening the faith of the newly converted, it may well belong to the early days of the religion. If this is so, its protagonist is presumably to be identified with the Viraza whose *fravaši* is among the earliest venerated in the *Farvardin Yašt*.[55] (There all names have the fixed epithet *ašavan*, Middle Persian *arda*, because their bearers were believed to have been just and therefore to have attained blessedness.[56]) These suppositions cannot be proved, since no Avestan version of the story exists; but it appears to have been current among the western Iranians from Achaemenian times, for strong influences from it have been traced in the Jewish apocalyptic work, the *Slavonic Book of Enoch*.[57] Many details of the existing Middle Persian version must be regarded as cumulative accretions; but the frame-story could be very old, with prominence given in it to the Gathic figure of the Daena (Middle Persian Den) at the Chinvat Bridge,[58] and with Viraz's spirit ascending thereafter, according to ancient cosmological ideas, first to the stars, and then to the moon and sun.

Most Avestan works have perished in their original forms, and of all the oral compositions which once existed in that tongue, of a religious or semi-religious nature, probably only a tiny proportion survived to be made part eventually of the canonical "Great Avesta" of Sasanian times. There are indications, however, of the activity of priestly schools in the Young Avestan period, with much attention being given, naturally, to Zoroaster's own words.

Throughout the existing Young Avesta the *Gathas* and *Yasna Haptanhaiti* are cited, imitated and invoked,[59] proof of their being constantly studied. Most of the resulting exegetical work survives only shrouded in the additional difficulties of the Middle Persian *zand*, but there is a notable exception in a long commentary on the *Yatha ahu vairyo*, with brief ones on the also very holy utterances, the *Ašəm vohu* and *Yenhe hatam*,which had come to be recited with it before the *Staota yesnya*. These commentaries were incorporated in the extended *yasna* liturgy, as *Y.* 19-21, and they thus constitute "the only remnants in Avestan language of a once extensive commentary on the holy *Gāthās* of Zarathuštra and related texts, somewhat comparable to the Old Indian commentaries on the Rigveda".[60]   They present naturally their own problems, and still await a close study both of their technical vocabulary and of their manner of exegesis, which appears to be a seeking of deeper meanings and symbolic implications rather than a straightforward attempt at direct clarification of linear thought.[61]   Unfortunately the Young Avestan period produced, it seems, no grammarians, and already by this time (as the awkward construction of the *Yenhe hatam* itself shows) niceties of Old Avestan grammar were no longer understood. Yet (as again this *manthra* attests) essential meanings were not therefore betrayed, the tradition of belief and worship being a living one.

Zand translations show that there was a great deal of other priestly activity during the Young Avestan period. The works thus represented include a hagiographic life of the prophet, with an exalted birth-legend which, while retaining his humanity, made him glorious above other men.[62] It also acknowledged him as the founder of a religion in which it is a virtue to rejoice and be glad, with a tradition that he had laughed when he was born. There were in addition works on cosmogony and cosmology, and others which gathered together the knowledge of that time about the natural world, all such knowledge being arranged on a dualistic pattern. It is in these expository works that the relationship of the Heptad to the seven creations is set out systematically, in contrast to the allusive and incidental treatment of this doctrine in the devotional and purity texts.[63]

Zoroastrianism evidently developed considerably in this period, growing from a new, revolutionary and imperilled missionary faith into the dominant religion among the eastern Iranians. This religion had intellectual, visionary, ethical, poetic and practical strands, and, while providing sustenance for thinkers and mystics, was able evidently to satisfy the needs of people at large. It furnished its adherents with daily devotional exercises and firm rules of conduct, and gave them the hope that by observing these they could attain eternal bliss. Meanwhile it enjoined them to seek happiness and well-being in this life, in gratitude to their Creator, and provided them with regular occasions for joyous communal celebrations. It was thus both a "this-worldly" and an "other-worldly" religion, and had the double strengths which this double nature conferred. In this it was following the teachings of its prophet; indeed, although it had grown in complexity, absorbing a number of popular and traditional elements, the religion of the Young Avesta appears in essentials strikingly faithful to the doctrines and vision of its founder, who is so greatly venerated in its surviving texts.

NOTES

1 The term "Young Avestan" is used here for want of a better one for the long period of the religion's development between the first generation or two after the prophet's own lifetime and its entry into history under the Achaemenians, for which materials have in the main to be derived from Young Avestan texts. The term is thus not linked here with the pace of development of the Avestan language (cf. above, p.46 n.14), for in an oral literature the linguistic stage at which a text is finally preserved often tells little about its time of origin or its evolution down to that point.

2 Cf. above, pp. 84-5.

3 See Nyberg, *Rel.*, 273-5.

4 Cf. above, p.55.

5 Cf. *Y.* 51:22 (above, pp.70-1), *Y.*39:3 (above, p.93).

6 *Y.* 12:8-9. (In v.9 there is what seems an obvious interpolation in support of *khvaetvadatha.*)

7 See below, p.138. The value of repetitive daily prayers is acknowledged with regard to the similar and (it is thought by scholars) partly imitative Muslim observance.

8 *Y.* 12:11-7.

9 On the distribution of the *gahambars* in the reformed 365-day calendar (see below), and their links with the creations see *GBd.* Ia 16-21; and on the links of the creations with the Heptad, ib., III 7, 12-19. On the dedication of No Roz to Aša Vahišta (partly blurred in later times by calendar changes, and the prolonged extensions of this festival) see Boyce, "Rapithwin, Nō Rūz and the feast of Sada" in *Pratidānam, Studies presented to F.B.J. Kuiper,* ed. J.C. Heesterman and others, The Hague, 1969, 201-15, esp. at pp.204-5.

10 Details of the celebration of the seven feasts come only from the Sasanian period and later, and no doubt some of the symbolic customs then attested not only for No Roz but also for the sixth *gahambar* had grown up in course of time; but the YAv. names of the *gahambars*, the great holiness attributed to these feasts, and the fundamental doctrinal significance of their dedications, taken together support the supposition that they and their essential observances belong to the early days of the faith.

11 Above, p.91.

12 Above, pp.58-9.

13 Widespread acceptance of the spurious 6th-century dating for Zoroaster led many scholars to suppose that the "Young Avestan" and Achaemenian periods were almost synchronous, and that the creation of the Zoroastrian calendar took place under one or other of the Persian Great Kings. It now seems (see p.110, above, with nn.18, 21) that the original Zoroastrian calendar, that is, one of 360 days, with the 30 month-days dedicated to 30 Yazatas,

was created in "Young Avestan" times, and that it is its modification by the addition of 5 days which is to be attributed to the Achaemenian period, together with the dedication then of 3 month-days to Ahura Mazda as Creator. The present writer once argued (in "On the calendar of Zoroastrian feasts", *BSOAS* XXXIII, 1970, 513-39) that the 5 days were added under the Sasanian Ardašir I, the main grounds for this being the evidence in Pahl. texts of enormous popular bewilderment attending the change, and of priestly resistance, resulting in duplications and other complexities in the keeping of festivals. However, no specialist in calendrical or chronological matters accepted this late dating for the 365-day calendar (in particular Professor Pingree argued privately against it with the writer from the first); and recently Professor B. I. Marshak has taken up the matter on the basis of the eastern Iranian forms of the Zoroastrian calendar, see his article "Istoriko-kul'turnoe znachenie sogdiyskogo kalendarya" in *Mirovaya kul'tura. Tradicii i sovremennost*, ed. T. B. Knyazevskaya, Moscow 1991, 183-97. In this he convincingly upheld the generally accepted dating, proposed by Markwart and Taqizadeh, of the 365-day calendar to the Achaemenian period. *HZ* II 243 ff. has accordingly to be revised. One way to reconcile the apparently conflicting data is to assume that some of the texts attributed to the Sasanian period are in fact older, that is Achaemenian, in substance, having evolved orally from Old into Middle Persian before being written down. Part at least of the difficulties and controversies which they reflect could then be assigned to the earlier epoch. This would accord with the suggestion made below (pp.131-2) about the possible linguistic evolution in this way of certain "Middle Persian" dedications and prayers. Yet even if this explanation is sound, considerable problems obviously remain about the religious calendar in "post-Avestan" times.

14   Cf. above, p.60, n.7.

15   On this divinity see *HZ* I 81, 117, 150; Duchesne-Guillemin, *ZDMG*, Suppl. IV, 1980, 64 f.; Narten, *YHapt.* 249.

16   *Yt* 19:16-18, on which see further below.

17   Above, p.75 with n.65.

18   For a change of this kind to be made in a religious calendar it seems necessary to postulate some more pressing motive than a mere desire for approximation to the Semitic week (which was wholly irrelevant to Zoroastrian devotional life); and Nyberg's suggestion ("Questions de cosmogonie et de cosmologie mazdéennes II", *JA* 1931, 68 ff., esp. at p.128 ff., = *Acta Ir.* 7, 1975, pp.260 ff., 320 ff.) that it was made so that the four dedications to Ahura Mazda should also honour, esoterically, the tetradic god Zurvan, acknowledged, it seems, by the later Achaemenians, appears to have much to commend it. The Zurvanites joined the orthodox (to judge from one of their myths) in worshipping Ahura Mazda as Creator, hence the new dedications of these three days to him under this aspect could satisfy them while in no way offending the orthodox.

19   See *Siroza* I 30. Here the three follow the *hamkars* or helpers of Anagra Raochå, namely the Mainyus of Garonmana (the highest heaven) and the Chinvat Bridge.

20   See Modi, *CC*, 450-1.

21   The present writer suggested previously (*HZ* II 247) that this was the result of debate and irreconcilable wishes at the actual creation of the 360-day Zoroastrian calendar, attributed to the Achaemenian period; but this was implausible, since all other displays of similar tenacity had behind them many years of usage, which the priests sought loyally to maintain. There could hardly be instant conservatism of this kind.

22   See Boyce, art. cit. in n.13.

23   *Yt* 10:137, 138. On *mainya* "having authority, authoritative" see *Air. Wb.* 1896, with (for Sogdian cognates) E. Benveniste, "Notes sogdiennes", *BSOS* IX, 1938, 513; W.B.

Henning, "A Sogdian fragment of the Manichaean cosmogony", *BSOAS* XII, 1948, 309; and on the use of the phrase *nar mainya* I. Gershevitch, *AHM*, 17.

24   For the Av. text see Geldner, *Avesta*, I 227, as *Y.* 68:11.

25   E.g., *Yt* 10:55, 8:23-5, cf. *Yt* 14:42.

26   E.g., *Yt* 10:6. For a commentary on the words see Narten, *Aməša Spəntas*, 140 n.19.

27   Cf. above, p.71.

28   This is attested by Indian practice, by Herodotus, and by Zoroastrian observances maintained into the 20th century in rural Iran; for references see *HZ* I 168-9, nn.144-9.

29   *Yt* 8:10, 10:73.

30   Cf. above, p.93.

31   These verses occur also in *Yt* 13:82-4. "Floating" verses which a reciter introduces now into this text, now into that, are characteristic of oral literature.

32   E.g., *Yt* 5:13.

33   See Gershevitch, "Old Iranian literature", 22.

34   B. Heimann, *Indian and Western Philosophy*, London 1937, 35. See further *HZ* I 270.

35   The most extreme are the instances in which Ahura Mazda himself is said to have worshipped a Yazata, those concerned being Tištrya (*Yt* 8:25), Mithra (*Yt* 10:123), Aši (*Yt* 17:61), Aredvi Sura Anahita (*Yt* 5:18), and Vayu (*Yt* 15:3). The verses in question are regarded as late, some being betrayed as such by bad grammar as well as bad theology; but their point is to exalt these Yazatas by describing this act of graciousness towards them by the supreme Deity, and also (explicitly in the case of Tištrya) to set mankind an example thereby. Inept and regrettable though the lines are, there is therefore no reason to suppose that those who composed them intended any heterodoxy.

36   E.g. *Yt* 5:21.

37   See, very strikingly, *Yt* 14:34 ff., where the magic is to be the sole decider of victory between two armies, with no question of the rightness or not of their cause.

38   For a detailed analysis of the *Yašts* from this angle see Sarah Stewart, *Some aspects of the devotional life of the Zoroastrian laity*, London Ph.D. thesis (in preparation).

39   On this Zoroastrian concept see, with references, *HZ* III 414 with n.236.

40   Cf. the late text, *Saddar Bundaheš* 10:1-2 (Dhabhar, ed., pp.78-9, tr. in *Riv.* p.511): "Why should the rich undergo more trouble than the poor? God the Most High answered: "For this reason, that the Amašaspands require good works from the rich and they wish (only) that the poor may not commit crimes".

41   *Vd* 8:73-8.

42   *Saddar Bd.* 75:1 (ed. Dhabhar, p.146, tr. Dhabhar, *Riv.*, p.556).

43   See Bailey, *Zor. Problems,* 131 ff.

44   *Yt* 13:2. The adj. *khvaēna*, of uncertain meaning, occurs only here and in the Gathic verse *Y.* 32:7.

45   The writer has long since abandoned the theory (put forward in *HZ* I) that a main reason for the change was the gradual substitution of metal for stone weapons, since this was not a matter which closely affected priests.

46   *Y.* 22:2. (The phrase occurs also in the *Visperad* and *Nirangestan*, see *Air.Wb.* 156.)

47   *Vd* 18:63-4.

48   *Vd* 9:10, 17:6..

49   *Vd* 16:6.

50   Bartholomae, *Air.Wb.* 1082, n.3 to *nitəma-*.

51 *Vd* 19:23-5; cf. *Pahl. Vd*, ed. B.T. Anklesaria, 380-1; Darmesteter, *ZA* II 267-8.

52 *Vd* 14:8, 18:2.

53 *Vd* 16:12, 17:3, 14:5.

54 See Chadwick, *Growth of Literature*, III 848 ff.

55 *Yt* 13:101.

56 For the scholarly literature on the use of the term *ašavan* and its cognates for the blessed departed see most recently P. Gignoux (ed.), *AVN*, 8-10 with nn. The word has never, however, been restricted to the righteous dead, but at all known epochs has remained the standard one for the Zoroastrian concept of a good person, one who lives according to *aša*, see Gnoli, *EIr* II 705-6.

57 See *HZ* III 416, 427-32.

58 So Gignoux, o.c., p.5 n.1. The figure is, however, still called the Den in a vision of the fate of one man's soul set down in Middle Persian in the 3rd century A.C., see P.O. Skjaervø, "Kirdir's vision", *AMI* 16, 1983, 269-306 at pp.276-7, 300-1.

59 See, for a table of such usages with reference to the *Gathas*, Darmesteter, *ZA* I xcviii.

60 P.O. Skjaervø, "Bag nask", *EIr*. III 400.

61 This has laid them open to the accusation by some philologists of wholly misunderstanding the holy texts.

62 *Dk.* VII:2:3-52; Molé, *Légende*, 14-23; excerpted in *Sources*,72-4. (It is in this legendary life that the malign activities of the *karbs* Durasrab and Bratrores are recounted, cf. above, p.14 ff.)

63 Notably *GBd.* Ia, III. In *Sources*, 48-9, an attempt is made to render in English the *zand* translation shorn as far as possible of later extensions and glosses; but it is not possible to excise all evidently later materials, for some have been too closely interwoven with earlier matter.

CHAPTER SEVEN

The Religion of Empires

Zoroastrianism, as we have seen,[1] had probably established itself on a firm basis in western Iran by the eighth century B.C., with its adoption there by some of the leading Median priests, the famed magi; and it entered recorded history with the founding, in the mid sixth century, of the Achaemenian empire. Vast and splendid though that empire was, more is known of the Persians' military achievements then than of their religious and cultural lives; but enough facts emerge, from a variety of sources, to show that the eastern Iranians instructed their western cousins thoroughly and well, so that in all essentials the "Avestan" and "Persian" religions were one. There are, moreover, indications that the "Ahuric doctrine", *ahura tkaeša*, had been a dominant element in the old religion of the western Iranians also, so that for them too Zoroaster's teachings had the strength of embodying with what was new a number of already cherished beliefs and observances.

One of the two chief sources for knowledge of the Persian religion is the inscriptions of the early Achaemenian kings. These are mainly political in intent, but some - notably those over the tomb of Darius the Great - contain considerable religious matter. The other main source is observations by foreigners, mostly Greeks, about the beliefs and ways of the Persians. There is a little supporting evidence to be had from material remains - sculptures, seals, coins and temple ruins - and more from collections of administrative documents, especially those in Elamite, while others in Aramaic yield various theophoric names.

The salient religious fact to emerge from Darius' inscriptions is that the only divine being whom he names is Zoroaster's God, whom he knows as Ahuramazda, his name and title having evidently become fused for the Old Persians through centuries of cultic invocation. Further, the king venerates him in all orthodoxy as the Creator of this world and what is good in it: "A great

God is Ahuramazda, who created this earth, who created yonder sky, who created man, who created happiness for man".[2] The mention here so prominently of "happiness" is moreover strikingly Zoroastrian, since in that religion happiness is regarded as a positive good, to be consciously fostered against the Evil Spirit's weapons of grief and sorrow.[3] This special emphasis appears again when Darius instructs his people: "Whoever shall worship Ahuramazda as long as he has strength, he will be happy, both living and dead".[4] That ethical elements were required in this worship is brought out in the similar declaration by his son Xerxes, who made use of the significant word *artavan*, the Old Persian equivalent of Avestan *ašavan* "just, righteous". "The man who has respect for the law which Ahuramazda has established, and worships Ahuramazda with due order and rites, he both becomes happy while living and *artavan* when dead".[5] *Artavan* is evidently used here for one to be blessed hereafter because only a just person can hope to attain that state. This appears to have been one of Zoroaster's great innovatory doctrines, and Xerxes' words reflect closely (although with the terms inverted) a *Vendidad* passage where it is said of an offender: "Living, he is not *ašavan*. Dead, he does not enjoy the Best Existence [that is, blessedness in Paradise]". [6]

Darius moreover followed Zoroaster's teachings in perceiving Ahuramazda the Creator as having divine helpers. These lesser beings the king refers to as "the other gods who are"[7] (presumably an established Old Persian cultic formula equivalent to Zoroaster's "those who were and are"[8]), or simply as "all the gods".[9] Thus he declares: "For this reason Ahuramazda bore me aid, and the other gods who are, because I was not disloyal, I was not a follower of Drauga [Av. Drug], I was not a doer of wrong - neither I nor my family. According to righteousness I conducted myself".[10] From this declaration alone it could be deduced that "the other gods who are" of Darius' veneration were Zoroaster's beneficent Yazatas, rather than all the beings of the old pantheon; and it is significant that among the numerous theophoric Old Persian names now known not one is compounded with that of a Daiva (Avestan Daeva) - that is, of warlike Indra or his fellows. Thereafter Xerxes left an inscription in which he recorded: "There was (a place) where previously Daivas were worshipped. Then by the will of Ahuramazda I destroyed that sanctuary of Daivas, and I proclaimed: 'Daivas shall not be worshipped.' Where earlier Daivas were worshipped, there I worshipped Ahuramazda".[11]

It was perhaps the need still in the early Achaemenians' reigns for such forceful missionary work among their Iranian subjects which caused these kings to name Ahuramazda alone in their inscriptions (copies of which were sent all over the empire). They thereby declared themselves unambiguously to be "worshippers of Mazda" and, following their prophet, put full stress on their God's unique greatness. The names of a few of "the other gods who are" were allowed, however, to appear more privately in the Elamite tablets of

Persepolis, the oldest of which belong to Darius' reign.[12] These provide further evidence for the veneration of the Ahuras among the ancient Persians, for Ahuramazda appears there both alone and with "Mithra-(and-the)-Baga", the two latter divinities being also worshipped together but apart from him. Baga, as we have seen,[13] was one of the Iranians' cult-names for Varuna, and the pair-compound "Mithra-Baga" appears as the Old Persian equivalent of Avestan Mithra-Ahura-berezant and Vedic Mitra-Varuṇa. The tablets and Aramaic documents yield, through theophoric names, evidence for the veneration of a few other Yazatas of Avestan worship, among them Vohu Manah, Aša and Khšathra.[14] The absence of the three other lesser members of the Zoroastrian Heptad is not surprising, since they are female Yazatas, and relatively few women's names are recorded from this time. Much later in the period Artaxerxes II broke with the usage of his forefathers by invoking in his inscriptions[15] two lesser divinities as well as Ahuramazda, namely Mithra and "Anahit", the goddess of composite origins who was peculiarly beloved by the Persians. "Mazda worship" was evidently firmly established by then among Iranians throughout the empire, and so this development would no longer have created any doctrinal confusion. His son, Artaxerxes III, reverted thereafter to the invocation attested on the Elamite tablets, seeking the protection of "Ahuramazda and Mithra-(and-the-)-Baga"[16] - presumably the traditional Old Persian equivalent of the traditional Avestan "Mazda-and-(the-other)-Ahuras" which Zoroaster himself had used.[17]

A Greek poet of the time of Artaxerxes II made a fleeting reference to Anahit's worship, joyously celebrated with much sweet music;[18] and, earlier, Herodotus gave brief accounts of the Persians' religious rites - how they had no temples or statues or altars, but "call the whole circle of heaven Zeus [that is, Ahura Mazda], and to him they offer sacrifices on the highest peaks of the mountains; they sacrifice also to the sun and moon and earth and fire and water and winds"[19] - that is, to the Mainyus of these created things, venerated under Mazda. Herodotus also tells how individual laymen offered worship,[20] and the rites which he records resemble quite closely, though on a modest and realistic scale, those ascribed with epic exaggeration to kings and heroes in the *Yašts*.[21] Thus he says that a man wanting to sacrifice to one of the gods - the *nar mainya* of the Avesta - would lead a sacrificial beast to an open space and call on the gods; and a magus would chant a "theogony" (presumably, that is, appropriate *Yašt* verses) "for no sacrifice can be offered without a magus." Herodotus stresses that "to pray for himself alone is not lawful for the sacrificer; rather he prays that it may be well with the king and all the Persians, for he reckons himself among them." This accords with living Zoroastrian usage, in which prayers are never said for the *framadar* alone, but always first for the local ruler or ruling authority, and for the community; for the obligation to care for Ahura

Mazda's especial creation, man, means that an individual should always be concerned for his fellows, and never simply self-regarding.

Herodotus expressly says that those who offered such sacrifices did not "kindle fire", and this accords with usage at such rites in modern times. Conceivably this is because this simple act of worship belongs to an age-old tradition, going back far beyond even Zoroaster's distant day, and untouched therefore by the especial symbolic importance which he gave to fire. That fire had this importance for the Achaemenian Persians is, however, attested in diverse ways, and most strikingly by the carving which Darius the Great had set above his tomb. This carving was repeated above each of his successors' tombs also, an unchanging declaration of the dynasty's faith. It shows each Great King standing in an attitude of reverence before a brightly blazing fire raised in an altar-like holder. Above there are sun- and moon-symbols, since sun, moon and earthly fire are the three icons before which a Zoroastrian should pray.[22]   Blazing fire in such a holder, often with a worshipper or worshippers represented beside it, became from then on a standard element in Zoroastrian iconography. It appears on minor Achaemenian carvings and seals,[23] in a famous tomb-carving of (probably) the Seleucid period, and on coins of Persis from that same epoch; and it was to be the fixed device on the reverse of all Sasanian coins. Another recurrent device, also used from Achaemenian times onwards, was of a worshipper with the *baresman* (Middle Persian *barsom*), the bundle of rods held during many acts of worship both by priests and by well-instructed lay people.[24]   The *baresman* was apparently by origin a handful of the herbage on which the sacrifice was laid, and its use goes back (as Brahmanic parallels show) to proto-Indo-Iranian times. So the iconography newly created for Zoroastrianism in western Iran, under the influence of the art of some of the Great Kings' Near Eastern subjects, embodied two age-old elements of Indo-Iranian observance which had been retained by Zoroaster: the ever-burning wood fire and the *baresman*.

In contrast to these developments, which were thus a blend of innovation and profound traditionalism, there is one belonging to later Achaemenian times which was wholly unprecedented. This was the founding of temples to house cult statues of the Yazatas. The step appears to have been taken under influences from Babylonia, Persia's subject and neighbour,[25] and it brought Zoroastrianism, the state religion of the greatest of the Near Eastern powers, into line in this respect with the usages of most other Near Eastern religions. It was imposed on the whole Zoroastrian community by Persian Great Kings, and constituted a complete breach with the ancient tradition of open-air worship with natural phenomena as icons. it seems accordingly to have swiftly provoked, as a more orthopractic counter-measure, the founding of other temples in which fire was the cult object, raised in an altar-like holder such as that before which the Achaemenian kings stand carved in prayer above their tombs. The purpose of these foundations was apparently to maintain the essential act of private Zoroastrian devotion - prayer before fire - in as traditional a form as possible, even when it was now to take place with public solemnity in a specially constructed "house of fire" (as these new sanctuaries were factually called).[26] Thus temple fires were ever-burning wood fires, like hearth ones, and were maintained with the same observances as hearth fires, namely with offerings, made with recitation of the *Ataš Niyayeš*, of dry wood and incense, and, less regularly, fat from the sacrifice, five times in the twenty-four hours.[27] Those who visited them prayed before them as they would have done before their own hearth fires, reciting their regular obligatory prayers and performing thus an individual, not a communal, act of devotion; and priests continued to solemnize the ancient high rituals (with which the cult of the hearth fire had no connection) in a quite separate precinct, the "place of rites" (Old Persian *brazmadana*,[28] in Middle Persian the "place of worship", *yazišn gah*). Thus fire temples were intended solely to offer the people generally a familiar icon before which to perform traditional acts of devotion, being founded, it seems, to defend the faith against innovation in worship.[29]

It was nevertheless inevitable that temple fires, established with elaborate rites of purification and consecration,[30] set within a consecrated building, and served by priests with rituals which natural grew to be more solemn and extended, should have come to be regarded as imbued with an exalted sanctity. Even so the ritual fire, consecrated by the solemnization of the *yasna*, had been apprehended by Zoroaster himself as being of peculiar holiness.[31] Unlike a ritual fire, however, the temple fires were abiding presences, which came, like any other icons, to attract devotion to themselves - indeed, perhaps more than most other icons, since fire is a beautiful, apparently living thing, visibly dependent on its devotees and visibly responding to their service. Though apprehended by the well instructed as a manifestation of the creation of fire, and hence of great Aša, each sacred fire became invested accordingly with individuality, and its Mainyu was loved and cherished as a being of great purity and power. This power (as is attested subsequently) was believed to extend to the granting of petitioners' prayers, as other Yazatas were held to be able to do;[32] and so the great fire temples drew many worshippers and pilgrims. All this gave fire a new prominence in Zoroastrian devotional life; and it was only after the founding of temple fires that observers began to apply to Zoroastrians terms such as "fire-kindlers" and "fire-worshippers". (Herodotus, living earlier, had barely remarked on their veneration of it.[33])

The fairly meagre indications given by Herodotus about the Persians' beliefs, as distinct from their usages, were later amplified by Theopompus or by Eudemus of Rhodes, both of whom lived in the fourth century B.C. Their works are lost, but there is a succinct summary by Plutarch.[34] According to this, Zoroaster taught a dualism in which a god, Horomazes, is opposed by a rival, a spirit (*daemon*) called Areimanius, with whom he is at war. Horomazes is "especially akin, among objects of perception, to light", and Areimanius "to darkness and ignorance". The former has created six gods, of whom Plutarch names the first as the "god of good will" (evidently Vohu Manah) and the second as the "god of truth" (that is, Aša).[35]   Areimanius created six rivals to these. Thereafter Horomazes created other gods within "an egg" (that is, the stone shell of the sky), and Areimanius created an equal number of spirits, who pierced this "egg", and "so it comes about that good and evil are mixed. Then will come the destined time when Areimanius, the bringer of plague and famine, must needs be utterly destroyed and obliterated by these. The earth shall be flat and level and one way of life and one government shall arise of all men, who shall be happy." If in the last sentence the qualification is added of "just" to "all men", and the expectation is made clear that the "one government" will be that of Ahuramazda, then this highly condensed epitome is very close to the expositions of doctrine preserved in the translation-*zand* and other sources, and testifies to the Persians' sound grasp of the theology of their religion. Further, Theopompus is elsewhere cited as stating that "Zoroaster prophesies that some day there will be a resurrection of all the dead".[36]

Greeks testified also to the ethical principles of the Persian religion, their witness in this regard supporting statements in the royal inscriptions. We have already met Darius' claim to have conducted himself "according to righteousness", and Herodotus tells of an incident in this king's life which suggests that in administering justice he kept in mind the model of how divine justice is dispensed at the Chinvat Bridge. He once, it seems, condemned one of his judges to be crucified because he had taken a bribe; but then, reviewing a reckoning of the man's good services, decided that these outweighed this one offence, and had him taken down from the cross.[37]   Herodotus further states that it was a general principle among the Persians that "not till the offender's wrongful acts are more and greater than his services" might he be severely punished.[38]   He also notes that "of what they may not do neither may they speak" - an allusion surely to the doctrine that words weigh with deeds in the scales of divine judgment. He was struck too by the immense importance which they attached to truthfulness, saying (doubtless with some exaggeration) that they taught their boys "three things only, riding and archery and truth-telling", and that they held "lying to be the foulest act of all."[39]   In this he was supported by the unknown author of *Alcibiades*, a work emanating from Plato's Academy, who wrote of the Persian princes: "When the boy reaches fourteen years of age [that is, was nearing the time for being invested with the sacred cord] he is taken over by the royal tutors ... The first teaches him the Magian lore of Zoroaster, ...that is the worship of the gods. ... [Another] teaches him to be truthful all his life long ... ."[40]   Xenophon too, who served as a gentleman adventurer with Cyrus the Younger in 401, made a number of observations on the behaviour of the Persians, which complement those of Herodotus in giving some idea of how their religion actually shaped their lives;[41] and the writings of these two Greeks, in conjunction with the royal inscriptions, testify to considerable degrees of piety, self-discipline and moral energy among the Zoroastrians of western Iran in the Achaemenian era.

Greeks were also struck, as foreign onlookers were to be down the centuries, by the Persians' observance of the Zoroastrian purity laws. This was evidently strictly instilled in them, for Herodotus records: "Rivers they chiefly reverence; they will neither make water nor spit nor wash their hands therein, nor suffer anyone so to do."[42]   These are standard orthopractic usages, to protect Haurvatat's pure creation of water: water to wash in is to be drawn off in a small receptacle, so that only a little is sullied, not the living stream itself. Herodotus also noticed with astonishment the zeal with which "the magi kill with their own hands ... all alike, ants and snakes, creeping and flying things, and take much pride therein"[43] - as was only proper for those who believed that they were thereby reducing the ranks of *khrafstra*, the evil creatures of Anra Mainyu.   He further remarked that they, and already in his time a number of the laity also, exposed the bodies of their dead to be "mangled by bird or dog".[44]   Even if their own distant forbears had once followed this practice of the steppe peoples, the western Iranians (as excavations have shown) had abandoned it long before Zoroastrianism reached them.[45]   The magi presumably grasped from the first the doctrinal reason for it - to protect the earth, Armaiti's pure creation - and adopted it strictly, with the laity following more slowly. The rite is, however, attested among the Persian nobility later in the Achaemenian period;[46]   and Herodotus himself notes the number of dogs which accompanied Xerxes' great army into Greece, possibly partly in connection with it.[47]

It is improbable that any of the instruction which bore this good fruit of sound doctrine, conscious moral endeavour and the disciplined observance of purity laws was given in Avestan, which, as we have seen,[48] appears to have been a dead language by the time the faith was brought to western Iran. The early missionaries from the east had presumably to master Median and Old Persian, preaching the faith in those cognate tongues; and thereafter instruction would have been passed on in these, the local languages, with Avestan used only for devotional purposes. The laity would presumably then, as at other better known periods, have learnt their Avestan prayers by rote, and only scholar-priests would actually have studied the sacred language. It seems likely, moreover, that a number of western Iranian usages, designed to help the laity to understand their devotions, go back to this time, such as that of preceding every religious service with a colloquial rendering of its Avestan *khšnumaine* or dedicatory formula.   This, spoken out loud and clear (as has remained customary down to modern times), and with other vernacular contributions in the course of "outer services", enabled all those attending to be fully aware of the intention of the devotional act, and to take part in it.[49]   It is also possible that already in the Achaemenian period some words in the vernacular were added to the sacred-cord prayers to help each worshipper to be fully alert to their significance; but none of this can be proved, because no religious texts were committed to writing at this time. It was not until long after Old Persian had evolved into Middle Persian - quite far, that is, into the Sasanian period - that any Zoroastrian devotional works were written down, all the vernacular additions naturally in their Middle Persian forms. How long a history these vernacular texts had by then there is thus no means of knowing; but common sense suggests that the orthodoxy and orthopraxy of the Achaemenian Persians are likely to have been supported by at least some basic religious texts which could be understood by the many; and it seems reasonable to suppose that oral vernaculars were used in this way in most areas of the Zoroastrian world.

With regard to the Persians in particular, it appears significant in this connection that the religious vocabulary of the Achaemenian and early Sasanian inscriptions differs in a number of particulars from that of the Avesta, and that Avestan words and expressions apparently entered Middle Persian on a large scale, replacing traditional Persian ones, only in the later Sasanian period. This was very probably connected with the writing down then of the Avesta, and in consequence its ever more intensive study. The fact that most western Iranians - and probably from about the eighth century B.C. most eastern Iranians also - must have believed in, practised and understood their religion without comprehending Avestan is no more remarkable than that for many centuries most Christians had no direct knowledge of the Bible, being innocent of Latin or Greek, let alone Hebrew and Aramaic. Zoroaster's own words, with the rest of the devotional texts, were evidently venerated as sacred utterances of great power, whose recital was both obligatory and profoundly beneficial; but their literal comprehension was not needful for an understanding of his teachings, because his followers had access to these through a living tradition of faith and observance, transmitted down the generations in unbroken continuity.

This continuity was not interrupted by Alexander's conquest of the Achaemenian empire in the late fourth century B.C., nor by the subsequent period of Seleucid rule.[50] Zoroastrianism came then for the first time under alien domination, and proved its vitality by surviving sturdily not only in Iran itself (where it had the support of numbers) but also in outlying lands of the Achaemenian empire now permanently lost to the Iranians - to the east in the Indian borderlands, to the west in Asia Minor and Syria, Palestine and Egypt.[51] The last of these expatriate communities only finally disappeared from all records in the sixth century A.C. - nearly a thousand years after Alexander's conquest. For most of this time they flourished under religiously tolerant polytheistic rulers, first Macedonian, then Roman; but for the last two or three centuries they had to withstand not only Christian proselytizing but also Christian persecution. The tenacity of these isolated communities is a potent attestation of the inner strength of Zoroastrianism. It is also striking that still in the fourth century A.C. the Zoroastrians of Cappadocia are recorded to have been transmitting their faith in the traditional way, that is, orally and by customary usage, from parent to child, without recourse to books.[52]

In Iran itself the Parthians of the north-east, under their Arsacid kings, gradually won back power from the Seleucids, and from the mid second century B.C. all Iran, with Babylonia, was once more under Zoroastrian rule. Even less is known of the internal affairs of the Parthian than of the Achaemenian empire, but such information as there is shows uninterrupted progression in religious matters, with both fire temples and image shrines flourishing, the Zoroastrian calendar attested for the first time in use for general dating purposes, and the legends of the faith being piously cultivated.[53]   The kings were advised by two councils, one made up of their own family members, the other of sage laymen and priests;[54] and it was presumably at the prompting of his priestly counsellors that late in their epoch one of the kings sent out an order to the provinces of his empire, bidding them "to preserve ... in the state in which they had come down in (each) province, whatever had survived in purity of Avesta and Zand"[55] - that is, presumably, of *zand* as composed in each local tongue. The order was apparently effective, and illustrates both the supreme authority wielded by the Parthian kings, and yet their readiness to let each province to a large extent manage its own affairs.

The contrast in this was sharp with the Sasanians, who overthrew the Parthians early in the third century A.C. and founded the second Persian empire. Over half a millennium had passed since the downfall of the Achaemenians, but memory of a time of Persian dominance had evidently persisted, and the speed with which the Sasanians and their priests began to act in both the religious and secular spheres suggests an eagerness to reassert what they felt to be their traditional, and hence rightful, authority. Thus the very first Sasanian king took up, but more strenuously and imperiously, the work of preserving Avestan texts. He commanded "that all those scattered teachings should be brought to (his) court" - which at that time could only mean, as far as the Avestan texts themselves were concerned, that those who knew them by heart should come there and recite them. His high priest then "selected those which were trustworthy and left the rest out of the canon."[56]   So, after many centuries, an authorized body of Avestan works was at last established, forming the great Sasanian Avesta.

The chosen works were presumably carefully learnt and transmitted orally thereafter by Persian magi, until some two centuries or so later the priestly authorities finally decided to permit them to be written down in a specially invented alphabet which made it possible to record the Avestan sounds with great exactness. Most Avestan texts, it appears, had customarily been recited in the priestly schools together with their *zand*, each short passage of Avestan having been memorized with its "interpretation", and this was the way in which they were now set down. Since it was Persian priests who did the setting down, from dictation by other Persian priests, the *zand* was naturally written in Middle Persian; but *zands* in other Middle Iranian languages were evidently drawn on, especially for the glosses and commentaries.[57] In general, the zealous endeavour of Sasanian scholastics was to preserve and compile, and many streams of Zoroastrian tradition met therefore and were at last given fixed form not only in the *zand* but in Middle Persian literature generally; for the Sasanian period saw a slow, steady transition from an oral to a written culture, with, from the fourth century onward, Middle Persian being, it seems, the only permitted written language.[58] This means that, apart from the Avestan texts themselves, all extant Zoroastrian literature is in that tongue (or, later, in Persian or Gujarati); and, because of the dominance of textual studies in the Western approach to Zoroastrianism, this gave rise to the extraordinary conception of Zoroastrian history as virtually one huge gap between the "Avestan" and Sasanian periods, with little thought being given as to how the religion remained alive during the supposedly blank centuries, or how its texts were transmitted then.

The writing down of the Avesta would have had no direct consequences for the great mass of Zoroastrians, for it was not for well over another thousand years, when it was finally printed, with translations in Gujarati and Persian, that the laity in general had immediate access to their holy works. Till then, most of them went on learning their obligatory prayers and other short texts by heart, and living their religious lives as before, without benefit of books. Most priests too must have continued for some time to memorize the liturgies in the age-old way, from oral instruction, for multiplying manuscripts of even the basic devotional works and bringing these into general use must have been a slow process, however lavishly the wealthy Sasanian church employed copyists, and sent instructors to priestly schools to teach the new Avestan alphabet. It would have been natural, moreover, for this innovation, so long resisted, to have been regarded generally with profound mistrust, so that several hundred years later even a scholar-priest could still declare that "it is reasonable to consider the living spoken word more essential than the written one (*zindag gōwišnīg saxwan az ān ī pad *nibišt mādagwardar hangārdan čimīg*).[59] Nevertheless, ability to read the Avestan script was so well taught that by the end of the Sasanian period, in Persia itself at least, it appears to have become part of the professional equipment of every fully-qualified priest.

The recording of the Avesta moreover effected the whole community indirectly. The holy texts had evidently been piously studied during the many centuries of their oral transmission,[60] but the written word clearly gave new scope and impetus to their detailed scrutiny. This, combined with Sasanian priestly zeal (which shows no signs of having slackened in later reigns) brought about some striking developments in observance. These, it is safe to assume, were not considered to be innovations, but were seen rather as old, neglected usages being revived through recovered understanding of how things should be done if the fight against evil was to be fought properly. This way of looking at things is likely to have received support from the Sasanians' propaganda that their predecessors, the Arsacids, had been unworthy protectors of the faith, and had allowed many of its practices to fall into disuse.[61]

Several of these developments appear to have come about through intensive study of the *Vendidad*, with its many prescriptions for right conduct, mostly aimed at smiting the demons of impurity. These and other evil powers were felt to be strongest during the hours of darkness; and by a bold step a "Vendidad" service was instituted to be solemnized at night, when the power of this holy text, "Against the Devs", was thought to be most needed.[62] The service consisted of a *Yasna* of 72 sections in its yet more extended form, the *Visperad* "(Service of) All the Masters" (itself created, it seems, primarily for the celebration of No Roz and the *gahambars*). During this service the entire text of the *Vendidad* - all twenty-two chapters - was recited by the celebrant priest, being interpolated bit by bit at various stages.[63] The *Visperad* proper, like the *Yasna*, may only be celebrated during the morning hours;[64] but a "Vendidad" is to be solemnized only between midnight and dawn, that is, during the Ušahin Gah, which is watched over especially by Sraoša (Sroš). This Yazata had come to be regarded as man's chief protector against the evil powers, which were particularly dreaded also at the time of death. A short service (the *Yašt i dron*) was accordingly performed with his *khšnuman* in each of the five *gahs* or watches of the three days after death, and a more complex *dron* service was solemnized in the Ušahin Gah of the third night, to aid the soul further just before it was believed to depart for judgment at the Chinvat Bridge. These usages together may have suggested the creation of the "Vendidad" service, to be solemnized with the *khšnuman* of Sroš during each of the three nights as a powerful additional weapon to ward off the demons believed to lurk then round the disembodied soul, eager to drag it down to hell. In orthodoxy it was of course the sum of its own thoughts, words and deeds which was held to decide its fate, and this doctrine remained immutable. Nevertheless, the ordinary human dreads and impulses which had led in the "Young Avestan" period to the revival of pre-Zoroastrian rites for the dead[65] later brought about an increase in the number of specifically Zoroastrian ones also. The "Vendidad" service was among the most elaborate and costly of these, and it came to be regularly performed for the souls of those whose families could afford it, and then, presumably by extension, for other beneficial purposes also.

The laity were involved in this mainly to the extent of commissioning and paying for the service, and providing the offerings; but other innovations affected them more closely. Study of a particular passage of the *Vendidad* (18:19 ff.) apparently led some zealous and influential priests to conclude that demon-haunted night brought pollution on all, and that some special measure was needed to remove this from believers before they embarked on the activities of a new day. They accordingly required everyone to make use on rising of the ancient and universally available disinfectant, *gomez* (cattle urine), rubbing this over the exposed parts of the body before applying the pure element of water, and then saying the first of the five daily sacred-cord prayers.[66] Further, it was enjoined in the *Vendidad* that for what was regarded as a unique case of gross inward pollution - a woman having carried a dead baby within her - the sufferer should imbibe a mixture of *gomez* and wood-ash (the other regular daily cleanser).[67] This form of purification was now greatly extended, it being prescribed that, before any act for which perfect purity was sought, a tiny ritual quantity of *gomez* should be imbibed, with a pinch of ash from a sacred fire. This then was made the regular practice before taking the ritual bath which is a preliminary to initiation into the faith and to marriage; and also before undergoing the *barašnom i no šaba*. Moreover, to purify the *gomez* for such use, and to strengthen its efficacy, it was first consecrated by a "Vendidad" service, which, when solemnized for this purpose, came in the post-Sasanian period to be known as the *Nirang-i din*, the "Ritual of the religion", for it was felt to provide the basis on which all ritual purity ultimately rested.

The absence of any authority for these usages in the *Vendidad* itself, and of any Avestan names for these particular rites, contributes to the near certainty that they were innovations of the late Sasanian period, when priestly zeal, fuelled by intensive study of the written Avesta, had the backing of strong kings, so that new extensions of ancient practices could be generally enforced.[68] The same reasons, together with the lack of any reference to such a conspicuous custom by foreign observers of Achaemenian times, makes it likely that this was true also of "taking the *waj*".[69] *Waj*, "word", was used in this connection as a Middle Persian equivalent of *manthra*; and in daily life the rite consisted of protecting an action by saying an appointed Avestan *manthra*, thus "taking the *waj*", performing the action in silence (so as not to break the power of the holy words), and then "leaving the *waj*" with more recitation of Avestan. The two *manthras* thus framed the action protectively, just as the two groups of *Gathas*, together with the *Ahunvar* and *Airyema išyo*, originally framed and protected the rituals accompanied by the *Yasna Haptanhaiti* . The concept appears in fact to have originated in the solemnization of priestly rites, and the existing *Yasna* contains many "*waj*-takings" which guard individual rituals within the extended service. The application of the usage to secular activities appears part of the zealous striving to find ever more means of strengthening good actions generally and so thwarting the aggressions of evil. Its observance clearly required constant self-discipline; and it too must have been vigorously instilled, for "taking the *waj*" became so regular an observance that a Jewish writer of post-Sasanian times gave it as the distinguishing mark of Zoroastrians.[70] As a secular observance the practice was probably developed - and was therefore the more readily acceptable - from the almost certainly ancient one of saying the Old Avestan *Itha at yazamaide* before a meal, in gratitude to Mazda and his bountiful creations.[71] This "grace" became the opening *waj* for eating and drinking, and in this particular case the silence which followed it was seen as a sign of respect also for two of the Heptad, revered through their creations. Thus among the souls declared to be suffering in hell is "the soul of that sinful man who in the world devoured Hordad and Amurdad, water and plants, while chattering, and ate unlawfully and did not keep the *waj*. And ... as he despised Hordad, water, and Amurdad, plants, so this soul must undergo heavy punishment".[72] A whole group of other "*waj*-takings" had for their opening *manthra* the invocation of Sroš, the great protector. Indeed the *Sroš Waj* was taken so often and regularly that it came to be among the Avestan texts to be learnt by heart before the ceremony of first putting on the sacred cord.

The priestly authorities thus appear to have prescribed at this time more and more prayers and rites for the community at large, as well as extending the religious services which priests alone performed. A text which is assigned to the late Sasanian period suggests that they also laboured to develop and systematize a widely ramified code to govern all possible circumstances in daily life in which a believer could become impure or ritually transgress (much use being made of the Pahlavi commentaries on the Avesta). This work, the *Shayest ne-shayest*, "Allowed and not-allowed", is the oldest extant specimen of an important group of Zoroastrian texts which later became known by the Arabic term *rivayat*, in the sense of a treatise dealing with miscellaneous traditional matters.[73] It appears from the *Shayest ne-shayest* that ritual "sins", whether incurred wilfully or carelessly, could be atoned for by penitential acts, by money-payments, or by having religious services performed; but true contrition was also required, good thoughts being thus joined to good acts. Hence another development which appears to belong to this period was a much reiterated demand for the confession of sins, preferably to a chosen priestly confessor.[74] In general, later developments suggest, a substantial number of the laity obeyed priestly directives and adopted new observances, accepting, presumably, that these were meritorious, and would, if properly carried out, help to save one's own soul, aid the creations, and bring about Frašegird; but there seems to have been effective resistance to this particular demand, perhaps because it did not accord with the spirit of Zoroastrianism, and the deeply instilled belief that each individual is responsible for his or her own conduct and fate. There is at any rate no later evidence for such a practice being generally adopted. Instead the community accepted the impersonal one of the recitation, on certain fixed occasions, of a *patet* or confessional formulary, recited aloud on behalf of another person by a priest, and covering in general terms a comprehensive array of sins.[75] There are four such formularies, all in Middle Persian and all doctrinally instructive. Thus all begin with general contrition for offences against the Heptad and their creations, starting with those "against Ohrmazd the Lord, and against men and all manner of men" and ending with those "against Amurdad, and against plants and all manner of plants". Thereafter more particular sins of omission and commission are enumerated. Some are distinctively Zoroastrian (such as that of not keeping No Roz and the *gahambars* holy), others are universal in character (such as those of deceit, slander, lust, etc.). The *Patet i xwad* then ends: "For all the sins which the wicked Evil Spirit brought into existence to assail the creatures of Ohrmazd and which Ohrmazd declared to be sins, through which men become sinners and must go to hell, if any stand to my account, I do penance for them. ... This penance I have performed ... with this intention ... that I may sin no more, but do meritorious acts, some to atone for sins, as far as is needful, some (purely) for the love of righteousness. I am opposed to sin, I assent to virtue, I am grateful for good fortune, and I do not repine at the assaults of evil."[76] The confessional thus embodies essentials of orthodox belief - uncompromising dualism, reverence for the Heptad, the need for moral striving, personal responsibility, and staunchness in the face of adversity - all set out in plain terms to be generally comprehended.

A penitential element was also introduced into the sacred-cord prayers.[77] According to the existing rite, as the worshipper unties the cord, thus losing its protection briefly, he recites the *Kemna Mazda*,[78] the Gathic verses having had added to them at some stage *Vd* 8:21: "Protect us from the foe, O Mazda and Spenta Armaiti! Begone, daevic Drug! Begone the one of Daeva-origin, begone the one of Daeva-shaping, begone the one of Daeva-begetting! Begone O Drug, crawl away, O Drug, disappear, O Drug! In the north shall you disappear. You shall not destroy the material world of Aša!" The cord is then retied with recitation of a Middle Persian prayer, the *Ohrmazd Khoday*, which begins: "Ohrmazd is Lord! Ahriman he keeps at bay, he holds him back", and contains the words: "O Ohrmazd, Lord! I am contrite for all sins and I desist from them, from all bad thoughts, bad words and bad acts which I have thought, spoken or done." The obligation was almost certainly older than the Sasanian period to recite with the day-time sacred-cord prayers the Avestan *niyayeš* or supplications to the Sun and Mithra, and with the night time ones, thrice monthly, the *niyayeš* to the Moon; but it was perhaps in this late Sasanian epoch that special prayers were created out of selected Avestan passages for the Menogs of the five watches or *gahs*,[79] and that it was made obligatory to recite whichever one was appropriate (or at least its dedicatory formula or *khšnuman*) in each watch. The daily *bandagi* (obligatory service to God) of the believer was thus extended well beyond reciting the Gathic verses which presumably alone originally accompanied the sacred-cord rite. Those who found it hard to memorize the extra prayers were allowed to do the same service - and so acquire the same merit - by reciting, rosary-fashion, a fixed number of *Ahunvars*.[80]

As the vernacular prayers and confessionary texts show, the priestly authorities were concerned that the members of the community should be well-informed, able to perform their devotions and conduct their lives with good understanding; and family priests must have been hard-worked at this time, both in mastering the new observances themselves, and in teaching these to the laity, presumably in carefully organized campaigns of instruction. For lay people with means and leisure there were moreover schools, *frahangestan*, which existed, it seems, independently of those for priests and scribes; and to judge from what has survived, a considerable religious literature was brought into being in the colloquial language for such educated persons to read - and probably also for family priests to read aloud in the homes of the well-to-do. Much of it was still traditional in form, with the use of question and answer in a manner common in didactic oral works; and the subject matter too was largely traditional, ranging over doctrine and ethics, ancient lore and correct observances.[81] A salient fact is that morality was still taught in terms which belong, unchanged, to the world of Gathic thought. The *ašavan* person, it was declared, should strive constantly to bring the lesser members of the Heptad (with whom Sroš was regularly associated) into his own person, so as to bar the way to their demonic adversaries. One passage runs: "There is none born of woman over whom these six Menogs do not struggle: Vahman and Akoman ('Evil Purpose'), Sroš and Khešm (Av. Aešma, 'Wrath'), Spendarmad and the demon Taromad ('Arrogance')".[82] The text goes on to illustrate the effects of the indwelling of one or other of these. For example, "He in whose body Vahman dwells has this for his mark: he is ardent in good works, has good relations with good people, makes peace readily, intercedes for the virtuous poor and is himself generous. He in whose body Akoman dwells has this for his mark: he is cold in good works, has bad relations with good people, makes peace reluctantly, is hostile to the virtuous poor, and is himself niggardly ...". In general it is said: "Being on one's guard is this, one makes this body like a fort, and sets a guard over it, and keeps the Yazads within it, and does not let demons (*devs*) enter."[83] This way of understanding mental states and impulses was old before Zoroaster was born, an ancient inheritance from animatism which he developed through his dualistic understanding of the world;[84] and it continued to be a vivid and effective way of interpreting conduct and teaching morality.

That this was so must have been due in large part to tradition; for clearly what chiefly enables the teachings of any prophet to remain effective is continuity of transmission - the fact that believers become familiar with them in childhood, accept them unquestioningly, and pass them on in their turn to their children. Stable social conditions can also help; and for Zoroastrianism it was clearly very important that, despite the fact that the Iranians had changed from tribal pastoralists to an imperial people, they had known no profound break in the pattern of their lives such as the industrial revolution was later to impose on much of mankind. In ancient and medieval times even those who inhabited the small cities and little towns remained of necessity close to the natural world. There had to be fields and gardens and streams all around them, to yield the daily necessities of life. Animals were abundant, and some were still stabled and stalled close to humans. There was always fire burning on the hearth, and space out of doors to stand and pray before the sun, with one's feet on earth and an unpolluted sky above. Hence awareness of the "creations" remained unforced, and the service of their Mainyus, linking the visible and the invisible worlds, was an obligation which could still be readily understood and accepted, by rich and poor.

The doctrine of the Heptad, with all its implications, thus continued central to the faith; and the changes and developments in belief which took place in Sasanian times appear minor or ancillary ones, affecting largely the learned and the leisured. Thus, as we have seen, much of the newly written-down literature appears wholly traditional in content, and is essentially impossible to date. But late in the period individual voices began to be heard, and some contemporary trends of thought found expression, showing that there was no stagnation. New knowledge was having to be confronted by those scholar-priests who laboured on translating foreign works into Middle Persian, mainly, it seems, from Syriac (Syriac literature including by then a number of translations of Greek philosophical writings). Some of the knowledge thus acquired was added to the *zand* commentaries, which together with the *zand* as a whole attained great importance as an authority, equal indeed to the Avesta itself.[85] Yet other priests worked on creating the great prose chronicle, the *Khwaday Namag*, "Book of Kings". This strove to be a history both of the Zoroastrian religion and the royal dynasties of Iran, with the Sasanians, under whose patronage it was composed, figuring as the worthy heirs to an immensely long tradition and the legitimate defenders of the faith. Much of the early material was drawn from Iranian minstrel traditions, which lent it vigour and poetic richness; and it was probably from among these that the story comes of "Arjasp's" assault on Balkh, and the slaughter of the priests who tended the great Bactrian fire of Adar Noš.[86] In the later parts of the chronicle some foreign works were again used.

Although there is no direct evidence, there are grounds for supposing that much of this varied scholarly work went on in libraries and schools attached to the greater fire temples. Many fire temples were founded at this time, partly in consequence of another manifestation of Persian priestly vigour, namely a long drawn-out and ultimately wholly successful iconoclastic campaign.[87] This was conducted from early in the Sasanian period till very near its end, when cult statues were still being removed, presumably from small, remote temples which had previously escaped official notice. Such statues, introduced in late Achaemenian times, had probably been set up in increasing numbers during the Seleucid and Parthian periods; and devotions paid to them over generations must by this time have made them seem very holy and very potent. Their destruction would thus undoubtedly have caused distress to many of the devout. The authorities were not only ruthless, however, in removing statues, but energetic in educating people against them, declaring them to be "dens of demons", empty forms into which *devs* slipped in order to misappropriate offerings. So successful was this double onslaught of vigorous action and steady propaganda that by the seventh century, when the Sasanian empire fell to the Arabs, not a single cult statue appears to have remained in place.[88] This was a remarkable achievement, the total sloughing off of an alien but long-established observance and a return to the earlier ways of the faith. Thereafter Zoroastrians again venerated the Yazatas as their distant forefathers had done, through natural phenomena only.

Even apart from the conversion of image shrines to fire temples, the zeal of the Persian clergy and nobles led to many new fire temples being founded at this period, both large and small, especially in Persia proper and the neighbouring regions. Where information exists, it shows that such foundations were made for the sake of the benefactor's soul, or that of a relative. The person named would be remembered in the priests' prayers, while the act of establishing the fire was itself meritorious, and would benefit the donor's soul at judgment day. Written records and excavations show further that the three greatest sacred fires - Adur Gušnasp, Adur Burzen Mihr and Persian Adur Farnbag - were by this time enormously wealthy and profoundly revered. Venerated liturgically through a carefully compiled verse added to the *Ataš Niyayeš*,[89] they drew many pilgrims, being regarded as of legendary antiquity and holiness. Devotion to temple fires generally was naturally encouraged by priests, since no worshipper came without some gift, however humble.[90] Further, charitable foundations of all kinds, characteristically designated as *pad ruwan* "for the soul", were abundantly endowed at this period, to such an extent that a ministry, the *Dewan i Kardagan* "Office for (Religious) Acts", was established to register and look after them,[91] the command to serve Ohrmazd through his creation, man, leading to a generous philanthropy.

A pious and joyful duty, which like temple worship and pilgrimages brought the community together, was the celebration of holy days, which were by now many. Through calendar changes, with consequent confusions, it had come about that all major festivals by now lasted officially for five days, and some even longer. Thus at the end of the old year and the beginning of the new there was a festive period which embraced the sixth *gahambar*, the feast of the Fravašis, and No Roz, and which was extended, in the enchanting Persian season of spring, to over three weeks. Naturally only the well-to-do and leisured could celebrate at such length; but the evidence is that at least the main holy day in each cycle was kept generally, with even the poorest eating well and making merry at the communal banquets which regularly followed the religious ceremonies.[92] Such banquets were always graced with wine, music and song, for the greater the pleasure and happiness then engendered, it was held, the greater would be the gratification of the Yazads and the strengthening of the forces of good.

During its long history as the religion of empires, Zoroastrianism inevitably developed sects and heresies and variant local forms. A little of this is recorded for Achaemenian times, but it is only for the comparatively well-documented Sasanian period that it is possible to gain any real sense of the varieties of religious experience and belief which existed within it, as within any other major religion. Only two major sectarian movements are, however, known. One, Zurvanism, originated under the later Achaemenians, and remained an important heterodoxy within the state religion for many centuries. This was a monism, which postulated a single eternal Being, the Mainyu of time (Avestan *zurvan*), who "begot" both Ahura Mazda and Anra Mainyu, that is, both good and evil.[93] The other, Mazdakism, was a Sasanian movement which, though keeping Zoroaster's fundamental dualism, was much influenced by gnostic thought, in the light of which its followers claimed new insights into the inner meaning of the Avesta.[94] After gaining a considerable following, it was suppressed by the power of the Sasanian throne, aided by the nobles and clergy, whereas Zurvanism lived on well into Islamic times and then disappeared without trace, leaving orthodoxy to hold the field alone - another striking proof of the inherent strength of Zoroaster's own doctrines. Various nameless minor movements have been detected within Middle Persian literature[95], and there is even a streak of asceticism in a few Zoroastrian writings of the late Sasanian period, which some have ascribed to Indian influence, others to that of Gnosticism or Christianity.[96] This again did not survive.

In addition to Zoroastrian sectarians and deviants, there were in the land adherents of a number of alien religions, whom Kirdir, the second Sasanian high priest, listed as "Jews and Buddhists and Brahmans and Aramaic- and Greek-speaking Christians and Baptizers and Manichaeans."[97] It is not known how many of these were represented at the theological disputations said to have been encouraged by Shabuhr II (309-379). At these the Zoroastrian high priest, Adurbad, is reputed to have triumphed, establishing the truth of Mazda-worship, whereupon the king declared his resolve to uphold it ever more zealously.[98] Indeed, despite all increase of knowledge and encountering of faiths at this period, only one modification is known of a teaching of Zoroaster's which became a part of standard belief, apparently from this time. This concerns his doctrine that sinners will perish, body and soul, in the molten metal of the river at Judgment Day.[99] Instead, it came to be held that they will experience only excruciating pangs through that immersion, and be purged thereby of their wickedness, and so be able to enter into the kingdom of Ohrmazd together with the righteous.[100] This softening of the prophet's teachings, over a millennium and a half after he lived, can be compared with the modern abandonment by various branches of the Christian church of the stern Gospel teaching of everlasting hell-fire for sinners.[101]

The Zoroastrian development is at odds, both in its mildness and its doctrinal concern, with the general conception of Sasanian Zoroastrianism as harsh and narrowly focussed on ritual. The harshness was one facet of Sasanian priestly zeal, as is admirably illustrated in the inscription of Kirdir just cited. He rejoices in being able to declare that "in every province and every place of the whole empire the service of Ohrmazd and the Yazads was exalted, and the Mazda-worshipping religion and its priests received much honour in the land. And the Yazads, and water and fire and cattle, were greatly contented, and Ahriman and the devs suffered great blows and harm." But as a corollary of this he states that the adherents of other religions "were assailed in the land." Some of them invited resentment by being active and diligent proselytizers, and the Christians and Manichaeans are known to have suffered in consequence from sporadic and sometimes severe persecutions. There was also an inquisition set up by the state to discourage apostasy among Zoroastrians.[102] The measures taken were, however, essentially defensive, not aggressive, and at the end of the epoch all the religions which Kirdir named at its beginning still existed within Iran, and some had gained in numbers. This was strikingly true of Christianity (which had been helped early in the period by the influx of Christian prisoners of war); and some scholars have even suggested that its growth within Iran was sufficiently vigorous to be the beginning of a possibly serious rivalry to Zoroastrianism. This idea is based on the statistics of bishoprics and congregations, whose numbers suggest a remarkable toleration in the main by the Persian authorities. It is nevertheless wholly improbable that it or any other alien religion could of itself have offered any real challenge to the state religion, upheld as this was by the king and the nobility, served by a large and evidently disciplined body of priests, and commanding, it is reasonable to suppose, the unquestioning loyalty of most of the peasants, as the familiar faith of their forefathers.[103]   As Firdausi has the last great Sasanian king, Khosrow Parvez, exclaim: "Let none dare hide the faith of God [that is, of Ohrmazd]. From Gayomard and Jamshid to Kay Kobad there was no word of Christ. Heaven forfend that I should abandon the faith of my forefathers, chosen and pure lords of the earth, and go over to the faith of Christ!"[104]   The indications are that to the end of the epoch Zoroastrianism was energetic and effective,[105] and there is no reason to suppose that, in spite of its antiquity, it did not have the strength, given an ordinary sequence of events, to have evolved gradually in accordance with its own nature, undergoing reforms and making modifications to correspond with general advances in thought and knowledge.   One thing was needed to cut off this possibility of organic growth and to cast the faith down from its secure worldly position, and that was the force of alien arms. Rome failed, but the Arabs were to succeed, conquering in the name of Islam.

NOTES

1   Above, p.28.

2   Darius, *Naqš-i Rustam* a 1-4 (Kent, *OP*, 138).

3   Cf. above, pp.96, 104-5, 120.

4   Darius, *Behistun* V 18-20 (Kent, 134).

5   Xerxes, *Persepolis* h 46-8 (Kent, 152).

6   *Vd* 5:61, cited in connection with Xerxes' words by J. Kellens, see *HZ* II 176-7 with n.67. On these uses of *ašavan* cf. above, p.119 with n.56.

7   Darius, *Behistun* IV 61 (Kent, 132).

8   Cf. above, p.71.

9   Darius, *Persepolis* d 14 (Kent, 136).

10   Darius, *Behistun* IV 61-5 (Kent, 132).

11   Xerxes, *Persepolis* h 35-9 (Kent, 151).   For references to discussion of these lines see *HZ* II 174-7.

12   See R. T. Hallock, *Persepolis Fortification Tablets,* Chicago 1969; and for detailed references to this work for what follows, *HZ* II 132 ff.

13   Above, p.60 n.7.

14   For such names see M. Mayrhofer, *Onomastica Persepolitana,* Vienna 1973.

15   Artaxerxes II, *Susa* a 4, d 3-4; *Hamadan* a 5.

16   Artaxerxes III, *Persepolis* a 24-5.

17   Cf. above, pp.56, 71.

18   The fourth-century Diogenes, cited by Athenaeus, *Deipnosophists*, XIV.636. (See further *HZ* III 204 with n.28).

19   I.131.

20   I.132.

21   Cf. above, pp.110-11. It seems likely that Herodotus depended for his description on what he was told by Persian friends rather than on personal observation, and that some details were therefore not clear to him. Thus he says that the layman sacrificed the beast before the magus came, which is against other attestations of Persian usage, which show it to have accorded in this with general Zoroastrian practice (namely that the priest, as the purest of men, was the sacrificer). See most recently *HZ* III 272-3, 295-7.

22   For fine photographs of all the royal tomb-carvings see E. Schmidt, *Persepolis* III, Chicago 1971; and on the three icons of fire *HZ* II 113-14.

23   For references see *HZ* II 145-8 (modified with respect to the Istanbul relief from Dascylium, and the Bünyan altar, in *HZ* III 103 n.172, 265).

24   See *HZ* II, III index s.v. *baresman*, and especially *HZ* II 38-9, *HZ* III 101.

25   See *HZ* II 201-2 and *HZ* III s.v. "temples, Zoroastrian".

26   Persian terms for them, with this meaning, are first recorded in Middle Persian literature, see *EIr.* III 9, s.v. *ātaškada*.

27   Cf. above, p.85.

28   See *HZ* II 184-5.

29   Veneration of Yazatas was of course in itself as traditional as that of fire, but offering it through man-made images was wholly alien, and brought with it new and alien observances, see *HZ* II 256, III 228 with 270.

30   These rites, although first attested in the post-Sasanian period, are traditional by nature, being developed from those enjoined in *Vd* 8 for purifying a sullied fire (cf. above, p.117).

31   Cf. above, p.91.

32   The parallels between boons sought of the Mainyus of sacred fires and those asked in the *Yašts* of Yazatas have been studied by Sarah Stewart, *Some devotional practices of the Zoroastrian laity*, Ch.4. Already in what appears to be one of the oldest "pagan" verses of the *Ataš Niyayeš* (v.16) the Mainyu of the hearth fire is represented as calling down on one who tends the fire well an abundance of "cattle and men", an active mind and spirit, and life-long joy.

33   It was merely incidentally that he observed (III.16) that "the Persians hold fire to be a god".

34   *Of Isis and Osiris*, 46, ed. and tr. by J.G. Griffiths, Cardiff 1970, 191-3. *Sources*, 108.

35   The other correspondences are less exact.

36   Aeneas of Gaza, *Theophrastus*, 77. See Jackson, *Zoroaster*, 248. *Sources*, 108.

37   VII.194.

38   I.137.

39   I.136, 138.

40   Clemen, *Fontes*, 22; Jackson, *Zoroaster*, 231; Fox and Pemberton, *Passages*, 22. *Sources*, 107.

41   See *HZ* II 211-16 for relevant excerpts from his *Anabasis* and *Cyropaedia*.

42   I.138.

43   I.140.

44   Loc.cit.

45   Cf., e.g., Sialkh cemetery B, above, p.42. This, and the fact that the "Kambojas" (a name given to ancient Iranian settlers in India) are also known to have killed *khrafstras* (insects, snakes, worms and frogs) as a religious duty (see *HZ* III 130) alone suffice to disprove the academic theory that both practices originated with the magi, and were adopted

into Zoroastrianism only after it reached western Iran. This theory evolved from the respectful wish to keep everything in Zoroastrianism which seemed uncongenial as far from Zoroaster himself as possible.

46   For references see *HZ* II 210-11.

47   VII.187. These dogs may have had more than one function to perform, see *HZ* II 169, and cf. above, p.100 n.56.

48   Above, pp.27-8.

49   How effective the use of such vernacular contributions could be for involving the laity in an act of worship is vividly shown by Khudayar Dastur Sheriyar in two articles in the *Sir J.J. Madressa Jubilee Vol.*, ed. J.J. Modi, pp.304-5, 312-14.

50   See *HZ* III, esp. Ch.4.

51   See ib., Chs. 6, 8-10.

52   See the *Collected Letters of St. Basil*, Loeb ed., Vol.IV, Letter 258, pp.46/47.

53   Cf. above, p.10 ff.

54   Posidonius, cited by Strabo, XI.9:3.

55   *DkM* p.412.5 ff., tr. M. Shaki, "The Dēnkard account of the history of the Zoroastrian scriptures", *Archív Orientalní* 49, 1981, 114-25. *Sources*, 114.

56   Ibid.

57   See Ch.1, above, passim, for the incorporation of diverse and often conflicting local materials in the Middle Persian *zand*.

58   See generally Boyce, "Middle Persian literature", *HdO* IV.2.1, 31-66.

59   *DkM* 460.7-8, cited by Bailey, *Zor. Problems*, 163.

60   Cf. above, pp.119-20.

61   Cf., e.g. the *Letter of Tansar*, ed. Minovi, p.12, tr. Boyce, p.37.

62   It cannot be proved that the "Vendidad" service was instituted in the later Sasanian period, but, in the light of the other developments which can reasonably be assigned to that time, this seems highly probable. In the Pahl. text *Khosrow ud Redag*, para.9 (ed. J.M. Unvala, Vienna 1917, p.14) a nobly-born page of the time of Khosrow II (591-628) is represented as claiming that, as part of his schooling, he had learnt by heart, "like a priest" the main Avestan liturgical texts, with which he names the *Vendidad*. On the practice of reading the *Vd* from a book see below, p.154.

63   See Modi, *CC*, 331-2.

64   Cf. above, p.87.

65   Cf. above, pp.106-7.

66   On this as a development of the later Sasanian period see Boyce, "Cleansing in Zoroastrianism", *EIr.* V (in press); "*Pādyāb* and *nērang* : two Pahlavi terms further considered", *BSOAS* LIV, 1991, 281-91.

67   *Vd* 5:51.

68   This is true also of the funerary rite of *sagdid*, see J.C. Tavadia, *Shayest ne-shayest*, p.17, and in more detail Boyce, *EIr.* , under "corpse, disposal of in Zoroastrianism" (in press).

69   On this rite see in detail M. Boyce-F. Kotwal, "Zoroastrian *bāj* and *drōn*,", *BSOAS* XXXIV, 1971, 56-73, 298-313.

70   See D.N. MacKenzie, "An early Jewish-Persian argument", *BSOAS* XXX, 1968, 260.

71   Cf. above, p.94.

72   *AVN* 23:7-9 (ed. Gignoux, pp.76/77, 176/177).

73   See Tavadia (ed.), *Shayest ne-shayest*, intro., p.1.

74   See, e.g., *Shayest ne-shayest*, 8:8-12.

75 For the occasions on which a *patet* is regularly recited see Modi, *CC*, 50, 66-7, 75, 76, 91, 93, 123, 166, 182.

76 *Patet i xwad* 11, 13. For the whole text see *ZXA*, ed. Dhabhar, pp.78-84, tr. Dhabhar, pp.149-56; Asmussen, *Xuastvānīft*, 90-8 (text and tr.); tr. Zaehner, *Teachings of the Magi*, 120-3. Excerpted, *Sources*, 60-1.

77 For these prayers see *ZXA*, ed. Dhabhar, pp.3-4, tr. Dhabhar, pp.5-8. *Sources*, 58-9.

78 Cf. above, p.85.

79 On their construction see Darmesteter, *ZA* II 710.

80 For a table of equivalences see Modi, *CC*, 322-3.

81 The best surviving example is the *Dadestan i Menog i khrad*, "Judgments of the Spirit of wisdom", attributed to the 6th century.

82 *Dk.* VI 77-8, ed. Shaked, pp.28/9 (text and tr.), 251-2 (commentary). The translation given above differs from his only in being a little freer. Although *Dk.* VI was incorporated in a mainly post-Sasanian work, "there can be ... little doubt that much of the material contained in [it] ... is based on oral traditions, possibly also on written documents, of the Sasanian period, while some of it seems to go even further back in antiquity" (Shaked, intro., p.xvii). In another, undoubtedly post-Sasanian, work all six lesser members of the Heptad are named with Sroš in this way, see Shaked, o.c., p.251 n.1.

83 *Dk.* VI E34a, ed. Shaked, pp.202/3.

84 Cf. above, pp.53, 66-7.

85 Cf. Bailey, *Zor. Problems*, 162-3, 167. The *zand* was not only relied on in prescriptive matters such as extensions to the purity laws, but even, in one known instance, affected the ritual invocation of a Yazata, see Boyce, "Dahm Yazad", *EIr* VI (in press).

86 See above, p.12 ff.

87 See Boyce, "Iconoclasm among the Zoroastrians", *Studies for Morton Smith at sixty*, ed. J. Neusner, Leiden 1975, 93-111; "On the sacred fires of the Zoroastrians", *BSOAS* XXXI, 1968, 63-4 (where for "idol" read "image"); and *HZ* III 66 n.71.

88 Clay and wood figurines have, however, been excavated in quantity in Central Asia from early Islamic times. For these at an earlier period see Grenet in *HZ* III 184 ff.

89 *AN* 5, cf. above, p.5.

90 This natural expression of devotion had also a scriptural basis in *AN* 7.

91 See A. Perikhanian in *CHIr.* 3(2), 661-5, who is among those scholars who consider that the Sasanian system of pious endowments made according to established laws was the model for the Muslim one of *waqf*.

92 See, e.g., the story of the magnificent feast provided by Khosrow I one year for all his subjects, high and low, to celebrate the sixth *gahambar*, *Riv.*, Unvala, I 436-9, Dhabhar, 325.

93 On it see most recently *HZ* III index s.v. Zurvan, Zurvanism. This heterodoxy contributed fundamentally to the formulation of the "European heresy", see above, p.81 nn.50,54.

94 On it see most recently E. Yarshater, *CHIr.* 3(2), 991-1024; and P. Crone, "Kavad's heresy and Mazdak's revolt", *Iran* XXIX, 1991, 21-42.

95 See, with references to other discussions, M. Molé, "Le problème des sectes zoroastriennes dans les livres pehlevis", *Oriens* 13-14, 1961, 1-28; S. Shaked, "Esoteric trends in Zoroastrianism", *Proceedings of the Israel Academy of Sciences and Humanities* III, 1969, 175-221, and "Dualism in transformation, varieties of religion in Sasanian Iran", *Louis H. Jordan Lectures in Comparative Religion* 1991 (publication in preparation).

96 That sometimes asceticism has been seen where in fact none exists has, however, been argued by Molé, "Un ascétisme moral dans les livres pehlevis?" *RHR* 155, 1959, 147-9.

97   Kirdir's inscription on the Ka^{c}ba-yi Zardušt, lines 6-7;   see M. Back, *Die sassanidischen Staatsinschriften, Act. Ir.* 18, 1978, 412-15. *Sources,* 112.

98   Loc.cit. in n.55, above.

99   Cf. above, p.77 with n.72.   The stern old doctrine is still attested in the Seleucid-Parthian period, see *HZ* I 243, *HZ* III 393-4.

100   *GBd.* 34:19 (*Sources,* 52);   *PRDd.* 48:70.   The original doctrine is alluded to in another passage of the latter work, Ch.32:5.   There it is said that Ahriman and the demons are only content in their triumph over a man "when they make his soul wicked and annihilate it" (*ka-š ruwān druwand ud abaydāg kunēnd),* see Williams, *PRDd,* II, commentary, p.186.

101   On a possible theological, rather than merely humane, reason for the modification of the Zoroastrian doctrine see however below, pp.169-70.

102   See *Letter of Tansar,* ed. Minovi, p.17, tr. Boyce, p.42.

103   A perhaps not wholly irrelevant analogy is to be sought in the religious situation in England in the latter part of the 20th century. There statistics of the number of Hindu and Buddhist temples, Sikh gurdwaras and Muslim mosques (in addition to older Jewish synagogues), and of the growth in numbers of their congregations, partly through proselytizing, can certainly give the impression of Christianity under siege. Yet many English people have never seen one of these places of worship, or met any of their supporters; and that any of the religions concerned, however thriving, should displace Christianity as the established state religion remains inconceivable, centuries of tradition being solidly against it.

104   *Shahnama,* ed. Beroukhim, IX pp.2793-4, Warner, VIII p.310.

105   Many fire temples, for instance, are said to have been founded during the last long reign of the dynasty, that of Khosrow II;   Adur Gušnasp's temple, sacked in 623 by a Byzantine army, was swiftly restored;   the iconoclastic campaign was successfully concluded;   the compiling of the *Khwaday Namag* continued almost till the downfall of the dynasty, and there are no indications of a falling off in other scholarly work;   and most of the ritual developments adopted throughout the community apparently took place late in the period.

CHAPTER EIGHT

The Faith under
Islamic Rule

The idea that the first Arab armies imposed Islam by the sword on all whom they conquered has long been abandoned. Arabia itself was the only land where no religion but Islam was tolerated, while elsewhere the object of subduing those of certain other faiths "was not the philanthropic one of saving ... souls - since the Unbeliever was permitted to compound - but the purely religious one of vindicating God's honour".[1] Conquest was undertaken, that is, in the spirit of *Qur'an* 9:29 "Fight those who believe not in God and the Last Day, and do not forbid what Allah and his messenger have forbidden - such men as practise not the religion of truth, being peoples of the book - until they pay tribute out of hand and have been humbled". The result was that, despite the strong religious element, the Arab conquest of Iran in the seventh century mirrored in a number of ways that of the Macedonians nearly a thousand years earlier. In each case the invaders were a poor people, hungry for land and spoil; and in each case two or three hard-fought battles brought them victory over the imperial armies and, by shattering the king's power, opened the way for the piecemeal conquest of the country. In each case too the local campaigns which followed were often bitter and bloody; and the Arabs, like the Macedonians before them, gained for themselves a fearful reputation, appearing to the Iranians as the hosts of Ahriman.[2] After the earlier conquest the Zoroastrians had developed an apocalyptic literature in which the rule of the Macedonians was seen as the last kingdom on earth,[3] an evil time when non-Iranians, infidels, were to exert lordship and rule, destroying "property and greatness ... fidelity to the faith, moderation, security, joy", and when Ahriman would be "very oppressive and tyrannical". Then at last the Saošyant would

come, and, with the righteous, would defeat the wicked and "make creation
pure again, and there will be the resurrection and the final body".[4] This
literature now underwent a revival, with the Arabs cast in the Macedonians'
role; and as one local defeat followed another, it seems to have induced in
some Iranians a sense of the inevitable, an acceptance of what had been
foretold, while some Arabs were evidently happy to exploit the terrors of the
devilish part assigned to them. This is to judge from a single striking incident
in the conquest of Seistan.[5] This took place in 651, nearly a decade and a half
after the first major Arab victory, an Arab army then appearing in this remote
region for the first time. A fierce battle was fought, in which more Arabs fell
than Iranians. Nevertheless, the next day the Persian margrave, Iran son of
Rustam, called a council of nobles, attended by the chief magus, and agreed
with them to make terms, since, he said, "though we are not powerless to make
war, for this is a land of brave men and heroes", yet "this is not an event that
will end in a day or a year or a thousand years. This is revealed in texts". The
Arab general, Rabi' ibn Ziyad, made careful preparations for the resulting
parley, being undoubtedly aware, after all the years of campaigning, that
Zoroastrians regarded corpses as the worst of all pollutions. Accordingly he
"gave orders to have the slain covered by garments, and a mound made of their
bodies, and above the mound, a place to sit, also of their bodies. Rabi' went
atop, and sat down.   Iran son of Rustam arrived accompanied by the nobles
and the chief of the magi. When they entered the army camp and approached
the mound, and saw Rabi' seated in this fashion, they dismounted and stood
there. Rabi' was a tall man, dark, with large teeth and thick lips. And when
Iran son of Rustam saw both Rabi' and his mound of the slain, he glanced back
and said to his companions: 'It is said that Ahriman is not visible in the
daytime. Behold, Ahriman became visible, there is no doubt about it'". Rabi'
asked for this to be translated, and laughed most heartily. Iran then greeted him
from where he stood, and he and his companions seated themselves on the
ground and parleyed from there. The terms which were agreed evidently
allowed them freedom of worship and protection for their fire temples, on the
payment of a large tribute twice yearly to the Caliph.

The making of separate local treaties on terms of this sort was general, with
only details varying. (Thus the Zoroastrians of Azarbaijan stipulated that the
conquerors should not "hinder the people of Shiz [that is, of Adur Gušnasp's
great temple[6]] in their particular custom of dancing on their festal days nor in
observing their usual observances."[7]) Yet it is said in one of the apocalyptic
works: "These *devs* are great deceivers. ... No treaty or pact is to be made
with them ..., and the treaty which they make, they do not keep."[8] The Arabs
were the victors, and power was in their hands. They came in different bands,
and governors and commanders changed and might pursue different courses.
Thus in Seistan the treaty terms were quickly threatened when an Arab

governor arrived with orders from his superior, Ziyad ibn Abih, in Iraq, to "kill Shabur the chief of the priests of the fire temples and stamp out their fires."[9] The Zoroastrians determined to resist; and the Muslims of Seistan (a minority then, with probably no desire for fresh strife) wrote to the Umayyad Caliph and received this reply: "You must not (harm them) because they have made a treaty of friendship with us and those places of worship are theirs." The new governor accordingly did not carry out his orders, but administered the whole community lawfully. Little is known in detail of the Zoroastrians there after this; but they were able to maintain the greatest of their sacred fires, that at Karkuye, in dignity and safety for several more centuries.[10]

Yet many sacred fires were evidently extinguished under the Umayyads (661-750); and indeed 'Ubaid Allah, son of Ziyad ibn Abih, as governor of Iraq followed in his father's footsteps by sending a commissioner to supervise the destruction of all fire temples in Iran,[11] in total disregard of treaty obligations and the earlier ruling from Damascus. His real aim seems, however, to have been to get money by threatening the Zoroastrians at this most vulnerable point, for those temples were spared whose congregations could collect a sufficient ransom for them. The sum of 40 million dirhams is said to have been thus raised, and although this is hardly a reliable figure, it gives an idea both of the number of fire temples which had survived the conquest and of the devotion of their congregations. But the money thus extorted bought no lasting security, and sacred fires were to be steadily put out. Zoroastrians could take some comfort from the belief that the Menogs of these fires did not perish, but simply withdrew elsewhere;[12] but the threat to the community's devotional life was clearly great, while on the material plane 'Ubaid Allah's blackmail was just one of the measures which helped to bring about the community's steady impoverishment.

Other Arabs harassed Zoroastrians out of religious zeal. Fierce proselytizing is well documented for the north-east, where in the late seventh century the Arab armies were commanded by the devout but ruthless Qutaiba. The local history of Bukhara records how he established Islam among its citizens "with much difficulty. He ... made (their own religion) difficult for them in every way ... He imposed the religious laws (of Islam) on them. He built mosques and eradicated traces of unbelief and the precepts of the fire-worshippers". The grand mosque was raised where a Zoroastrian temple had stood, and Qutaiba bribed the poor to attend Friday prayers there. Muslims were quartered on Zoroastrians within the city, so that they could be subjected to constant surveillance, and the well-to-do who lived outside its walls were made targets for mob intimidation.[13]

It was in the cities, now the centres of Muslim administration, that such pressures were most easily and strongly applied; and once the conquest of the whole land had been achieved, and Arab rule established everywhere, then worldly advantage could be generally seen to lie in embracing the Semitic faith. Hopes of government employ, civic position, trading opportunities, patronage for scholars and poets, freedom from harassment and humiliation, and relief from poverty could all be most readily realized by taking this way. Nevertheless, the pace at which Islam advanced was uneven,[14] and under the Umayyads many small towns and villages remained predominantly Zoroastrian. Yet even some Iranists still write of the "collapse" of Zoroastrianism at the coming of Islam, with all sorts of reasons being suggested for it. In fact the Iranian religion never collapsed, but survives to this day through the courage and tenacity of generations of its adherents. In the past these faithful ones belonged to that minority in any society who are prepared to put loyalty to their beliefs before all worldly considerations; and if in time their numbers were whittled away to a saving remnant, this was not peculiar to Zoroastrianism, but has been the general fate of religious communities everywhere which have found themselves ruled by those committed to a proselytizing and different creed. Thus when Christianity became the state religion of the Roman Empire, it rapidly reduced all other religious communities in the eastern Mediterranean area to harassed and persecuted minorities; but when through the Arab conquests Islam replaced it as the dominant faith in almost the whole of this region, most Christians in their turn converted, were killed or fled, leaving it overwhelmingly Muslim; and later the Ottoman Turks brought about the same state of affairs in Anatolia. Of all the countries conquered by the Arabs only in Spain were Christians able to maintain themselves in substantial numbers, and this was because of particular circumstances there. The Zoroastrian case is thus in no way exceptional, and the only reason why it has seemed to be so is that the Arabs conquered all the Zoroastrian lands - that is, the whole Sasanian empire (the small expatriate communities to the west having by then disappeared from sight under Christian rule). There were therefore no Mazda-worshippers anywhere who could maintain their religion in freedom, preserve its books and places of worship without threat, and develop its theological schools.

Nevertheless, despite the new uncertainties and harshnesses, the Umayyad period appears to have been one of relative tranquillity for many Zoroastrians. Pars (now Fars on Arab lips) had suffered as much as anywhere during the actual conquest, but was subsequently fairly fortunate for several centuries, being remote from frontiers and frontier wars. The head of the Zoroastrian community (recognized as such by the Muslim authorities) lived there, in succession to the Sasanian high priest; and among his co-religionists he took the title of *Hudinan pešobay* "Leader of those of the Good Religion". *Hudin*, "of the good religion", or, more commonly, *behdin*, "of the better/best religion", was from now on the standard term used by Zoroastrians for themselves[15], it would seem as a firm declaration of faith. The little that is known of the *Hudinan pešobayan* shows them to have been men of ability and courage, who strove as best they could to defend their faith and their community. One form which this defence took was theological debate. The main points of Muslim attack were those which had been made earlier under the Sasanians by Jews and Christians, namely dualism, apparent polytheism, and veneration of physical things, notably fire and the sun. On dualism orthodox Zoroastrians never wavered, holding it to be a doctrinal strength, but the charge of polytheism was strongly rejected, with stress being laid on the worship of Ohrmazd as God alone, and on the subordinate character of the lesser Yazatas. This was emphasized by the adoption as an alternative name for these beings of the Persian word *ferešte* "one sent, angel". As for the accusation of sun and fire worship, they simply stated: "It is not the sun and the fire ... that we worship: on the contrary, they are ours in the same way that the *mihrab* (of mosques) are yours" - that is, objects to which to turn in prayer.[16]

As this comparison shows, Zoroastrian priests studied Islam and its ways, with some among them learning Arabic (as their remote forbears had once learnt Greek), and seeking to understand the religion of their new rulers. Pahlavi writings of this and early 'Abbasid times show knowledge of the Qur'an and of the main Muslim tenets, of Mu'tazalite thought, and of "wholly technical terms of Islamic dialectic theology."[17] Learned Zoroastrians entered into debate with Muslim men of learning, but the records of these debates naturally deal only with the particular points of doctrine then discussed. "Mazdean theology" (it has been observed) "suffers from not being expounded anywhere as an ordered whole. Its works of the Muslim period show, however, a system of thought both mature and refined. Had favourable circumstances been granted it for another century or two, it would doubtless have evolved to produce a monument of the human spirit comparable to the intellectual edifice of Islam. One may cite the anthropology of *Dēnkard* III:292, the profound theory of knowledge in *Dēnkard* III:253, the development of reason in *Dēnkard* III:77 and *'Ulamā-yi ālam* 77:10 ff., finally the theology properly so called. There is but one God, and he alone is the Creator ... . God is absolutely good. This goodness-of-itself desires (*Dēnkard* III:147) the good of others: God wishes that men should comply in knowing Him nearly."[18]

In the course of defending their own faith, Zoroastrian priests of this and the early 'Abbasid period made a number of critical comments on Islam, more or less safely shrouded in the little known Pahlavi script; and in the ninth century a layman drew on these priestly works to compile a treatise of his own, which - intended for general enlightenment - is distinguished by its clarity of thought and orderly arrangement. He called it the *Shkand-gumanig Vizar*, the "Doubt-destroying Exposition", concern for truth having led him to inquire into the doctrines of the five major religions known to him (his own, and Judaism, Christianity, Manichaeism and Islam), as well as to consider the position of sophists and atheists.[19]   His conclusion (the book would clearly not otherwise have been preserved) was that his ancestral faith embodied the truth, essentially because it taught the existence of a good God to whom was to be attributed nothing but good, all evil being ascribed to a different source. His analysis of Zoroastrianism acknowledged the essential doctrine of the Heptad and the seven creations; but he made no reference to the ancient myths and legends to be found in parts of the Avesta and zand, or to the body of curious lore preserved through the latter, an inheritance from ancient schools of oral wisdom. Such matter was plainly irrelevant to the living Zoroastrianism of his day, and indeed would have been unfamiliar to the community at large at any time, since it represents a store of archaic knowledge, the science of its day, which simply happened to be transmitted by Zoroastrian priests as the learned men in their society. They organized it according to dualistic doctrine, and attempted in some respects to bring it up to date; but it remained quite outside the beliefs and concerns of the main body of the faithful, and so, as this work shows, placed no burden on their credulity as they confronted Islam.

Other scholar-priests continued the same pursuits as their forefathers under the Sasanians, studying the Avesta with its *zand* and extending the commentaries; but they no longer enjoyed the same security of life as their predecessors, and it may have been from among their ranks that a suggestion came of a way to strengthen their community's vital but disputed claim to be a "people of the book", and hence exempt from the choice of conversion or death. This was that during the *Vendidad* service[20] the text of the *Vendidad* should be read from a manuscript instead of being recited by heart. The intention in this may partly have been to take off this extra burden on priests' memories, relatively recently imposed; but it would also have justified a declaration by the Zoroastrians that they, like the Jews and Christians, read from their holy book at a regular act of worship. The usage, maintained to this day, represented a striking break with tradition; and the innovation was only practical because virtually no ritual is performed as the scattered *Vendidad* chapters are read. It appears to have been introduced (as one would expect) in Fars, and may not yet have become familiar to those priests of Khorasan who were among the small body of migrants who left Iran in the late ninth century, and, as "Parsis", found religious freedom in India.[21]

By that time conditions were deteriorating fast for Zoroastrians in the northeast, where the first Persian Muslim dynasts arose, nominally still subject to the 'Abbasid caliphs, but in fact largely independent. They joined Persian pride with Muslim zeal, and this was a deadly combination for Zoroastrianism. Antagonism had by then largely ceased to be between Iranian and Arab, and had grown instead to be between Muslim and non-Muslim. Only the latter now had to pay the poll-tax, *jizya*, imposed at first on all non-Arabs, and collected harshly, with deliberate and public humiliations; and Islam was being promoted generally with vigour. It is recorded of one of the new dynasts that he "ordered that wherever in his territories any ... book of Magian authorship might be discovered it should be destroyed", because he considered such books accursed, and because the *Qu'ran* and *hadith* were sufficient reading for all.[22] Some scholars have doubted the truth of this, but it appears entirely reasonable conduct on the part of a zealot, and history provides many parallels, with Christians destroying Muslim and Jewish books, Muslims those of Buddhists and Manichaeans, and so on. The widespread and deliberate destruction of Pahlavi manuscripts, and the rarer Avestan ones, must moreover have been furthered by Zoroastrian priests converting to Islam, for burning their own collections of texts would have been one obvious way of signalling, to themselves and others, their decisive abandonment of their old religion.

Pressures on Zoroastrians to convert were generally greater under the 'Abbasids, with some devout Muslims conceiving the desire to bring all the Caliph's subjects to Islam. Missions went out from the Iranian cities into the smaller towns and villages, and earnest preaching was at times supported by mob violence, persistent harassment and occasionally officially sanctioned force. Many mosques were built, some in place of fire temples, and as the numbers of Zoroastrians dwindled, the ability of the remainder to resist intimidation and injustice also became less, as did their limited freedom to manage their own affairs. Some of the Pahlavi texts of the ninth and tenth centuries indicate the daily struggles of Zoroastrians, and "attest at the same time the tenacious vitality of the principles of Mazdean law and the growing impotence of its adherents when it came to applying that law."[23] State enactments pressed on them with deliberate harshness, one being that if any member of a Zoroastrian family converted to Islam he could in due course claim the entire family heritage. Through this and other measures the community was deprived of means as well as numbers, and the material inducements to convert were increased. It was able to hold out most strongly, it seems, in Fars, probably not only because of the strength of the religious tradition there, fostered by the zeal of Sasanian priests, but also because of the depth of national pride in what had been the cradle of both the Achaemenian and Sasanian dynasties. So still in the early eleventh century some of the towns of Fars were strongly Zoroastrian, and there were fire temples in most places, although Islamization was proceeding apace.

It was from the eleventh century onwards that disasters came thick and fast, and swept away many of the remaining Zoroastrians. This came about through the dominance of Iran by successive waves of Turks and Mongols, penetrating the land from the steppes. They brought many changes to Iranian society[24], and, some of them being newly converted, displayed a freshly vigorous Islamic zeal. Some areas of Iran now became as completely Muslim as Arabia itself, with all minorities eliminated. How this was brought about in the case of the

Zoroastrians - how many converted, willingly or on pain of death, how many chose martyrdom, how many were simply killed in the course of fighting - there is no means of knowing. Azarbaijan is a striking example of such an area, for Christians and Zoroastrians had been relatively numerous there, and in the mid tenth century Adur Gušnasp still burned in its hill-top sanctuary, "a greatly respected fire temple", as a Muslim traveller noted.[25] But the region's pasture-lands attracted Turkish settlers, all religions but Islam came to be banned, and the minorities disappeared without trace. Adur Gušnasp's great temple was reduced to ruins, and eventually a petty Turkish khan built himself a palace among them.

In Seistan in the far south-east the Zoroastrian community survived for several more generations, and its most sacred fire, at Karkuye, was still housed in an imposing temple, where it was reverently tended with silver implements down into the thirteenth century;[26] but then, it seems, the tide of Mongol destruction made an end of it, and probably of every other still stately Zoroastrian building in the land. Thereafter there was to be little new building, for once the Mongol rulers of Iran had embraced Islam, the best hope for the remnant of the community to survive lay in being as unobtrusive as possible.

The most likely way of achieving this was plainly to withdraw to poor country areas, remote from frontiers and from centres of power and wealth. Such places existed notably around the desert cities of Yazd and Kerman in central Iran. At the latter place particularly a harsh climate and limited water supplies meant that there was little to attract newcomers, whether Arab, Turk or Mongol, while a stubbornness and hardihood that went perhaps with these conditions had, it seems, kept most of the inhabitants Zoroastrian. There must have been anxious deliberations and much careful planning, before at some unknown date the high priest of Fars, with a number of his priests and probably lay followers, accordingly found refuge there. The particular haven chosen was two small villages, Sharifabad and Turkabad, at the northern end of the Yazdi plain - as far as possible, that is, from the city of Yazd itself, with its Muslim authorities and largely Muslim population, and distant from any other town of note. They bore with them not only precious manuscripts, but also the two most sacred fires of Fars.[27] These were installed in Sharifabad, in buildings outwardly indistinguishable from the other small mud-brick village houses, while the high priest himself took up residence as modestly in neighbouring Turkabad.[28] Members of the community paid regular visits, as a pious duty, to him and to the sacred fires, and from their gifts and offerings he was able to make the generous "presents" to the local Muslim authorities which allowed this small citadel of the faith to survive.[29] The first report by a European traveller, through which the West was made aware of the existence still in Iran of adherents of the "ancient Persian religion", was of Zoroastrians near Yazd, with a reference, it seems, to the greater of the two Sharifabadi fires.[30] This was in 1604.

Other Zoroastrians from the north and east - that is, from Khorasan and Seistan - found refuge among their co-religionists of Kerman.[31] They had their own high priest, who acknowledged the pre-eminence of the Yazdi Dastur dasturan (as he was now usually called, or the Great Dastur); and the two communities were able to maintain close ties, this being the easier because there were Zoroastrians also in the villages strung out between them. It was through the labours of priests of Yazd and Kerman, supported by their often hard-pressed communities, that almost all the surviving Avestan and Pahlavi manuscripts were copied and recopied and so preserved, some of the copies fortunately being taken or sent from time to time to the Parsis in India. In Iran itself at moments of mob violence Zoroastrian manuscripts continued to be sought out for destruction by Muslim zealots down to late in the nineteenth century, and were all too difficult to keep safely hidden.[32] Yet the Zoroastrians are still sometimes reproached by scholars for having "lost" so many of their writings, as if this were due to carelessness or indifference on their part.

For centuries after the coming of Islam groups of Zoroastrians managed to survive also elsewhere, and still in the mid seventeenth century there were individuals who were relatively well-to-do. This appears to have been particularly true of the Kermani community, where some were able to engage in the wool trade, and where in 1644 a certain Rustam son of Bundar had the means to build a fire temple at his own cost - and presumably to give the necessary presents to the Muslim authorities to obtain permission to do so. This pious act was recorded on a marble tablet which has survived.[33] At about the same time a European traveller wrote of a large market town some four leagues from Isfahan which, he said, was inhabited entirely by Zoroastrians, who produced the finest raisins in the district - a side-product, apparently, of their skilled cultivation of grapes for wine.[34] In general, however, those of the good religion lived obscure and poverty-stricken lives, their presence known only from some casual mention, and the date of a local community's extinction passing usually unremarked. Notably, a European traveller recorded in the seventeenth century a large number of them, all wretchedly poor, in the Afghan city of Kandahar, which had a very old Zoroastrian tradition - much older than that of Fars.[35] Yet others are known to have lived scattered in country areas in central and southern Iran. But, again in the seventeenth century, another European observed: "These ancient inhabitants of Persia, faithful to the religion of their fathers, have been exterminated by Muslim fanatics; and the numerous villages which they inhabited to the south of Isfahan have been destroyed in the last civil wars of Persia."[36] He noted further that Islam was "extremely hostile" to the old Persian religion, and that the Zoroastrians "would long since have been utterly destroyed, were it not that their poverty and simplicity prevent them being thought of."[37]   One hapless group, of several hundred households, lived then, however, in circumstances of especial conspicuousness and therefore danger. They had been settled by the Safavid Shah 'Abbas I in 1608 on the outskirts of his new capital, Isfahan, to provide it with cheap and reliable labour. They and their descendants were allowed to pass their hard-worked lives in comparative peace for nearly a hundred years, but in 1699 Shah Sultan Husayn was persuaded to sign a decree for their forced conversion. A Christian archbishop happened then to be in the city, and he left an account of the terrible events which followed.[38] Numbers of the Zoroastrians yielded, but many others chose martyrs' deaths, which were often of extreme brutality; and Yazdi tradition tells of the river of Isfahan running red with the blood of stabbed and mangled corpses.[39] A few escaped to carry the fearful news to their co-religionists in the Yazdi villages, but the Isfahan community itself was obliterated in a single day, with a mosque being swiftly raised on the ruins of its fire temple. On a smaller scale similar events must often have taken place, unrecorded, elsewhere, the last known instance of a forcible mass conversion of Zoroastrians being that of the villagers of Turkabad in the mid nineteenth century.[40]

Even in the larger Zoroastrian centres living for the faith could be both hard and perilous; and the tiny old mud-brick houses of the Zoroastrians of Yazd, dark, cramped and built like miniature fortresses, bear witness to the beleaguered lives spent in them.[41] There was little security for any non-Muslims, and the mildness of the legal penalties incurred by their oppressors meant a constant threat of hooligan attacks, with robbery, rape and sometimes murder.[42] At times mob fanaticism was unleashed, and there were remorseless official pressures - the annual harsh exaction of the *jizya*, erratic demands for unpaid forced labour, the passing of petty local laws to make life ever more burdensome for the "unbeliever".[43] Occasionally the whole community mourned some gross and arbitrary injustice, as when Shah 'Abbas demanded from them a fabled book in which all the greatest events to come had been foretold, it was said, by Abraham, and when they could not produce any such work, took revenge for his disappointment by having two of their leading priests put to death.

News of this calamity was conveyed to the Parsis by the Dastur dasturan of Yazd, writing from Turkabad,[44] for the two Zoroastrian communities had long established a warm fraternal relationship, maintained irregularly by lay messengers travelling, sometimes perilously, between them by land or sea.[45] It proved of the greatest importance for the ultimate survival of the faith that the ancestors of the Parsis chose exile as their way of continuing to uphold it, with all the difficulties and dangers that this entailed. They had evidently entered with only very modest resources on their new life in Gujarat, early in the tenth century, and they lived there humbly for generations, as petty farmers, weavers and the like, increasing in numbers rather than in wealth; and in 1628, when this particular letter was written to them from Yazd, their time of great prosperity still lay well ahead. Nevertheless, even then they were flourishing compared with their oppressed Irani brethren, and one reason why the Dastur dasturan wrote was to thank them for a gift of a thousand dinars, sent from the offerings made to their Ataš Bahram. The Parsis were experiencing at that time something of the same troubles as the Iranis, since the fifteenth-century Muslim conquests in Gujarat had brought them back under the Islamic rule which their ancestors had fled, and they too were then paying the *jizya* and being subjected to exclusions and discriminations. But these they underwent together with their Hindu hosts, who formed the vast majority of the population; and this meant that the Parsis were never exposed to the intense harassment known by their co-religionists in Iran, or called on to suffer as they did. Indeed, only one Parsi is known to have died for his faith at Muslim hands, choosing martyrdom rather than enforced apostasy.[46]

It is therefore above all the tribulations of the Irani community which evoke the question: what in fact, at this late stage in its long existence, was the nature of the religion for which uncounted numbers chose to die, and others to live lives of unrelenting hardship, generation after generation, when the gate to escape - acceptance of Islam - was always open? Had its adherents, as some foreign observers thought, lost in the grinding poverty of their lives all real knowledge of the teachings of their prophet, or was it indeed the strength of those teachings which impelled them to endure as they did? The next and final chapter of this book will be devoted to seeking an answer to this question.

NOTES

1 D. S. Margoliouth, *Mohammedanism*, London 1911, 144.

2 Cf. Frye, *Golden Age*, 96, with n.51; and for the Macedonians *HZ* III 375.

3 See *HZ* III 375 ff.

4 *ZVYt* 4:7, 66, 9:23.

5 *Tarikh-i Sistan*, ed. M. Bahar, Tehran 1935, 81-2; tr. Milton Gold, IsMEO, Rome 1976, 64-5. On the passage see J. K. Choksy, "Conflict, co-existence and co-operation: Muslims and Zoroastrians in eastern Iran during the medieval period", *The Muslim World* LXXX, 1990, 216 (with modification needed about the date of Zoroastrian apocalyptic). The story is more briefly told by Baladhuri, *The Origins of the Islamic State*, tr. Hitti and Murgotten, II 142-3, who gives the margrave's name as Abarwiz.

6 On Shiz as the name for the hill on which Adur Gušnasp was installed in the late Sasanian period see *HZ* III 77-8.

7 Baladhuri, II 19-20. On other such treaties see, concisely, P. Schwartz, *Iran im Mittelalter*, VII, 858.

8   *ZVYt* 4:11.

9   *Tarikh-i Sistan,* ed. Bahar, pp.92-4, tr. Gold, pp.74-5. (On Ziyad see Gold, ib., pp.63, 72 ff.; and on his sending "an expedition that penetrated to Seistan, putting out the sacred fires", see A. S. Tritton, "Islam and the protected religions", *JRAS* 1931, 331, citing Jahiz.)

10   An account was given of it in the early 13th century by Qazvini, see Schippmann, *Feuerheiligtümer,* 38-9. *Sources,* 63-4.

11   See A. von Kremer, *Culturgeschichte des Orients unter den Chalifen,* Vienna 1877, II 164-5 (citing Ibn Hamdun).

12   Cf. above, p.16.   The belief was still held by Zoroastrians of the Yazdi area in the 20th century.

13   Narshakhi, *History of Bukhara,* tr. R. N. Frye, Cambridge Mass., 1954, 20-1, 47-8.

14   See generally, with references, Frye, *Golden Age.* R. W. Bulliet has made detailed studies of some early Muslim societies in the north-east from which indications about Zoroastrian conversions there can be derived, see his *Conversion to Islam in the medieval period,* Cambridge Mass., 1979. Also J. K. Choksy, art.cit. in n.5, and "Zoroastrians in Muslim Iran: selected problems of co-existence and interaction during the early medieval period", *Iranian Studies* XX, 1990, 17-30.

15   The expression *vaŋhvī- daēnā-* recurs in the *Gathas* (*Y.* 53:1, 4), and can be understood to mean "good religion".

16   *Tarikh-i Sistan,* l.c. in n.9.

17   G. Monnot, "L'implantation de l'islam en Iran: la réponse mazdéenne", *Annuaire de l'Ecole pratique des Hautes Etudes, Section des Sciences Religieuses,* XCVIII, 1989-1990, 285. See also J. de Menasce, "Problèmes des mazdéens dans l'Iran musulman", *Festschrift W. Eilers,* ed. G. Wiessner, Wiesbaden 1967, 220-30, esp. at p.220, where the author observes that several of the Pahl. texts "shed much light on the vitality of Mazdean thought during the early centuries of Islamization".

18   Monnot, art.cit., pp.284-5.

19   On the book see the remarks by its editor, J.-P. de Menasce, in *CHIr.* III 560-1.

20   On this service cf. above, p.135.

21   Copies of the *Vd Sade* (without Pahl. *zand*) became accordingly much needed.   In a letter written in 1515 the Irani dasturs expressed themselves puzzled as to why the Parsi priests did not teach the *Vd,* especially because this was easy, since it had only to be recited from the book.   "Certainly" (they declared) "you should not omit teaching and consecrating *Vd*" (*Riv.,* ed. Unvala, I 428. 9-13, tr. Dhabhar, 327). But still a century later, in 1618, they were concerned at an apparent scarcity of *Vd* mss. among the Parsis, and prepared a copy for them (*Riv.,* ed. Unvala, II 160.7-9, tr. Dhabhar, 594). This is the ms. now known as MF 2 (see K. F. Geldner, ed., *Avesta,* Stuttgart 1896, I xxii ff.).   Thereafter through the labours of Parsi copyists *Vd* mss. became numerous in India. - Khorasan was ancient Parthian territory, but from the time of the Achaemenian Empire all Iranians were known abroad indiscriminately as "Parsis" or Persians (i.e., those from Pars).

22   See E. G. Browne, *A Literary History of Persia,* London 1902, repr. 1929, I, 346-7 (citing Dawlatshah); cf. A. S. Shahbazi, *Ferdowsī,* 120. The story was current in the 19th century among the Zoroastrians of Yazd, see Jackson, *Persia past and present,* 359.

23   Menasce, art. cit. in n.17, p.230.

24   See Frye's admirable study, *Golden Age,* Ch.11, "The Turkish ascendancy".

25   *Abū-Dulaf's Travels in Iran (circa A.D. 950)*, ed. and tr. by V. Minorsky, Cairo 1955, 32; cited by Schippmann, *Feuerheiligtümer*, 321.

26   See above, n.10.

27   See *Stronghold*, 1-4.

28   A remote parallel can be seen here with the withdrawing of the Median high priest from Raga, newly made a Greek polis, to remote Azarbaijan, which took place probably some 1500 years earlier, cf. above, pp.7-8.

29   See Chardin, *Voyages*, II 183; G. Drouville, *Voyage en Perse fait en 1812 et 1813*, 2nd ed., Paris 1825, II 210 (referring to the duty to visit the high priest); *Stronghold*, 1-4 with nn.8, 9. The last extant letter written by a Yazdi high priest from Turkabad is dated 1681, see Hodivala, *Studies*, 339-40. Sometime after this the Dastur dasturan with his priests moved - either voluntarily or by order of the Muslim authorities - to the city of Yazd, where the holder of this office was found residing by travellers in the 18th century.

30   *The Travels of Pedro Teixeira*, tr. by W. F. Sinclair and D. Ferguson, Hakluyt Society, London 1902, 196-7, cited by Firby, *European Travellers*, 24. Teixeira evidently depended in this on Muslim reports.

31   See, with further references, Boyce, "The fire-temples of Kerman", *Acta Orientalia* XXX, 1966, 51-72; "The Zoroastrian villages of the Jupar range", *Festschrift W. Eilers*, ed. G. Wiessner, Wiesbaden 1967, 148-56.

32   On the hiding-places created by Zoroastrians within their small fortress-like houses see Boyce, "The Zoroastrian houses of Yazd", *Iran and Islam: in memory of V. Minorsky*, ed. C. E. Bosworth, Edinburgh 1971, 125-47, at pp.130-1, 141, 142.

33   See Boyce, *Acta Orientalia* XXX, 70-2.

34   Chardin, III 337.

35   J. de Thevenot, *Travels*, Pt II, *The relation of Indostan*, Ch.33 (Eng. tr. by A. Lovell, London 1687), who reported this on the authority of the Superior of the Capuchins of Surat, who had made a tour of the region. See Firby, *European Travellers*, 70. On Zoroastrianism in the region of Kandahar in ancient times see *HZ* III 125 ff.

36   Chardin, o.c., X 242.

37   Ib., II 180.

38   Abbé Martin Gaudereau, *Relation d'une Mission d'Ancyre à Ispahan en Perse*, Paris 1702, 134-9 (cited by L. Lockhart, *The fall of the Safavid dynasty*, Cambridge 1958, 73).

39   In the course of retelling, the massacre has come to be attributed to Shah 'Abbas II, of whom it is in fact known only that he had the whole Isfahan settlement moved to a different site to make room for a pleasure garden. The new site had its own bridge, so that Zoroastrians coming into the city to work should not be in contact with Muslims.

40   See *Stronghold*, 7, and ib., pp.7-8, on the erosive effects of persistent petty harassment.

41   See Boyce, art.cit. in n.32. The former life of the Kerman community cannot be so readily traced in this way because of special disasters which it suffered, above all in 1719, when the Zoroastrian quarter, which was outside the city walls, was overrun by an Afghan army and almost all its inhabitants slaughtered. (See further Boyce, *Zoroastrians*, 191.) It was never rebuilt, and still in the 1960s the ground plans of some of its small houses and shrines could be made out from the footings of their mud-brick walls.

42 For references see Boyce, "The vitality of Zoroastrianism attested by some Yazdi traditions and actions", *Corolla Iranica, Papers in honour of D. N. MacKenzie*, ed. R. E. Emmerick and D. Weber, Frankfurt-am-Main, 1991, 15-22.

43 On harassment by such laws in Yazd still at the end of the 19th century see Napier Malcolm, *Five years in a Persian town*, London 1905, 44-53. Some of these laws were indeed petty, intended merely to humiliate; but others (such as the ban on Zoroastrians building wind-towers for their houses, which made life tolerable in the burning summer heat) were harshly oppressive.

44 For this letter see Hodivala, *Studies*, 330-1. Cf. Chardin, *Voyages*, VIII 362 (who erred slightly, however, in saying that the high priest himself was among those executed). Chardin heard that 26 Zoroastrian works were handed over to the king in response to his vain quest.

45 Thus one luckless Parsi, arriving in Fars around 1635, was enslaved by a Muslim, who blinded him before demanding a ransom for him from his co-religionists. See Hodivala, o.c., p.333.

46 See Boyce, *Zoroastrians*, 186.

CHAPTER NINE

Fidelity and Endurance

The history of the Zoroastrians in Iran can thus be traced only very sketchily after the coming of Islam, with many gaps, and sudden lasting silences descending locally. Despite this, a surprising amount can be learnt for the later centuries about their beliefs and hopes and practices, their chief religious concerns and the conduct of their lives. For this there is a variety of sources, different in character and complementing one another usefully. The last flourishing of Pahlavi literature was in the early tenth century, but all literary activity did not then cease. Zoroastrian priests drew thereafter on Pahlavi writings to compile for the instruction of the community a number of works in the contemporary Persian idiom, using the easier Arabic script but avoiding in the main Arabic loanwords. Among the most important of such works are the *Saddar* and the *Saddar Bundaheš*. It is not known when these were composed, but the older, the *Saddar*, was in existence in 1496,[1] and may well have been written two or three centuries earlier. The two texts, which are very similar, are in character *rivayats*,[2] treating simply and clearly of a miscellany of beliefs and observances, myths and legends, in a wholly traditional manner. Their anonymous authors drew on such sources as the *Pahlavi Vendidad* and the *Shayest ne-shayest*, and in the case of the later compilation, on the *Bundahišn*; and their books became standard texts of reference for working priests, being easily accessible and of recognized authority.[3] They thus made a valuable contribution to maintaining continuity in the religious life of both branches of the community. The original Parsi migrants had apparently taken few manuscripts with them to India, probably indeed only those containing essential devotional texts; and the Irani priests gradually supplied them with others over the years. Copies of the *Saddar* and the *Saddar Bundaheš* are known to have been sent from Yazd to Gujarat in

1559,[4] and there these works were subsequently diligently copied and recopied and much used.

The date when these particular manuscripts were sent is known from one of the letters written by Irani priests to the Parsis at irregular intervals between the fifteenth and eighteenth centuries.[5] They were in response to letters brought them from the Parsis, which contained many questions about religious observances, some put in pursuit of knowledge, others simply seeking verification of their own practices. These questions were dealt with by the Irani dasturs in long answers which, because of their nature and scope, are known as the *Persian Rivayats*. In them the dasturs drew on older authorities, notably the *Pahlavi Vendidad*, the Pahlavi *rivayat* literature, and the Persian *Saddars*; but what gives their own writings a unique importance is that in them are to be heard the voices of individual priests writing at precisely known dates and expressing their personal beliefs, as well as describing rituals which were actually being performed and practices which were actually being followed at those dates by their own community.

The *Persian Rivayats* were carefully preserved at the chief Parsi religious centre, the little town of Navsari, and have been almost completely published and translated.[6] They partly overlap in time with another important source, namely the observations made by a number of Europeans who, as merchants, missionaries, diplomats, soldiers, scholars and adventurers, made their way to Iran from the beginning of the seventeenth century, and there came across members of the small Zoroastrian community, whose survival under Islam had been previously unknown in the West. In setting down what they learnt about them, these foreigners were following in the footsteps of ancient observers, from Herodotus onward, and it is striking to what an extent their notices agree over a space of some two thousand years; but whereas their distant predecessors had recorded the beliefs and ways of an imperial people who dominated their own known world, these later travellers were noticing those of a small and deeply oppressed minority, identified to them contemptuously by their rulers as *gabr* (*guebre, gor*) - a general Muslim term for "infidel", in Iran used characteristically of the Zoroastrians - or *ataš-parast*, "fire worshipper". The Europeans' reports vary greatly in value, a few being first-hand and full of detail, others mere brief reworkings or marked with strong Christian prejudices; but taken together, and judiciously assessed[7], they furnish a valuable body of evidence, again precisely datable, whose particular contribution lies in showing how, to outsiders, the Zoroastrians' beliefs appeared to have affected their characters and way of life. Thereafter, in the nineteenth and twentieth centuries, a few Western scholars sought out the Zoroastrians of Yazd and Kerman to learn more of their beliefs and ways.

A little knowledge can also be gleaned from the attitudes - mostly, but not uniformly, hostile - of Iranian Muslims to the "gabr". Finally there are descriptions of the traditional usages of their own community published from early in this century by Irani Zoroastrians themselves. These show that a strong conservatism existed in some Zoroastrian villages down to the late 1960s, that is, to just before Iran's "economic miracle", which made great changes in the life of the country in the following decade. These changes brought modern urban ways into the Zoroastrian villages, and this made the community more generally susceptible to the reformist tendencies which had already been reaching it through various channels for over half a century from Bombay.[8]

These diverse sources thus cover, if erratically, over five hundred years or seventeen generations - a stretch of time which by an odd coincidence is roughly the same in length as that other period of Zoroastrian history which has also been generally ignored by scholars, namely the combined Macedonian-Parthian eras. The earlier period has been widely neglected because of the meagreness of the sources, the later one because it holds little attraction for the philologists who in the main dominate the academic study of Zoroastrianism, and whose professional interest tends to wane with the waning of Pahlavi. For students of the religion this half-millennium is, however, of particular importance, for this is the first epoch for which the records are full enough to show in any detail how Zoroastrianism was actually lived, and how it directed the lives of its devout adherents.

Information of some abundance becomes available for the Parsis also from the seventeenth century; but for the present study the Iranis have a special importance for three reasons: first, continuing to live in their homeland, they retained some ancient elements of belief and practice that were weakened or actually lost among the Parsis as they made their way in a new country; second, as we have seen, they maintained their faith under duress, and so bore the more telling witness to its strength, generation after hard-pressed generation; and third, the Parsis were earlier influenced by modern (mostly Christian European) ways of thought, with the result that the religious unity of their community was sooner shattered, with the vigorous contests of reformists and counter-reformists tending to obscure the traditional orthodoxy and orthopraxy which persisted quietly among them also.

During the later centuries of their separation the Parsis grew very prosperous, while the Iranis were reduced to ever greater poverty and distress; but in the fifteenth century inequalities in wealth and worldly position were not yet so marked between them. There were, however, leading Parsis then who were already comfortably off, and who had the means and the desire to raise the standards of religious observance in their community; and for this they looked to the priests of Yazd and Kerman for authoritative rulings, seeing them as guardians of the ancient traditions of the faith, preserved in purity on ancestral soil. This attitude is exemplified by a recorded instance of money being sent from Gujarat for ceremonies to be performed by the Irani priests for the donors' souls, in the belief that they would be solemnized by them more efficaciously.[9] The Irani dasturs responded with self-deprecating courtesy, and except when they felt absolute certainty about some matter, showed no disposition to assume authority over their distant co-religionists.[10]   This emerges with particular clarity from a letter written from Turkabad in 1635 by the "Great Dastur" of Yazd. Here he is responding to a question from the Parsis about the month's difference between the Irani calendar and their own: "If they [the Parsis] are sure that a month has been forgotten by them", he wrote, "... they may now observe the months according to the Irani reckoning. But if that [reckoning of theirs] has descended to them from ancient times, they may allow it to remain."[11] In general the Irani priests evince a warm regard and respect for the Parsis, whom they greet as fellow "wearers of the sacred cord" (baste-kustiyan),[12] and as staunch upholders of the "good Mazda-worshipping religion", that "of Ormazd and Zartušt"[13], praising them for all the efforts they have made on its behalf.[14]   They welcome news of any good fortune that has befallen them, and share with them their own hopes and deep sorrows.

Plainly the Irani dasturs found no cause to instruct these devout co-religionists in the basic tenets of their common faith, and so here again there is no systematic treatment of theology. It emerges clearly from their letters, however, that they held to their religion through all afflictions because they were convinced that "there is but one path of righteousness",[15], namely that revealed by Ormazd to Zoroaster, and that it was only by following it that they could attain salvation, rescuing their own souls from hell and helping to save the world. As they declared: "When God the Most High sent Zartušt as apostle and conferred on us the Best Religion, Zartušt brought the 21 Nasks of the sayings of Ormazd [that is, the "Great Avesta" as written down in the Sasanian period], ... and made them manifest and explained their import to the people of the world; that is, he showed us the way to pass our lives in good thoughts, good words and good deeds ... saying 'Love virtue and abstain from vice'. We obtain reward and punishment in the other world for the obedience and disobedience that we practise".[16]   The opening words of this declaration are purely monotheistic, with the phrasing shaped, it would seem, by long years of defending the faith against Islam;[17] but that it was Zoroaster's own doctrine of a modified monotheism which the dasturs upheld is shown by their regular form of benediction on their Parsi brethren, namely that they might be "under the protection of Ormazd and the Amašaspands".[18]   It is impossible to be certain whether by "Amašaspand" they here meant the lesser Six of the Heptad, or the Yazatas generally. Both usages are attested in the Persian Rivayats, and both are consonant with Zoroaster's own uses of this term.[19]   Whichever is meant, the phrase is broadly in harmony with the expression employed by the early Achaemenians in their inscriptions, who spoke of "Ahuramazda ... and the other gods who are."[20]

Sometimes the Irani dasturs invoked longer blessings, of which the following is a striking example:[21] "In the name and with the praise and help of the Creator, Ormazd the radiant and glorious, and of the immaterial Yazads and material Yazads,[22] and of all the *fravašis* of the just, and of Mihr, Sroš and Rašn[23], and of the Glory of the pure and good Mazda-worshipping religion, which has been revealed for dispelling and annihilating the wicked Ahriman and all the *devs* and *drujs*, oppressors and sinners! May it not be possible for them to do any harm, injury or evil deed affecting the good Mazda-worshipping religion! May our wishes be fulfilled through thinking, speaking and acting in accordance with it, and may we keep off wicked persons from ourselves until we come to the time of Mihr of wide pastures [that is, to our own judgment day]." Every word of this benediction could have been uttered, unmodified as to content, by Zoroastrians of the "Young Avestan" period. It is, moreover, entirely faithful to Zoroaster's own teachings in the veneration of Ormazd as Creator, and of the lesser beneficent divinities; and in the expressed belief in judgment at death, the ethic of goodness in thought, word and act, and the great purpose of annihilating Ahriman. All that the prophet might not himself have countenanced would perhaps be the invocation of the *fravašis*,[24] and this had been part of general usage from probably very early in the existence of the faith.

The dasturs everywhere exalt Ormazd as God, but they strongly adjure their co-religionists (then like themselves under Muslim rule) never to think of him as the author of evil, and hence not to submit to misfortune as being sent by him. They cite in this regard the famed Sasanian high priest, Adurbad Mahraspand, of whom it was told that when trouble befell him he would thank God that this affliction brought on him by Ahriman was not greater and that he had the fortitude to endure it.[25] How much better, too, to suffer here in the body rather than hereafter in the soul. The dasturs evidently had constantly in mind the thought of judgment at death, when the soul ascends, at sunrise on the fourth day, to the Chinvat Bridge, there to stand before "the Judge Mihr Ized" (*Davar Mihr Ized*);[26] and this thought was undoubtedly a sharp spur to striving after virtue. One of the first rites to be described this century by an Irani priest was that of *Chaharom*, the "(Service) of the fourth (day)", at which the living bid the departing soul farewell;[27] and this ceremony is so close in detail to the parallel Parsi observance that it is evident that, as solemnized in the two communities, it goes back at least to Sasanian times. Its origins are almost certainly pre-Zoroastrian, so that basically the rite is likely to have been maintained from the prophet's own day. It is by its circumstances naturally impressive, for it is not difficult in the growing light to sense the soul's withdrawal, and to imagine its lonely ascent to the ordeal that awaits it, with heaven or hell as the award; and this accordingly is a moment for prayers to be devoutly prayed on its behalf, and acts of charity to be undertaken for its sake. Before this, many ceremonies had been performed for the departed, dedicated mostly to Sroš and some, it appears, instituted only in Sasanian times.[28] These, to which great importance is attached, are dealt with at some length in the *Persian Rivayats*.[29]

Should any individuals lack the imagination to picture for themselves the terrors which an unrighteous soul would face at death, or its sufferings thereafter in hell, this want could be made good from the ancient *Arda Viraz Namag*.[30] This had been set down in an adapted Pahlavi version of the ninth or tenth century, to strengthen waverers against Islam. The work was much copied and also illustrated, so that those who could not read the text could look at the pictures, and frighten themselves edifyingly with the thought of what might be to come. An illustrated copy was among the manuscripts sent from Turkabad to the Parsis in 1559,[31] and about a century later a French merchant noted that in Kerman the priests had "several books full of small pictures, ill done, representing how the several sins of man shall be punished in hell."[32] The work was translated into Persian and Gujarati, and in due course printed in Bombay; and it was a printed copy from there, with pictures, which in the 1960s found its way back to Sharifabad, where it was studied from time to time with a fearful interest by some of the villagers.[33]

Apart from the hope of happiness in heaven hereafter for the individual, to be attained through virtue, the Zoroastrians were sustained by the larger expectation of the ultimate victory of goodness here on earth, and with it the triumph of their own, the "Best Religion". This had evidently been looked for by Zoroaster himself, and had been foretold with vivid embellishments in later apocalyptic works.[34] In them the concept appears of a world-year of twelve "months" of a thousand years each. Zoroaster was supposed to have lived at the beginning of the tenth "month", and the end of his millennium was to see the coming of the first Saošyant or World Saviour, named Ukhšyat-ereta (Middle Persian Ušedar or Hošedar), "He who will make righteousness flourish".[35] The belief had moreover developed (probably after the Macedonian conquest[36]) that evil would grow very powerful before the Saošyant's coming, that is, before its final overthrow. This was contrary to the orthodox expectation (which persisted side by side with it) that, through the efforts of each *ašavan*, evil will be steadily weakened to the point when it can be finally destroyed; but it seems a natural development (fostered in earlier days by Babylonian and other influences) among those who had been brought to live under infidel rule. Once the tenth millennium had come to be perceived as an evil age, indeed as the "millennium of Ahriman"[37], it was possible for the Zoroastrians subjugated in these later times to detach it from its link with their prophet and to see it simply as that of the Arabs, the Evil One's agents; and so they came to date its beginning to that of their own current era, namely 631, the enthronement-year of the last Sasanian king, when Arab armies were already in the field. Accordingly the Irani dasturs convinced themselves that it was in 1631 that the Saošyant and his helpers - the Yazata of victory, Verethraghna "of miraculous power" (Bahram Varjavand), and Pišišyaothna (Pišotan), the immortal son of Kavi Vištaspa - would appear, defeat the powers of evil, and gloriously vindicate faithful believers. True, at times, when their troubles were great and their oppressors strong, they found it hard to conceive how this could come about. Thus they wrote to the Parsis in 1559, when there was much turbulence in Iran: "In what manner he can come to us (we do not know), for in this quarter the Ataš Bahram and all the *behdins* are distracted and distressed, and in this wilderness it will not be practicable."[38] But as the year of hope approached, they grew confident, and in 1626 they wrote: "The millennium of Ahriman is ended and the millennium of Ormazd is near, and we hope to see the face of the victorious king [Bahram] Varjavand, and Hošedar and Pišotan will come, without any doubt or suspicion".[39] The firmness of these declared hopes was such that it discouraged an ardent Roman Catholic missionary from attempting at that time the conversion of the Isfahani Zoroastrians;[40] and the passing of 1631 without any sign of these longed-for happenings must have been correspondingly bitter for the oppressed Iranis. But though their calculations had proved wrong, the doctrine stood firm and continued to provide them with a lifeline of hope. As a European observer recorded some forty years later, "one of their most constant traditions is that their religion will again be paramount ... and that empire will once more be theirs. They sustain themselves and their children with this hope."[41] The community continued to pray regularly for the coming of Bahram and Ušedar and Pišotan,[42] and still in the twentieth century "Shah Bahram" visited the faithful in their dreams, appearing as a splendid figure on horseback, usually with two attendants clad either in white or green, and bringing promise of help and earthly salvation.[43]

The Zoroastrians spoke fairly readily, it seems, of their future expectations to Christian inquirers, one of whom recorded that, after telling him about the three Saošyants, their miraculous conception and saving acts, they went on to describe the last time, saying that then "shall all the mountains, and all the metals in the world be melted, and shall fill up the great chaos of hell, whereby the mansion of the devils shall be utterly destroy'd. After this the world shall be levelled, and men shall have every one their apartment answerable to the degree and quantity of the good which they did in their life time; but that their chief delight shall be to behold and praise God ... They also say that God will have pity upon the damn'd, and that they shall go into Paradise as having suffer'd enough".[44] This account is essentially true to original orthodox expectations as enshrined in *zand* translation and expounded to the ancient Greeks,[45] but the last statement represents a modification of Zoroaster's doctrine of the annihilation of sinners, reached, it seems, in the Sasanian period.[46] The idea of a gradation according to virtue among the inhabitants of God's kingdom is plainly linked with this modification, since it would be a discouragement to goodness to think that sinners would in the end be entirely equal with the righteous; and it is first found in a ninth-century book.[47] What seems truly remarkable is how widely the Irani dasturs were prepared to extend this doctrine, despite their community's sufferings; for when the Parsis asked if those of other religions (*juddins*) would live after the Resurrection they replied unflinchingly: "After the punishment of the Resurrection the creation of Ormazd [that is, mankind], doers of good and sinners, all will be alive" (*dām-i Ōrmazd, kirfevarzīdārān va vināhkārān, ba'd az pādefrāh-i ristākhēz, hame zīnde šavand*).[48] The phrasing of this answer suggests the possibility that a doctrinal rather than a simple humanitarian principle was in fact involved - that theologians of the Sasanian period may have come to think that Ahriman could not be allowed the lasting triumph of having diminished the creation of God.

The Zoroastrianism of this late period was thus as ardently a salvation faith as when it was first preached by its prophet, some three thousand years earlier. As to its theology in the strict sense of that term, Western inquirers learnt orally of the same beliefs which are to be found in the *Persian Rivayats*, and which, as we have seen, were likewise orthodox, that is, those taught by Zoroaster. To these inquirers individual Zoroastrians declared repeatedly and roundly that the God of their worship was one,[49] a Being whom they spoke of as the "Eternal Spirit",[50] the "Creator of heaven and earth, whom they adore with an adoration which is special to him".[51] Like the dasturs, however, they firmly maintained their dualism, avowing that "there are two principles of things, as it was not possible there could be only one, as all things are of two kinds or natures, that is to say, good or bad. These two principles are Light, which they call Ormous ... and Darkness, which they call Ariman".[52] This account, given by Zoroastrians in the seventeenth century A.C. to a Frenchman, is expressed in terms very close to those reproduced by Plutarch on the authority of a Greek inquirer of the fourth century B.C.[53] Such fidelity over more than two millennia is in no way surprising, since this is basic doctrine; but it is nevertheless a pleasing attestation of continuity in living belief, and hence of the strength of Zoroaster's teachings.

Zoroastrians of the seventeenth century also readily acknowledged to Christian inquirers their veneration of lesser divinities, whom some called "angels"[54], but others termed "lesser gods" (in a French rendering, *dieux subalternes*), ruled over by the Sovereign God.[55] This particular definition of belief comes close to that made to an earlier generation of Christians by a Sasanian king, who declared that he "acknowledged only one God. The rest were but as courtiers of the King";[56] and both seem very fair representations of Zoroaster's fundamental teaching in this vital respect.[57]

The Irani dasturs themselves in their communications occasionally used the ancient term Mainyu, in its Persian form Mino, for a divine being, and once the expression *hame mīnōyān*, "All the Spirits",[58] for the whole pantheon, from Ormazd himself and his Holy Spirit down to the humble Mino of a ritual sulphur drink. In Sasanian theology, it has been observed, the expression "the *menog* creation" included "not only created beings but also the Creator";[59] and this was in accord with ancient animatism in which all was perceived as being a Mainyu or possessing a Mainyu.[60] Although this theology was thus maintained by the dasturs in the Islamic era, within the world of "Minoyan" they stressed, again in full orthodoxy, the distinction in dignity between the lesser members of the Heptad (termed by them the Amašaspands) and the other subordinate divinities. "Know", they said in a rare doctrinal declaration, "that there are six Amašaspands."[61] This reflects the organization of the lesser divinities of the pantheon into "fellow workers" (*hamkars*) of the Six, which, it is generally accepted, took place some time after the creation of the Zoroastrian calendar. Their subordination to the Six is expressed in regular daily liturgical invocations,[62] and so was profoundly part of the theological awareness of every priest. That the Heptad was also at the heart of Zoroastrian ethical life is shown by the dasturs' response to the Parsis' question: "What is the law of the Creator Ormazd and the Amašaspands?"[63] They cited to them, in Persian translation, a passage from the *Denkard* [64]: "The law of the Creator Ormazd is the love of (one's fellow) man. The gift of Bahman is concord. The law of Ardibehešt is truthfulness. The gift of Shahrevar is the maintenance of relationships. The gift of Spandarmad is humility and complete mindfulness. The law of Khordad is charity and thanksgiving. The gift of Amurdad is consultation (with the wise) and moderation." The last two "gifts" or "laws" are substitutes (of activities or attributes highly valued by Zoroastrians) for those proper to these two Amašaspands, namely wholeness and immortality, which though so much desired by mankind do not have the moral dimension sought here.[65]

The ethical functions of the Heptad are set out at length, and more systematically, at the beginning of the *Saddar Bundaheš*;[66] and later in that work there is a long disquisition on how these divinities are to be served.[67] They are the guardians of the different parts of the world, it is stated, and if what they guard is not kept well, they are afflicted, and will challenge the soul of a neglectful person after death, saying: "You did not attend to us and did not take care of us."[68] In this and in what follows the doctrine of the immanence of the Heptad in the creations is clearly implied; and this doctrine appears as a part of daily assumptions in two documents among those which the Irani dasturs sent to India. These were two *Sogand Nama*, formularies for administering a judicial oath to a person accused of a breach of undertaking, this being still called by the ancient term *mihr-drujih* "betrayal of contract (*mithra*)". The oath was solemnly administered in the hall of a fire temple, and the accused was subjected to a fiery ordeal in the form of a drink to be consumed containing sulphur, which it was believed would burn him inwardly if he lied. (This form of trial was maintained in Kerman till the late nineteenth century,[69] one of the many manifestations of the profound conservatism of the Irani community.)   In both formularies the Amašaspands represent their creations in a manner which is truly Gathic,[70] each oath beginning with an invocation of the Heptad.   One is as follows: "I swear truly before the Creator, Ormazd the radiant and glorious, and before Bahman Amašaspand, and before Ardibehest Amašaspand [= fire] who is kindled before me, and before Shahrevar Amašaspand [= the metal vessel] who is placed before me, and before Isfandarmad Amašaspand [= earth] on whom I stand, and before Khordad Amašaspand [= the ritual drink] who is set before me, and before Amurdad Amašaspand [= the bread] who is before me and whom I must consume ...".[71]   In the other version Bahman Amašaspand is invoked through "the girdle of the religion" (*band-i dīn*) "which I wear around me",[72] for the sacred cord, being of wool, can represent his creation of beneficent animals, and hence also him.[73]   In this formulary, therefore, all six lesser members of the Heptad are systematically invoked through their creations.   After them Mithra is called on, as he must have been at such judicial ordeals for many generations even before Zoroaster lived; but in this profoundly Zoroastrian formulary he brings with him his regular companions at the heavenly trial after death, namely Sroš and Rašn.

The Amašaspands are here named through their creations because apparently of the solemnity of the occasion, with a man's life believed to be at stake.   The oath appears designed to impress on the accused the extreme seriousness of his action, with the greatest divinities being called on to bear witness, together with the pure creations which they inform - the "immaterial" and the "material" conjointly, so that he swears thus before the whole attendant world.

The other solemn occasion when the concentrated presence of the greatest divinities was similarly apprehended was at religious services, both the "inner" rituals and the "outer" ones which were regularly attended by the laity.   There was no cause for this to appear in the writings of the Irani dasturs to their Parsi co-religionists, for it was part evidently of the fabric of their religious consciousness, a wholly natural way of apprehending one aspect of their acts of worship.   Indeed, just how natural and therefore self-explanatory it seemed to them is shown by the fact that they felt no need to offer the Parsis any comment on, let alone interpretation of, the wording of the oath-formularies in this respect.   The doctrine was for them a living article of faith, handed down in the community from generation to generation, and an integral part of their way of looking at the world; and still in the 1960s conservative believers were ready to expound it, plainly and naturally, to well-disposed outsiders who showed an interest in their religion.[74]

The same reason - a general profound familiarity with the doctrine - explains why it does not figure in the few Pahlavi works which exist on ritual.[75] These were written by priests for priests, and are concerned with giving precise details of ritual actions, and not at all with expounding their significance. Hence there is no written record of this liturgical aspect of the doctrine of the immanence of the Heptad; and since through their professional training most scholars attach prime - sometimes indeed exclusive - importance to written texts, Western academics have in general doubted the antiquity of this belief (which they find in any case too strange to attribute to the "enlightened" Zoroaster), and the possibility of its having been transmitted orally from the time of the faith's foundation. But ritual can be a very effective transmitter of doctrine, witness for example the Christian mass, whose doctrinal significance can also appear archaic and strange to twentieth-century outsiders, and whose rituals have in the past embodied that significance for countless generations of illiterate believers, so that only the most ignorant and stupid among them would not have had some apprehension of it. In the case of Zoroastrianism, the survival of the Old Avestan texts - that is, of Zoroaster's own words - has depended on the regular consecration of the ancient *Staota yesnya* (which forms the core of the present *yasna*) from the time when he himself taught it to his first priestly disciples; and since there has thus been demonstrably no break in the solemnization of this service, there is no reason to suppose any break in the understanding of this aspect of it. There are on the contrary good reasons for accepting the soundness of the oral tradition, for this shows how the central act of Zoroastrian worship was imbued with the prophet's moral and doctrinal teachings, and helps to explain the dominant position of the Heptad in Zoroastrian devotional and ethical life. That it had this position is as solid and incontrovertible a fact as any textual datum, and one for which no satisfactory explanation has ever otherwise been found.

All that sets Zoroastrianism apart from other credal religions in respect of its tradition, laying its teachings open to untrammelled academic speculation, is the length of its purely oral transmission - in this particular matter it would seem fully three thousand years - and the great gaps in the recorded history of the faith. These have encouraged a wholly baseless - indeed rationally untenable - assumption that there were corresponding gaps in the transmission of its doctrines. At this late period of its existence, although still relatively little is known of events in the history of the community, it is possible to see that its religious life flowed on steadily through all vicissitudes; and the same must be true of earlier times also, or there would be no *Staota yesnya* and no Zoroastrianism today.

Even in the period of its secular power, as an imperial religion, its adherents lived, as we have seen,[76] close to nature, and had in general no reason to question the archaic assumptions which underlie the doctrine of the Heptad; and now in these Islamic times the Zoroastrians of Iran suffered many restrictions, which meant that most of them had to earn their living from the land, as peasant-farmers, field labourers, gardeners and the like. They thus spent their days very largely in direct service of the Amašaspands of earth and plants and water and beneficent animals, and so were able to make a virtue out of an often harsh necessity. Thus a European observer recorded that the "Guebres" held farming to be "not merely a good and innocent calling, but also meritorious and noble", believing it to be "the first of all vocations, that for which the Sovereign God and the Lesser Gods, as they say, have the most satisfaction and which they reward most amply."[77]   Another Western inquirer reported their belief that the way to salvation was "to work to purify the elements [that is, the creations]: to till the ground; to cultivate the gardens; to purge the water of insects [that is, *khrafstras*]; and to keep the fire alight".[78] This echoes a declaration by the dasturs in the *Persian Rivayats* that it was a duty of those of the Best Religion that they "should keep the water, the earth and the trees and plants pure and clean".[79]   In part this was to be done in simple if laborious ways, with all impurities being kept as far as possible from the good creations, either by being carried out to stony barren ground or destroyed by acid[80] - for naturally fire was never put to this polluting task. Ritual means were also however employed positively to increase the purity of water, by pouring consecrated libations into running streams, or to cleanse sullied fire (readily "rescued", at a price, from Muslim neighbours) by an ancient rite laid down in the *Vendidad*.[81]   Both observances were regarded as highly meritorious, and hence not only of service to the creation concerned, and pleasing to its Amašaspand, but also beneficial to the souls of those who had them performed.

An American scholar visiting Yazd at the beginning of this century was struck by how closely in general the Zoroastrians there still followed "the injunctions of the *Vendidad*".[82]   The sense of purity and impurity which imbues much of that work was deeply engrained in them, being strictly inculcated from childhood;[83] and impurity, like moral sin, was still firmly attributed, as in ancient orthodoxy, to the evil powers. One positive way of weakening these was by destroying *khrafstras*, a practice noticed centuries earlier by both Greek and Indian onlookers,[84] and now recorded anew by several Western travellers. Two of these learnt the doctrinal justification for it, for as one wrote: "What gives them so much aversion for these animals is the belief ... that they were not created by God, but by the devil"[85] - or as the other expressed it "by an Evil Principle and wicked Author".[86]   Another reported that "the greatest kindness that the Guebres think they can do to a dead man is to kill for his sake a great many frogs, serpents and other insects";[87] and indeed in a versified last testament, of which the Irani dasturs sent a copy to India, Dastur Noshirvan Marzban of Kerman specifically asked his son, among the pious acts he was to perform for him after his death, to kill all kinds of *khrafstras*, so that the dastur's soul might benefit therefrom.[88]

Another Zoroastrian observance which had caught the attention of Herodotus was the characteristic method of disposing of the dead, designed to protect the pure creations; and this again was now repeatedly commented on by European travellers. Some of their reports are plainly based on hearsay, and are inaccurate; but one seventeenth-century inquirer in particular took pains to learn all that he could at first hand, and left a detailed description of a *dakhma* or funerary tower near Isfahan, and of the "Guebres'" funerary rites there. These impressed him by their elaborateness, causing him to comment: "Since these people are very poor, and under the yoke of a hostile religion, one can judge by the things they still do now what they would have done when their religion was supported by the royal authority and sanctioned by the zeal of the multitude".[89] Some three centuries later a Zoroastrian layman wrote a full account of the traditional funerary rites of his community as they were then still observed in the most conservative of the Yazdi villages;[90] and this shows that the Irani usages were indeed even more elaborate than the closely similar Parsi ones. This elaboration appears to have come about gradually through ever more strenuous efforts being made to pen in and even as far as possible destroy the pollution from a corpse, which was believed to be deeply harmful to the creations.

As we have seen,[91] observing the purity laws was very much part of the striving to attain the world's salvation, that is, to bring about Frašegird, and it was natural that the Zoroastrians of these Islamic times, who were sacrificing all chance of present prosperity for the hope of future bliss, should seek to keep them with great strictness. They even in their zealousness increased or extended their application beyond what is required in the *Vendidad*, and also beyond the late Sasanian developments of *Vendidad* injunctions.[92] This process can be traced in the rites of purification[93], and also in the onerous restrictions on women at times of birth and menstruation. Many injunctions are laid down concerning these in the *Persian Rivayats*,[94] and foreign observers confirmed how harsh in some respects they were,[95] their gradual relaxation not beginning until the first quarter of the present century.

One development with regard to the *barašnom* purification was purely interpretive, and gave the nine nights' retreat which forms part of it an added and cherished significance. In Iran (largely, it seems, because of poverty combined with a desire for absolute cleanliness) the nights were austerely spent, lying on a hard surface with only a thin cotton sheet beneath one and another for covering; and this austerity came to be made more bearable through the belief that the retreat had been instituted in remembrance of Zoroaster's harsh imprisonment by the as yet uncoverted Vištaspa. Its discomforts were accordingly embraced as a link between the faithful and their revered prophet.[96] Outstanding incidents in the legendary life of Zoroaster were well known among them, the life having been made freshly accessible to the community in a Persian metrical version called the *Zaratušt Nama*, composed from Pahlavi sources in 1278 by a priest named Zardušt Bahram Pajdu.[97] Its main episodes were, it seems, readily communicated to European travellers, being linked with the prophecy of the coming of Zoroaster's sons, the Saošyants.[98] One of the earliest of these travellers had duly learnt from the "Gabrs" that "Zertoošt was their lawgiver",[99] while, as we have seen, the dasturs regularly invoked the prophet's name in their letters. His *fravaši* was venerated daily through the liturgy of the *yasna* and other services, and every year the whole community commemorated the day of his death, as this had come to be fixed in the Zoroastrian calendar.[100]

There is thus no question, on the combined evidence, but that the Zoroastrians of this late period remained staunchly *mazdayasna-* "worshippers of Mazda", *zarathuštri-*, "Zoroastrians", and *vidaeva-* "opposed to the Daevas", that is, to the forces of evil. As to the fourth term of self-identification of the ancient confessionary, *ahura-tkaeša-*"upholding the Ahuric doctrine", this, as we have seen [101], may be taken to mean upholding the moral aspect of *aša*, that principle of rightness guarded by the Ahuras, and striving thus to be *ašavan* in the full sense of that deeply significant word; and there is abundant evidence that the Zoroastrians of this time not only continued to pursue this aim, but as a community went far towards achieving it.[102] One of the basic principles of the Ahuric doctrine, it seems, was to tell the truth;[103] and we have seen Greeks impressed by how highly truthfulness was esteemed among the Achaemenian Persians, and how vigorously it was inculcated.[104] It appears prominently in the lists of virtues in the Pahlavi books, and now in their turn the Irani dasturs stress again and again the pre-eminence of this quality. The *behdin*, they admonish, "should utter truthful words day and night, and should practise truthfulness at all times, for Ormazd regards the truthful speaker as his friend".[105] In contrast "Ahriman has no dearer wish than this, that someone may tell a lie or take false oaths".[106] So a *behdin* should always be able to declare: "I do not say one thing with my tongue and another in my heart."[107] Further, to break a contract (*mihr*) even with one of another religion, a *juddin*, was a sin,[108] for honesty must govern all one's dealings. Stealing was obviously wrong, or misappropriating something given to one in trust; and so too was to do too little work while taking full payment.[109]

There is nothing very remarkable about these precepts themselves, except for their grounding in a clear-cut dualism; but what is remarkable is the extent, according to the testimony of *juddins* - Christians and Muslims alike - to which the Zoroastrians succeeded in putting them into practice. Early European travellers commented on the "simplicity and frank nature" of the oppressed Gaurs,[110] considering them, despite their harsh circumstances, to be "of better faith and more upright" than those who surrounded them, and far harder workers;[111] and later ones, who were able to meet them on closer terms, declared their deep respect for this "much-suffering people".[112] Qualities of theirs which are repeatedly praised are "honesty, integrity, and industry"[113], and these are attributed directly by one observer to "the teachings of Zoroaster, who made truth and honesty a watchword of the religion".[114] The testimony of Muslims is still more striking, because it comes from those who, if not hostile, were generally condescending towards the down-trodden Zoroastrians, whose poverty had become proverbial in the Yazdi area. There the saying "poor as a Gabr" was equivalent to the English "poor as a church mouse";[115] but another local saying was that one should "eat at the house of a Jew, but sleep at that of a Gabr" - implying that at the first one could expect to be well fed, while at the second one could trust one's hosts in all things. Muslims were very ready to employ Zoroastrians as gardeners, not only because of their skill and industry but also because of their honesty; and stories are told of Muslims going on a journey and leaving their savings in safekeeping with a Zoroastrian neighbour. This general reputation for strict honesty, acquired over generations, stood individuals in good stead when the restrictions on the community were at last relaxed, from the second half of the nineteenth century; for Zoroastrians then became Persia's chief bankers, and because of their acknowledged integrity were rapidly successful, gaining great wealth and influence in a society which still despised their co-religionists collectively.[116]

In general the Irani dasturs urged their fellow believers to be diligent in the pursuit of virtue, since "virtue is the destroyer of every vice".[117] They should practise good thoughts, words and acts steadily, and avoid delay in doing good, for Ahriman has made "two fiends, Tardy and Afterwards" which keep the soul from duty and good works.[118] Not surprisingly, hatred had become for them a great demon, of which they say: "for the destruction of hatred, much wisdom is needed ... because hatred is such that when they allow it entry into themselves, the path of religion is blocked."[119] They saw hatred between peoples as the cause of the devastation wrought on Persia by the Turks, and (serene in the religious unity of their own small community) attributed to it also the existence of the 72 mutually antagonistic sects of Islam.[120] "There should" they admonished, "be concord and peace amongst men and there should be no squabble or strife or quarrel, because the Creator Ormazd and the Amašaspands will thereby be pleased."[121] That the Zoroastrians succeeded in this to a very fair degree among themselves is attested by a foreign observer, who wrote: "the ancient Persians have gentle and simple habits (and) live very peacefully under the leadership of their elders."[122]

To maintain a fine ethic, with self-discipline and self-respect, through centuries of poverty and insult was a remarkable achievement; and what seems as remarkable is that the Zoroastrians also managed, with immense spirit and courage, to retain their gaiety, continuing to defy Ahriman through joyfulness and laughter. The Irani dasturs uttered a truly Zoroastrian blessing on the Parsis when they wrote: "May the upholders of the religion derive happiness from the faith."[123]   They also spoke in the spirit of their many forerunners when they declared: "Happy is that man who practises (virtue) for his soul".[124] The colophons of texts copied at Yazd and Kerman regularly contain some such words as "Finished with blessings, joy and delight,"[125] and in general there was welcome for everything which gave scope for contentment at least, and if possible for positive feelings of pleasure. Inevitably, circumstanced as the community was, there were times of general grief and disheartenment, as we have seen from the dasturs' letters, and private sorrows must often have been heavy. Nevertheless, a Western observer was struck by "the buoyant hope" characteristic of the faith, which kept up their courage.[126]   This hope was of the coming of Frašegird, and one tiny way of contributing to its realization was by curtailing demon-created sorrow as far as possible, and cultivating God-given joy in its place, the Spirit of one driving out and weakening that of the other. In his last testament, Dastur Noshirvan Marzban of Kerman specifically instructed his son that no one should weep for him when he was dead;[127]   and the many rituals for the departed gave activities to the living which to some extent helped to assuage their sorrow. Among these rituals was still the age-old one of providing consecrated food for the soul's benefit;[128]   and when a Western observer asked why a corporeal feast should be provided for incorporeal spirits, he was told that the souls received comfort from it, and sometimes came to rejoice.[129]   In fact there was a firm belief that, unless something untoward happened (such as quarrelling among the relatives[130]), the departed souls always came to the offerings, and would be distressed if they were met by grief. So funerary and memorial feasts were sometimes held on a generous scale, with abundant food, and with music and song, story-telling and the drinking of wine in the name of the departed, all this being for the purpose of *šād-ravānī* "gladdening the soul".[131]   Parallel usages in other Indo-European cultures suggest that this may have been a very old custom, surviving so strongly among the Irani Zoroastrians because it was reinforced by their faith's teachings about the positive need to cultivate joy in defiance of Ahriman, the bringer of death.

In every family there were usually funerary or memorial observances held each year, since the ancient, pre-Zoroastrian, custom was kept up of maintaining an annual ceremony for a departed relative for thirty years (that is, for roughly a generation).[132]   Thereafter he or she was still remembered by name in the great annual feast for the *fravašis*, the ancient Hamaspathmaedaya.

There were, moreover, plenty of family observances which provided occasions for small festive gatherings. *Jašans*, for which the family priest celebrated a simple religious service, were held in thanksgiving for all kinds of happenings - a recovery from sickness or escape from danger, a traveller safely returned or a crop successfully harvested; and also in petition for divine help or favour.[133] Sometimes a man would choose instead to go up to a sacred place and offer sacrifice there, thus unconsciously carrying on an age-old tradition celebrated in the *Yašts* and recorded by Herodotus.[134] Relatives and friends would accompany him and a feast would be held in the mountains, with some of the meat of the sacrifice always being set aside to be taken in charity to the priests and the poor.[135]

The great occasions for rejoicing were, however, the communal feasts, chief among which were the seven obligatory high festivals, namely No Roz and the *gahambars*. The latter had been celebrated, it is reasonable to assume, in unbroken continuity from the early days of the faith;[136] and calendar changes had led to their becoming five-day observances.[137] Hence a seventeenth-century onlooker recorded of the Zoroastrians: "They have ... thirty days in honour of their Saints which they keep very strictly, no man daring to work".[138] The *gahambars* are listed by their Avestan names in the *Saddar Bundaheš*, with the creation which each celebrates, and it is there declared (following the *Pahlavi Afrinagan i Gahambar*) that it is a great sin if a poor man does not attend the celebration of a *gahambar*.[139] This the dasturs expanded on in the *Persian Rivayats*: it is one of the six religious duties of a Zoroastrian,[140] they declared, to celebrate the *gahambars* by having the religious ceremony performed, or by attending it, or by giving something towards its performance.[141] The whole community was thus involved.

The *gahambars* were all celebrated in the same way, although in the Yazdi area there were special secular observances at the sixth *gahambar* in honour of Ormazd's acts of creation.[142] There on the first day of each *gahambar* all the priests gathered before sunrise at the Ataš Bahram of Yazd, and together celebrated the first part of a *Visperad* service. Then at a fixed point, while the celebrant priest and the servitor continued that long act of worship, the others left and dispersed to their own town or village parishes, there to conduct the "outer" *gahambar* services at individual homes. The *parahom* (Avestan *parahaoma*) consecrated at the communal *Visperad* was believed "to possess the great virtue and efficacy of giving health and strength to the body and mind", and many sought to partake of it during the festival.[143]

In the Yazdi area the individual *gahambar* ceremonies were all endowed for the sake either of the donor's soul or, more often, of the souls of departed relatives. Making such an endowment was held to be very meritorious, and it helped, moreover, to safeguard the property so used from passing into Muslim possession.[144] The endowments varied naturally in value, but provision was always made for the religious ceremony - essentially an *Afrinagan i Gahambar*, in which all those present took an active part[145] - and for food to be consecrated at this ceremony and distributed afterwards to those attending, as well as being taken to the sick and frail. Sometimes this food was simply freshly baked bread or a handful of *lurk*, that is, a mixture of seven kinds of nuts and dried fruits, but sometimes the endowment was sufficient for an animal sacrifice, and then meat too was given out. In the years of bitter poverty this festival food meant a few days without hunger, and it was this aspect of the festivals which led an Irani priest to say that "the very word *gahambar* conveys the noble idea of charity".[146] No invitations were given for the religious ceremonies, which any and every Zoroastrian who was in a state of purity was welcome to attend; but in addition there were private festivities during the five holy days, with dancing and singing, feasting and mime and merry-making, and, perhaps above all, the pleasant meeting together of relatives and friends. These joyous aspects of Zoroastrian observance awoke a measure of envy in some of their Muslim neighbours, who were ruefully aware of the gaiety with which the "gabrs" celebrated their holy days in contrast with the ritualized weeping and mourning which tended to mark their own.

The most joyful festival of all, however, No Roz (or No Ruz, in modern Persian pronunciation) the Muslims of Iran still in a measure share with the Zoroastrians, for when their forbears converted to Islam they refused to give up this most delightful of festivals, and no ruler since, however strict a Muslim, has succeeded in coercing them into doing so. They even celebrate it still with a rite which embodies the number seven, this being the seventh and last of the Zoroastrian feasts of obligation. For them it is, however, a purely secular, springtime holiday, whereas for the Zoroastrians, as well as being the most joyful of all their festivals, it is also the holiest. All their feast-days were kept with purity, but No Ruz demanded it in the highest degree. There was serious cleansing beforehand of everything in the house (even stalled animals were washed and scrubbed), and of the house itself, from the roof downwards. People bathed from head to foot, and many sought purity of mind by making an act of contrition the day before, either reciting or having recited for them a confessional, a *patet*.[147] The festival of the New Day itself was characterized by a sense of new life, and was the only one of the Zoroastrian year which was celebrated ritually wholly for the living,[148] since at the New Day of Frašegird there will be no more death. Especially at this festival people sought to drink the *parahom* consecrated at the *Visperad* (which was solemnized as at the *gahambars*), in order to gain new strength and vigour.[149] The secular observances also embodied the concept of renewal, through the wearing of new clothes, exchange of sprays of fresh greenery and the like. There was also a whole series of customs marked by the number seven, in honour of this seventh feast. These customs had become very varied and charming, supporting the Spirit of happiness which pervaded the day. This was a time too for special kindness towards one's fellow men, with the giving of presents, and above all of gifts to the poor, so that a seventeenth-century merchant observed of the festival, as kept by the then still relatively prosperous Kermani community, that it was "celebrated with an extraordinary pomp; besides, that then they bestow large alms".[150] Even in harsher times, it remained customary on that day for the slightly better off to give what they could to those in real need.

For centuries before the coming of Islam the festival of the *fravašis*, known to the Persians as Fravardigan, had been celebrated during the last ten nights of the year, the last five of which were the nights of the sixth *gahambar*.[151] Keeping it also was regarded as obligatory, and is given as one of the six duties of a Zoroastrian.[152] Its essential rite - setting out consecrated food for the souls of the dead - remained the same from immensely ancient, pre-Zoroastrian times, and had been only awkwardly adapted to the prophet's teachings.[153] Thus the great Muslim scholar, Biruni, writing around 1000 A.C., recorded of the Zoroastrians that they believed that "the spirits of their dead during these days come out from the places of their reward or their punishment, that they go to the dishes laid out for them, imbibe their strength and suck their taste. ... The spirits of pious men [that is, of *ašavans*] dwell among their families, children and relations, and occupy themselves with their affairs, although invisible to them."[154] Just before dawn on the last night the souls were bidden a formal farewell from the rooftops, with fire kindled and the chanting of Avesta, so that they should be gone before the sun rose on the festival of the living, No Ruz.[155]

Biruni names many other festivals of the Zoroastrian year, drawing, it seems, both on Sasanian sources and his own knowledge of the customs of the Zoroastrians of Khorasan in his day; and all the major ones which he gives were celebrated also by Zoroastrians of Yazd, and so may be presumed to have been generally observed throughout the community. Notable among them were the feasts held annually to honour a Yazad when both a day and a month were dedicated to him or her. Thus, for example, the festival (*jašan*) of Spendarmad was held on the day Spendarmad of the month Spendarmad. The month-names were probably not given before Achaemenian times; but, honouring as they did some of the greatest Yazads of the Zoroastrian pantheon, these name-day festivals were nevertheless fully in keeping with the spirit of the faith. The dedications were to all the members of the Heptad; to Mithra; to the Fravašis (the only one of perhaps doubtful orthodoxy); and to the Yazads of fire, the waters and rain.[156] Observances for the festival of the waters took place mostly by streams or springs, for that of fire in the fire temples which were the focus of the community's devotional life. Old Zoroastrian centres also had consecrated but empty buildings dedicated by name to individual Yazads, in which fire was kindled on special occasions - the successors presumably of the image shrines from which cult statues had been removed by the Sasanian authorities.[157]   (Here again there is evidence of the Zoroastrians' remarkable tenacity in observance, and their reluctance to abandon any way once practised of honouring a divine being.)   Mihr was one who had a number of such shrines; and his name-day festival was celebrated by the Irani Zoroastrians with great devotion and special rites.[158]   Shrines were also regularly built to Bahram (Verethraghna), who was much prayed to for protection, notably by travellers.[159]   Every shrine was regularly visited by priests and laity on the Yazad's festival day, when an act of communal worship would be performed; and individuals would go there at other times to offer the divinity their private prayers and petitions, very much as their remote forbears are represented as doing on mountain-top and at lakeside in the *Yašts*.[160]

One other major act of communal devotion was that of going on pilgrimage. The custom of doing so appears to have been deeply engrained among the Zoroastrians. Its practice can be established with reasonable certainty in the late fourth century B.C., and there are good grounds for thinking it to be very much older.[161]   The destruction of their great fire temples, and the occupation by Muslims of regions where their most sacred places were - notably the Kuh-i Khwaja in Seistan - cut the Zoroastrians off from their major pilgrim goals. It seems, however, that the custom of which Herodotus had learnt in the fifth century B.C. had been generally maintained in the community, namely that of going up at appointed times into the mountains to offer sacrifice in worship of the Yazatas.   It was natural that the same places should have been resorted to year after year, and that, sanctified by regular devotions, they should have come to be regarded as themselves holy, so that visiting them was seen as a form of pilgrimage.   There were six such places in the mountains which enclosed the long narrow Yazdi plain, each with its own particular character and beauty; and devotion to them was so great that some Yazdi Zoroastrians believed that their small community had been preserved by Ormazd against all human odds so that worship could continually be offered there.[162]   The earliest reference to them is in a letter written in 1626 from Turkabad by the Irani dasturs, reporting to the Parsis how one of their messengers, having cleansed himself of the pollutions of travel by undergoing the *barašnom-i no šaba*, had subsequently made his devotions at the mountain shrine of Banu-Pars, which they identified as a "place of pilgrimage" (*ziyārat gāh*)[163] .   In maintaining this practice of regular communal worship in high places the Irani Zoroastrians were probably continuing a very ancient, pre-Zoroastrian, observance, which had been incorporated in their religion from its earliest days.

It is not of course only the lofty and estimable aspects of Zoroastrian belief and practice which are to be found in the religion of this period.   Those other magical and semi-magical elements which make their appearance already in the

Young Avesta[164], and which can be traced in the Pahlavi books, persisted naturally in this small isolated community, whose intellectual horizons were so severely limited, and which lived surrounded by threats and dangers - not only from man's inhumanity, but also from nature, the menace of the desert beginning (for the Yazdi community) at the very edge of their fields. The *Persian Rivayats* give a handful of Avestan *manthras* (called in Persian *nirangs*) to be used virtually as spells to ward off evils.[165] Family priests regularly wrote such *manthras* on scraps of antelope skin to be worn as amulets, and children were protected against the evil eye by blue beads and other charms sewn on their caps.[166] Sometimes purification rites were undergone in the hope that they would free the candidate from ill luck,[167] and certain elaborate magical ceremonies were performed by women seeking cures for prolonged ill-health or barrenness.[168] These were frowned on by the elders of the community and the priests; but the priests themselves, as the *Persian Rivayats* show, were not guiltless of the tendency earlier manifest in the *Vendidad* and certain Pahlavi works, of laying such stress on the merit of having rituals performed that they almost appear to suggest that salvation could be bought by this means.[169]

All such practices and tendencies can be closely matched within different branches of the other great religions of the world; and the innate strength of Zoroaster's own teachings shows in the fact that despite these elements, and despite the normally degrading pressures of extreme poverty and prolonged insult, those who chose to live by them were able to remain informed about their faith, ethically strong, and self-respecting. Moreover, when at last repression was relaxed, individuals swiftly achieved remarkable worldly successes, as their Parsi brethren had done before them; and this suggests that there were excellent qualities of mind as well as character among those whose forbears had chosen to remain *mazdayasna, zarathuštri*, and that their religion had continued to nurture those qualities down the generations.

It is moreover notable that, despite the influences and pressures of the surrounding society, the Zoroastrian women retained the dignity which had been accorded their sex by their prophet. Girls continued to be initiated in the same way as boys, and women took their full part in the religious life of the community. Indeed the maintenance of many observances devolved largely on them, as well as the upbringing of the next generation in the ways of the faith.[170] The keeping of many of the purity laws was their responsibility, and even when these laws pressed harshly on them, they observed them with disciplined stoicism, as those who found themselves in the forefront of the battle against evil.[171] Together with their men they endured privation and insult without losing their pride and self-respect;[172] and an outward mark of their especial courage was that even those who lived in cities firmly refused to adopt the veil, though this put them at times in greater peril.[173] The basic equality of the sexes in their community was further marked by the fact that neither bigamy nor divorce were countenanced, except in especial circumstances.   One Westerner recorded his impression of the Zoroastrian women as being "dignified without reserve, and modest without diffidence",[174] and a seventeenth-century traveller has left a vivid account of a woman entering freely, with vigour and understanding, into a religious discussion between him and her husband, who had apparently a poorer command of words.[175]   The fact that Parsi women too were endowed with courage and strength of character suggests that these qualities were fostered among their sex also by their religion.

Clearly that religion had not remained unchanged from the time of the prophet. A believer of even the "Young Avestan" period would have found numerous strange elements in it, such as the existence of consecrated buildings and temple fires, the length of the acts of worship and of private prayers, the elaboration of purification rites, the complexity of funerary observances and the rich variety of festivals; but at the heart of all these things there would have been familiar elements, notably the fire-cult, the *Staota yesnya* and the Old Avestan parts of the daily prayers, the wearing of the sacred cord, the basic purifications and the seven obligatory feasts; and just as this core of observance was unchanged, so too was the core of belief, with Mazda as God, and the doctrines of the Heptad and dualism remaining at the centre of the faith's theology, and the salvation hopes vivid and enduring.   Zoroaster himself would plainly have found many things to reprove, not least the enormous importance which had come to attach to the *fravaši* cult, with the many rites to help the dead, and the regular invocation when speaking of them: *Khodā be āmurzad-ešān* "May God have mercy on them!", when it is justice, not mercy, that the true Zoroastrian should seek.[176]   But the prophet would surely have been moved to admonish and to reform rather than to repudiate these latter-day followers of his, who so loyally and valiantly maintained his essential teachings, and who testified very strikingly to their power to give dignity and fulfilment to human lives.

The history of the Irani Zoroastrians entered a new phase in the latter part of the twentieth century, as reform movements gathered strength among them,[177] contending with secularism and together with it bringing about the end of many old beliefs and observances.   Economic changes meant that they themselves gained a new mobility, migrating in numbers from the old centres of the faith to Tehran and abroad, and becoming thereby mainly city-dwellers, with urban skills and an urban outlook, and sharing in the general culture and knowledge of the times. With the scattering of the community there came a breakdown in social cohesion to match that in religious unity, and inevitably a much greater openness to outside influences; but the variety of current interpretations of doctrine and the energy with which each is promoted suggest that the ancient faith still has its vigour. To follow such developments in detail would, however, require another book.

NOTES

1   See B. N. Dhabhar (ed.), *Saddar Naṣr and Saddar Bundehesh,* v-vi.

2   Cf. above, p.137, and Dhabhar, o.c., pp.xvii-xviii.

3   See Dhabhar, o.c., p.v.

4   *Riv.,* Unvala, II 459 14, Dhabhar, 618.

5   Cf. above, p.158.

6   See *Riv.,* ed. Unvala, tr. Dhabhar. One or two unpublished letters are cited by Hodivala in his *Studies.*

7   See the admirable critical study by N.K. Firby, *European Travellers.*

8   On Parsi reformist movements see in outline Boyce, *Zoroastrians,* 199-206, 212-15. From the second half of the 19th century Irani Zoroastrian laymen began making their way to Bombay, from where some returned as prosperous merchants with "enlightened" ideas; and priests followed, also going out and returning. In the early 20th century some Irani boys were sent to be educated in Bombay, as potential leaders of their own community, and one of them, Kay Khosrow Shahrokh, came back to be a vigorous and influential reformist. See Boyce, o.c., pp.218-23. The deep conservatism of the Zoroastrians of Yazd, and especially of those in some of its outlying villages (notably Sharifabad with Mazra' Kalantar and Taft) was however only very gradually eroded.

9   See Hodivala, *Studies,* 313 n.61.

10   Cf. ib., p.318.

11   Ib., p.331.

12   *Riv.,* Unvala, II 158.16, Dhabhar, 593.

13   *Riv.,* Unvala, II 390.7, Dhabhar, 606.

14   E.g., *Riv.,* Unvala, II 380.6-8, Dhabhar, 600.

15   Cf. *Y.* 72:11. The declaration is reiterated in the letters, and appears also in the colophons of mss. copied by the Irani priests.

16   *Riv.,* Unvala, I 283.19-284.4, Dhabhar, 277-8.

17   Similar declarations are to be found generally in the Persian Zoroastrian writings of the Islamic era, e.g. *Zaratušt Nama,* line 10, ed. Rosenberg, p.1.

18   E.g., *Riv.,* Unvala, II 160.5, Dhabhar, 594.

19   Cf. above, pp.91, 93 with n.50.

20   Cf. above, p.126.

21   *Riv.,* Unvala, II 378.19-379.3, Dhabhar, 593.

22   *yazdān-i mīnōān va yazdān-i gētiyān,* cf. above, p.68. *Yazd/ized* are Persian forms of Av. *yazata.*

23   The three divinities who preside over judgment at death, cf. above, pp.75 with n.65, 109.

24   Cf. above, pp.106-7.

25   *Riv.*, Unvala, I 286.17 ff., Dhabhar, 280.

26   *Riv.*, Unvala, I.71.18, Dhabhar, 59.

27   Khodayar Dustoor Sheriar, "The funeral ceremonies of the Zoroastrians in Persia", *Sir J. J. Madressa Jubilee Vol.*, ed. Modi, 306-18, at pp.312-14.

28   See above, pp.135-6.

29   See *Riv.*, ed. Unvala, I 151-70, Dhabhar, 166-78.

30   Cf. above, p.119.

31   *Riv.*, Unvala, II 459.14, Dhabhar, 618.

32   Tavernier, I 166 (Firby, *European Travellers*, 46).

33   *Stronghold*, 21.

34   That is, in *Yt* 19:10-11, 88 ff., and in the later works of post-Achaemenian times.

35   See with references *HZ* I 284-5.

36   See *HZ* III 381-2.

37   Also termed by them "the millennium of Wrath (Hešm, Av. Aešma), and "the millennium of the Evil Spirit" (Gana Mino, Av. Anra Mainyu), see *Riv.*, Unvala, II 379.8, 383.12, Dhabhar, 598, 603.

38   *Riv.*, Unvala, II 460.7-8, Dhabhar, 619.

39   *Riv.*, Unvala, II 159.18-19, Dhabhar, 593-4.

40   Chinon, 480 (Firby, 38).

41   Chardin, VIII 371.

42   *Riv.*, Unvala, I 405 ff., Dhabhar, 318-19.

43   *Stronghold*, 71. (On the importance attached to dreams, as conveying divine messages, see, e.g., ib., pp.88, 90.)

44   Tavernier, I 164-5 (with the English translator's "minerals" altered in favour of the original French "métaux", so Firby, *European Travellers*, 43).

45   See above, p.77 with n.72.

46   See above, p.143.

47   *Dadestan i denig*, *Purs.* 31.10-13, ed. Dhabhar, pp.67-8, tr. West, *SBE* XVIII, 73-4 (as Ch. 32.12-16).

48   *Riv.*, Unvala, II 49.10-11, Dhabhar, 424.

49   Della Valle, II 106 (Firby, 27).

50   Chardin, VIII 364 (Firby, 64).

51   Chinon, 445 (Firby, 50).

52   Chardin, VIII 365-6. (On his confusion over the Zoroastrians' use of the term "Yazd", i.e. God, and the name "Ormous" see Firby, 64.)

53   See above, pp.129-30.

54   Della Valle, II pp.106-7 (Firby, 27).

55   Chardin, VIII 359, 365 (Firby, 64).

56   Vahram V, see G. Hoffmann, *Auszüge aus syrischen Akten persischer Märtyrer*, Leipzig 1880, repr. Liechtenstein 1966, 42.

57   Cf. above, pp.70-1.

58   *Riv.*, Unvala, I 52.15, Dhabhar, 49. On the forms Pahl. *mēnōg* (*mynwg*), Pers.-Pazand *minō*, see Nyberg, "Questions de cosmogonie et cosmologie mazdéennes", *JA* 1929, 242-9 [=*Acta Ir.* 7, 1975, 124-31].

59   Nyberg, art.cit., p.249.

60   Cf. above, pp.53-5.

61   *Riv.*, Unvala, I 575.4-5, Dhabhar, 346.

62   That is, as set out in the *Siroza*.

63   *Riv.*, Unvala, I 487.7-9, Dhabhar, 332-3.

64   See Dhabhar, 333 n.1.

65   The link of Shahrevar's concept with his "gift" here is not obvious, but has perhaps its basis in the idea (developed presumably from Seleucid times, when coinage came into use within Iran) that money belonged to his creation of metals (on which see above, pp.118-19), and was to be wisely used to help the good. Cf. *The Supplementary Texts to the Shayest ne-shayest*, ed. Kotwal, XV.18: "One should not give gold and silver to the wicked".

66   *Saddar Bd.* Ch.2.

67   Ib., Chs. 74-84.

68   Ib., Ch.74.4-5.

69   Information orally from Arbab Sorush Sorushian of Kerman.

70   Cf. above, pp.67-70 with nn.36, 42.

71   *Riv.*, Unvala, I 46.1-4, Dhabhar, 40.

72   *Riv.*, Unvala, I 52.17, Dhabhar, 50.

73   Cf. above, p.85.

74   *Stronghold*, 51.   In view of the importance of this late testimony for understanding this aspect of Zoroaster's doctrine of the Heptad, the writer should perhaps record that before going to live among Zoroastrians in Iran she had no preconceptions whatsoever in this matter, and hence was in no position to put any leading questions concerning it.   On one occasion she was simply waiting for a village *Afrinagan* ceremony to begin when a kindly farmer took it on himself to instruct the stranger in this aspect of the coming act of worship, speaking wholly matter-of-factly of the awaited entry of the Amašaspands into the consecrated objects. At another time she was instructed in the doctrine by a priest of the fire temple in Tehran.   At first she found it as hard to accept as most other Iranists were to do subsequently; but after nine months spent in a Zoroastrian village, where the constant presence of the Amašaspands in the surrounding natural world was taken for granted (see *Stronghold*, passim), the belief came to appear so fully integrated into general doctrine and awareness that it had indeed to be recognized as original to Zoroaster's own system of thought.   Afterwards study both of the *Persian Rivayats* and the Old Avestan texts from this aspect together confirmed this.

75   Essentially the *Yasna ba nirang*, that is, the *yasna* with ritual instructions (most readily accessible for non-Zoroastrians through Darmesteter's *Zend-Avesta* I) and the *Nirangestan*.

76   Above, p.140.

77   Chardin, VIII 359 (Firby, 60).

78   Sanson, *The present state of Persia*, 188 (Firby, 73).

79   *Riv.*, Unvala, I 291.13-14, Dhabhar, 283.

80   See *Stronghold*, 108.

81   See ib., pp.187-91, and cf. above, p.117.

82   Jackson, *Persia past and present*, 398.

83   See, e.g., *Stronghold*, 109.

84   Cf. above, p.131 with n.45.

85　　Tavernier (1724), II 107 (tr. Firby, 52, see her n.259).

86　　Chardin, VIII 377 (Firby, 66).

87　　J. de Thevenot, *Travels into the Levant*, Pt.II, 111 (Firby, 70). The intention of this act was as a vicarious atonement for the dead person's sins, this atonement being required of living people in *Vd* 14:5, 18:73.

88　　*Riv.*, Unvala, I 62.15-17, Dhabhar, 176.

89　　Chardin, VIII 380.

90　　A. Khodadadian, *Die Bestattungssitten und Bestattungsriten bei den heutigen Parsen*, doctoral dissertation, Freie Universität, Berlin 1974.

91　　Above, pp.116-118.

92　　On which cf. above, p.136.

93　　Thus in the *Persian Rivayats* the dasturs list some fairly minor pollutions for which the elaborate *barašnom* ceremony was required, and state most emphatically that every *behdin* must undergo the purification once before reaching 15 years, and that it is highly meritorious to undergo it yearly thereafter (*Riv.*, Unvala, I 606-8, Dhabhar, 388-92). It has, however, to be borne in mind that in these texts priests were setting down ideal rules. The laity, often with little means or leisure, had to do the best they could, temperament also playing a part; and they looked moreover to some extent to the priests, as professionally the purest of the pure, to act on their behalf, sometimes directly as their proxies. Cf. *Stronghold*, 120-1, 125-7. - One costly addition to the *barašnom* observance, unknown among the Parsis, was the solemnization of a *Vendidad* during each of the nine nights of the retreat (*Stronghold*, 119, 123). This is not mentioned in the *Persian Rivayats*, and may therefore be a late development.

94　　*Riv.*, Unvala, I 205-36, Dhabhar, 211-38.

95　　Tavernier, I 166 (Firby, 50-1); *Stronghold*, 100-7.

96　　*Stronghold*, 117-18 with 122-3.

97　　See Rosenberg (ed.), *Zaratušt Nama*, vi ff.

98　　Chinon and Tavernier, see Firby, 38, 42-3.

99　　Thomas Herbert, *A relation of some yeares travaile, begun anno 1626*, London, 1634, 168 (Firby, 31).

100　*Riv.*, Unvala, II 48.15-16, Dhabhar, 423. The day was kept with the regular observances for a death-anniversary (called *sāl-rōz* or simply *sāl*), but with a heightened sense of its importance. As regards to the circumstances of the prophet's death, the story of his violent end (see above, p.13 ff.) was unknown among the Irani Zoroastrians. As a 17th-century traveller recorded, they believed simply that he had disappeared from sight, "nor do they justly know what became of him", Tavernier, I 165 (Firby, 43).

101　Above, p.102.

102　There must naturally have been individuals who fell short; but generally speaking any Zoroastrian who was prepared to imperil his hope of heaven by recurrent bad actions might just as well turn Muslim, and so have at least an easier and more agreeable time in this life; and so there was probably a steady erosion of worse as well as weaker elements. There must, however, have been some dishonesty among Zoroastrians towards one another, or there would have been no litigation and no *Sogand Nama*.

103　Cf. above, pp.54-5, 95.

104　Above, p.130.

105　*Riv.*, Unvala, I 292.14-15, Dhabhar, 285.

106 *Riv.*, Unvala, I 48.8-9, Dhabhar, 44.

107 *Riv.*, Unvala, I 54.9, Dhabhar, 51.

108 *Riv.*, Unvala, I 57.9-10, Dhabhar, 54. Cf. *Yt* 10:2.

109 *Riv.*, Unvala, I 299.7, Dhabhar, 286.

110 Figueroa, 179 (Firby, 196).

111 Nicolas Hemmius and Sebastien Manrique, cited by Firby, 28, 32.

112 Browne, *A year amongst the Persians*, 401.

113 Ib., p.405; cf. Jackson, *Persia past and present*, 337.

114 Jackson, o.c., p.426. The fact that the same virtues were both highly valued and generally practised among the Parsis supports his assumption.

115 Drouville, *Voyage en Perse*, II 209.

116 See with references Boyce, "The vitality of Zoroastrianism attested by some Yazdi traditions and actions", *Corolla Iranica, Papers in honour of D. N. MacKenzie*, Frankfurt-am-Main 1992, 15-22 at p.19; Jackson, o.c., p.426; M. M. Murzban, *The Parsis in India*, Bombay 1917, Ch.2, "The Zoroastrians in Persia", 150 with n.154.

117 *Riv.*, Unvala, I 291.9, Dhabhar, 283.

118 *Kama Bohra's Rivayat* in *Riv.*, Dhabhar, 300.

119 *Riv.*, Unvala, I 291.4-5, Dhabhar, 382.

120 *Riv.*, Unvala, I 291.6 ff., Dhabhar, 283.

121 *Riv.*, Unvala, I 291.14-15, Dhabhar, 283.

122 Chardin, VIII (Firby, 62).

123 *Riv.*, Unvala, II 371.7-8, Dhabhar, 596.

124 *Riv.*, Unvala, II 371.10, Dhabhar, 596. Cf. above, p.126.

125 E.g., *Riv.*, Unvala, II 372.6, Dhabhar, 596.

126 Jackson, *Persia past and present*, 353.

127 *Riv.*, Unvala, I 162-4, Dhabhar, 175. In *AVN* 16 Viraz sees in the hereafter a dark river, formed from tears wept for the dead. The more that had been shed for an individual soul, the greater its difficulty in crossing this river.

128 Cf. above, pp.58, 106-7.

129 Chinon, 467-8 (Firby, 38).

130 Cf. *Stronghold*, 161 n.47.

131 See ib., pp.160-1.

132 See *HZ* I 120-1 (with "catholic" to be corrected to "chthonic", as in the 2nd printing).

133 In Yazdi usage such a *jašan* had come by modern times to be termed a *gahambar-i toji*, see *Stronghold*, 53-4 and ff.

134 Cf. above, pp.110-11, 127.

135 For an instance see *Stronghold*, 61-2.

136 Cf. above, pp.104-5.

137 See Boyce, "On the calendar of Zoroastrian feasts", *BSOAS* XXXIII, 1970, 513-39.

138 Tavernier, I 166 (Firby, 48).

139 *Saddar Bd.* 51 (tr. Dhabhar, *Riv.*, 541 with n.4).

140 Lists of these six chief duties first appear in works of the post-Sasanian period; but (conceivably in order to avoid any appearance of imitating the 5 duties of Islam) they do not

include such fundamental religious acts as saying the sacred-cord prayers or giving alms. The order in which the duties are given varies, and there are tiny differences in the duties themselves (although all of them are ones which were actually required of all believers).

141 *Riv.*, Unvala, I 304.12, 427.17, Dhabhar, 290,322.

142 See *Stronghold*, 48-9.

143 Khudayar Dastur Sheriyar, "The celebrations of the Gahambar in Persia", *The Sir J. J. Madressa Jubilee Vol.*, ed. Modi, 303.

144 See ib., and *Stronghold*, 32-3. The trusteeship of the endowment remained with the donor and his family, who thus continued to draw a (somewhat diminished) income from the property in question.

145 See Khudayar Dastur Sheriyar, art.cit., pp.303-6; *Stronghold*, 42-3.

146 Khudayar Dastur Sheriyar, art.cit., p.303.

147 Hence one Parsi name for this festival, *No Roj-i pateti*.

148 See *Stronghold*, 232, 233.

149 See ib., pp.231, 232, 233 with Pl.VIa.

150 Tavernier, I 166 (Firby, 48).

151 Cf. art.cit. in n.137 and *Stronghold*, 212-26.

152 Cf. above, p.179 with n.140.

153 Cf. above, pp.106-7.

154 Biruni, "On the festivals in the months of the Persians" in his *The Chronology of Ancient Nations*, tr. Sachau, 210.

155 *Stronghold*, 224-5.

156 Honouring the rain-Yazad, Tištrya, in this special way appears due to foreign (Babylonian) influence, see *HZ* II 35-6, 204-6; but veneration of the divinity of life-giving rain was in itself wholly Zoroastrian.

157 Cf. above, p.141, and on the later custom *Stronghold*, 81-91.

158 See Biruni, l.c., pp.207-8; Boyce, "Mihragān among the Irani Zoroastrians", *Mithraic Studies*, ed. J. R. Hinnells, Manchester 1975, I 106-18. Mihr was less actively venerated among the Parsis.

159 On the promotion of this Yazad from Seleucid times see *HZ* III 64-5.

160 Cf. above, p.116, and *Stronghold*, 84.

161 Cf. above, pp.8-9.

162 *Stronghold*, 241. In detail on the mountain shrines and the annual pilgrimages to them see ib., pp.241-70.

163 *Riv.*, Unvala, II 159.3, Dhabhar, 593.

164 Cf. above, p.115.

165 *Riv.*, Unvala, II 272-82.

166 See Jackson, *Persia past and present*, 378.

167 See ib., p.379; *Stronghold*, 111, 126.

168 See *Stronghold*, 62-7, 105-6 with n.14. Even after such ceremonies part of the offerings was regularly distributed in charity, see ib., p.63.

169 Often, however, an injunction to perform a rite for a quasi-magical purpose was given together with the instruction also to do some act of charity, see, e.g., *Riv.*, Unvala, I 283.11-12, Dhabhar, 277.

170   See *Stronghold*, passim.

171   See ib., p.100 ff., and esp. pp.106-7.

172   See for example the testimony of the Parsi emissary Hataria apud Boyce, "Manekji Limji Hataria in Iran", *K. R. Cama Oriental Institute Golden Jubilee Volume*, Bombay 1969, 19-31 at p.27.

173   A relatively minor assault on a beautiful Zoroastrian woman is recounted by Browne, *A year amongst the Persians*, 406-7.   The great threats were rape and abduction; and in the 1960s the older generation of Zoroastrian women still told of pretty girls begriming their faces and blackening their teeth when they had to leave their houses.

174   Jackson, *Persia past and present*, 386.

175   Della Valle, II 106 (cited by Firby, 27).

176   This usage, unknown among the Parsis, is presumably to be attributed to Muslim influence.

177   Cf. above, p.185 n.8.

SELECT BIBLIOGRAPHY

For works cited only once, bibliographical details have generally been given in the notes. Where the title of a work is cited in the notes by initials only, or in much abbreviated form, the initials or abbreviation are put at the end of the entry, in square brackets.

Anklesaria, B. T., ed. and tr., *Pahlavi Vendidād*, ed. D. D. Kapadia, Bombay 1949 [*Pahl. Vd*].

Anklesaria, P. K., ed., *A critical edition of the unedited portion of the Dādestān-i dīnīk*, London University doctoral thesis, 1958 [*Dd.*].

Anklesaria, T. D., ed., *The Datistan-i dinik* Part I, *Pursishn* I-XL, Bombay n.d. [*Dd.*].

Asmussen, J.P., *Xuāstvānīft, Studies in Manichaeism*, Copenhagen 1965.

Bahar, M. T., ed., *Tārikh-e Sīstān*, Tehran A.H. 1313/A.C. 1935.

Bailey, H. W., *Zoroastrian problems in the ninth-century books*, Ratanbai Katrak Lectures 1932, Oxford 1943, repr. 1971.

Bartholomae, C., *Altiranisches Wörterbuch*, Strassburg 1904 [*Air. Wb.*].

Basilov, V. N., *Nomads of Eurasia*, tr. M. F. Zirin, University of Washington Press, 1989.

Belenitsky, A., *Central Asia*, tr. J. Hogarth, London 1969.

Bidez, J. et F. Cumont, *Les mages hellénisés*, 2 vols, Paris 1938, repr. 1973.

Boyce, M., *A History of Zoroastrianism, HdO*, Vol. I, "The early period", 1975, corrected repr., 1989; Vol. II, "Under the Achaemenians", 1982; Vol.III, with F. Grenet, "Under Macedonian and Roman rule", 1991 [*HZ*].

- *A Persian Stronghold of Zoroastrianism*, based on the Ratanbai Katrak Lectures 1975, Oxford 1977, repr. Universities of America Press, 1989.

- ed., and tr., *Textual Sources for the Study of Zoroastrianism,* in *Textual Sources for the Study of Religion*, ed. J. R. Hinnells, Manchester 1984, paperback repr., Chicago 1990.

- (tr.) *The Letter of Tansar*, IsMEO, Rome 1968.

- *Zoroastrians, their religious beliefs and practices*, London 1979, 3rd revised repr., 1988.

Browne, E., *A Year amongst the Persians*, Cambridge 1893, 2nd ed. 1926, repr. 1927.

Chadwick, H. M., *The Heroic Age*, Cambridge 1912.

Chadwick, H. M. and N. K., *The Growth of Literature*, 3 vols, Cambridge 1932-40.

Chardin, J., *Voyages en Perse et autres lieux de l'Orient*, ed. L. Langlès, 10 vols, Paris 1811.

Chinon, G. de, *Relations nouvelles du Levant ...*, ed. L. Moréri, Lyon 1671.

Christensen, A., *Le premier chapitre du Vendidad*, Copenhagen 1943.

Clemen, C., *Fontes historiae religionis Persicae*, Bonn 1920.

Crouwel, J. H. see under Littauer

Cumont, F., see under Bidez

Darmesteter, J., tr., *Le Zend-Avesta*, Annales du Musée Guimet, 3 vols, Paris 1892-1893, repr. 1960 [*ZA*].

Dhabhar, B. N., ed., *Pahlavi Yasna and Visperad*, Bombay 1949.

- ed., *Saddar Naṣr and Saddar Bundehesh*, Bombay 1909.

- tr., *The Persian Rivayats of Hormazyar Framarz and others*, Bombay 1932 [*Riv.*].

- ed., *Zand-i Khūrtak Avistak*, Bombay 1927 [*ZXA*].

- tr., *Zand-i Khūrtak Avistak*, Bombay 1963 [*ZXA*].

Drouville, G., *Voyage en Perse fait en 1812 et 1813*, 2nd ed., 2 vols, Paris 1825.

Figueroa, G. de Silva, *L'Ambassade ... en Perssee*, tr. from Spanish by De Wicqfort, Paris 1667.

Firby, N. K., *European travellers and their perceptions of Zoroastrians in the 17th and 18th centuries*, Archäologische Mitteilungen aus Iran, Ergänzungsband 14, Berlin 1988.

Fox, W. S. and R. E. K. Pemberton, *Passages in Greek and Latin literature relating to Zoroaster and Zoroastrianism rendered into English*, JCOI 14,1929.

Francfort, H. -P., *Fouilles de Shortugaï*, 2 vols, Paris 1989.

Frumkin, G., *Archaeology in Soviet Central Asia*, HdO VII.3.1., Leiden 1970.

Frye, R. N., *The Golden Age of Persia*, New York 1975.

- ed., *The Cambridge History of Iran*, IV, "From the Arab invasion to the Saljuks", Cambridge 1975 [*CHIr.*].

- tr., *The History of Bukhara ... by Narshakhī*, The Mediaeval Academy of America, Cambridge Mass., 1954.

Geiger, W., *Civilization of the Eastern Iranians in ancient times*, tr. D. P. Sanjana, 2 vols, London 1885-1886.

Gershevitch, I., ed. and tr., *The Avestan Hymn to Mithra*, Cambridge 1959, repr. 1967 [*AHM*].

- "Old Iranian literature", *HdO* IV.2.1, Leiden 1968, 1-30.

Geldner, K. F., ed., *Avesta*, 3 vols, Stuttgart 1886-96, repr. 1982.

Ghirshman, R., *Iran, from the earliest times to the Islamic conquest*, Penguin books, 1954.

Gignoux, P., ed. and tr., *Le Livre d'Ardā Vīrāz*, Paris 1984 [*AVN*].

Gnoli, G., *De Zoroastre à Mani, quatre leçons au Collège de France*, Paris 1985.

- *Ricerche storiche sul Sīstān antico*, IsMEO, Rome 1967.

-   *The Idea of Iran*, IsMEO, Rome 1989.
-   *Zoroaster's Time and Homeland*, Naples 1980 [*ZTH*].

Gold, M., tr., *The Tārikh-e Sīstān*, IsMEO, Rome 1976.

Grenet, F., see under Boyce

Gupta, S. P., *Archaeology of Soviet Central Asia and the Iranian borderlands*, 2 vols, Delhi 1979.

Henning, W. B., *Selected Papers*, 2 vols, *Acta Ir.* 14 and 15, 1977.

-   *Zoroaster, politician or witch-doctor?* Ratanbai Katrak Lectures 1949, Oxford 1951.
-   *Memorial Volume*, ed. M. Boyce and I. Gershevitch, London 1970.

Hitti, P. K. and F. C. Murgotten, tr., *The Origins of the Islamic State (Kitāb futūḥ al-buldān of ... al-Balādhuri)*, New York 1968.

Hodivala, S. H., *Studies in Parsi History*, Bombay 1920.

Hoffmann, K. and J. Narten, *Der Sasanidische Archetypus*, Wiesbaden 1989.

Humbach, H., *A Western approach to Zarathushtra*, *JCOI* 51, 1984.

-   ed. and tr., *Die Gathas des Zarathustra*, 2 vols, Heidelberg 1959. [The revised English version, *The Gāthās of Zarathushtra*, 2 vols, Heidelberg 1991, appeared as the present book was about to go to press.]

Insler, S., ed. and tr., *The Gāthās of Zarathushtra*, *Acta Ir.* 8, 1975.

Jackson, A. V. W., *Persia past and present*, New York 1909, repr. 1975.

-   *Zoroaster, the prophet of ancient Iran*, New York 1899, repr. 1965.

Jettmar, K., *Art of the Steppes*, tr. A. E. Keep, London 1967.

Kellens, J., *Zoroastre et l'Avesta ancien*, Travaux de l'Institut d'Etudes Iraniennes de l'Université de la Sorbonne Nouvelle 14, Paris 1991.

Kellens, J. et E. Pirart, *Les textes vieil-avestiques*, Vol.I, *Introduction, texte et traduction* [*TVA*]; Vol.II, *Répertoires grammaticaux et lexique*; Vol.III, *Commentaire* (which appeared as the present book was about to go to press), Wiesbaden 1988, 1990, 1991.

Kent, R. G., *Old Persian, Grammar, texts, lexicon*, American Oriental Society, New Haven, Connecticut, 1950, 2nd ed., 1953.

Kohl, P. K., *Central Asia, Palaeolithic beginnings to the Iron Age*, Paris 1984.

-   (ed.), *The Bronze Age Civilization of Central Asia*, New York 1981.

Kotwal, F. M. P., ed. and tr., *The Supplementary Texts to the Šāyest nē-šāyest*, Royal Danish Academy, Historisk-filosofiske Meddelelser 44, 2, Copenhagen 1969.

Kreyenbroek, G., *Sraoša in the Zoroastrian tradition*, Leiden 1985.

Le Strange, G., *The lands of the Eastern Caliphate*, Cambridge 1905, repr. 1930.

Lincoln, B., *Priests, warriors and cattle*, University of California Press, 1981.

Littauer, M. A. and J. H. Crouwel, *Wheeled vehicles and ridden animals in the ancient Near East, HdO* VII.1.2B.1, Leiden 1979.

Lommel, H., *Die Religion Zarathustras nach dem Awesta dargestellt,* Tübingen 1930, repr. 1971 [*Rel.*].

Madan, D. M., ed., *The Dēnkard,* Bombay 1911 [*DkM*].

Malcolm, N., *Five years in a Persian town,* London 1905.

Markwart, J., ed. and tr., *Catalogue of the Provincial Capitals of Ērānshahr,* ed. G.Messina, Rome 1931.

- *Wehrot und Arang,* Leiden 1938.

Marquart, J., *Ērānšahr,* Berlin 1901.

Masson, V. M. and V. I. Sarianidi, *Central Asia, Turkmenia before the Achaemenids,* tr. R. Tringham, London 1972.

Meillet, A., *Trois conférences sur les Gāthā de l'Avesta,* Paris 1925.

Menasce, de, J.-P., *Une encyclopédie mazdéenne, Le Dēnkart,* Paris 1958.

Menant, D., *Les Parsis, Histoire des communautés zoroastriennes de l'Inde,* Annales du Musée Guimet, Paris 1898, repr. Osnabrück 1975.

Minovi, M., *Nāme-ye Tansar,* Tehran A.H. 1311/A.C. 1932.

Modi, J. J., *The religious ceremonies and customs of the Parsees,* Bombay 1922, 2nd ed. 1937, repr. from 1st ed., 1979 [*CC*].

- ed., *Sir Jamsetjee Jejeebhoy Madressa Jubilee Volume,* Bombay 1914.

Molé, M., *La légende de Zoroastre selon les textes pehlevis,* Paris 1967.

Monchi-Zadeh, D., ed. and tr., *Die Geschichte Zarēr's,* Uppsala 1981.

- *Topographische-historische Studien zum iranischen Nationalepos,* Wiesbaden 1975.

Mongait, A. L., *Archaeology in the U.S.S.R.,* tr. M. W. Thompson, Penguin books, 1961.

Murgotten, F. C., see under Hitti

Murzban, M. M., *The Parsis in India,* being an enlarged ... English ed. of D.Menant's *Les Parsis,* 2 vols, Bombay 1917.

Narten, J., *Der Yasna Haptaŋhāiti,* Wiesbaden 1986.

- *Die Aməša Spəṇtas im Avesta,* Weisbaden 1982.

- see also under Hoffmann

Nyberg, H. S., *Die Religionen des Alten Iran,* tr. from the Swedish by H. H. Schaeder, Leipzig 1938, repr. 1966.

Rosenberg, F., ed. and tr., *Le Livre de Zoroastre (Zarātusht Nāma),* St. Petersburg 1904.

Rudenko, S. I., *Frozen tombs of Siberia,* tr. M. W. Thompson, University of California Press, 1970.

Sachau, E., tr., *The Chronology of Ancient Nations ... of Al-Bīrūnī,* London 1879, repr. 1969.

Sanson, Father, *The Present State of Persia ...,* tr. J. Savage, London 1695.

Sarianidi, V. I. see under Masson

Schippmann, K., *Die iranischen Feuerheiligtümer*, Berlin-New York 1971.

Schlerath, B., ed., *Zarathustra*, Wege der Forschung CLXIX, Darmstadt 1970.

Schwartz, P., *Iran im Mittelalter nach den arabischen Geographen*, Vol.VII, Leipzig 1932.

Shahbazi, A. S., *Ferdowsī, A critical biography*, Harvard University Center for Middle Eastern Studies, Costa Mesa 1991.

Shaked, S., ed. and tr., *The Wisdom of the Sasanian Sages (Dēnkard VI)*, Persian Heritage Series, Boulder, Colorado, 1979.

Sinor, D., ed., *The Cambridge History of Early Inner Asia*, Cambridge 1990.

Stewart, S., *Some devotional practices of the Zoroastrian laity*, London University doctoral thesis (in preparation).

Taraf, Z., ed. and tr., *Der Awesta-Text Niyāyiš mit Pahlavi und Sanskritübersetzung*, Münchener Studien zur Sprachwissenschaft, Neue Folge Beiheft 10, Munich 1981.

Tavadia, J. C., ed. and tr., *Shāyast-ne-shāyast*, Hamburg 1930.

Tavernier, J. B., in *Collections of Travels through Turky into Persia and the East-Indies ... the travels of Monsieur Tavernier, Bernier and Other Great Men*, 2 vols, London 1684.

- *Suite de voyages, Les six voyages ...* 6 vols, Rouen 1724.

Thevenot, J. de, *The Travels ... into the Levant*, London 1687.

Unvala, M. R., ed., *Dārāb Hormazyār's Rivāyat*, 2 vols, Bombay 1922 [*Riv.*].

Valle, P. della, *The Travels ... into East India and Arabia Deserta*, tr. G. Havers, London 1665.

Warner, A. G. and Warner E., tr., *The Shāhnāma of Firdausi*, 9 vols, London 1905-1925.

West, E. W., *The Dādistān-ī dīnīk*, SBE XVIII, 1882, repr. New Delhi 1965.

Williams, A. V. W., *The Pahlavi Rivāyat accompanying the Dādestān ī Dēnīg*, 2 vols, Royal Danish Academy, Historisk - filosofiske Meddelelser 60, Copenhagen 1990.

Wolff, F., *Glossar zu Firdosis Schahname*, with Supplementband, Berlin 1935.

Yanine, V., G. Fédorov-Davydov, E. Tchernykh, D. Chélov, *Fouilles et recherches archéologiques en URSS*, Moscow 1985.

Yarshater, E., ed., *The Cambridge History of Iran*, III, "The Seleucid, Parthian and Sasanian periods", 2 vols., Cambridge 1983 [*CHIr.*]

Zaehner, R. C., *The Teachings of the Magi*, London 1956, repr. 1975.

INDEX

In the alphabetic order š is treated like sh. A word for which a range of forms occurs is indexed under the Avestan one (with an Old Avestan form taking precedence over a Young Avestan one as the key form), followed when relevant by the Old Persian, Middle Persian and Persian ones. Cross references to different forms are generally given.